Divine Violence and the
Christus Victor Atonement Model

To Ian & Zoe

with warmest regards.

Romans 12:2

Martyn :)

Divine Violence and the Christus Victor Atonement Model

God's Reluctant Use of Violence
for Soteriological Ends

Martyn John Smith

FOREWORD BY
David Hilborn

PICKWICK *Publications* · Eugene, Oregon

Pickwick Publications
An Imprint of Wipf and Stock Publishers
199 W. 8th Ave., Suite 3
Eugene, OR 97401

www.wipfandstock.com

PAPERBACK ISBN: 978-1-4982-3947-9
HARDCOVER ISBN: 978-1-4982-3949-3
EBOOK ISBN: 978-1-4982-3948-6

Cataloguing-in-Publication data:

Names: Smith, Martyn John (author) | Hilborn, David (foreword).

Title: Divine violence and the christus victor atonement model : God's reluctant use of violence for soteriological ends / Martyn John Smith, with a foreword by David Hilborn.

Description: Eugene, OR: Pickwick Publications, 2016 | Includes bibliographical references and index.

Identifiers: ISBN 978-1-4982-3947-9 (paperback) | ISBN 978-1-4982-3949-3 (hardcover) | ISBN 978-1-4982-3948-6 (ebook)

Subjects: LSCH: Atonement—Biblical teaching | Jesus Christ—Crucifixion | Atonement—History of doctrines | Violence in the Bible

Classification: BT265.3 S65 2016 (print) | BT265.3 (ebook)

Manufactured in the U.S.A.   09/15/16

For my wife Suzanne, without whom . . .

Contents

Foreword

I WAS VERY PLEASED to read and examine the original form of this book when Martyn Smith submitted it as a doctoral thesis at the London School of Theology in 2014, and I am very pleased to see it published now. As Smith himself attests, in temporal terms at least, violence is an inescapable political and theological reality, yet it has come into distinctive focus in both spheres more recently.

Politically, while the immediate threat of a "Third World War" appears to have waned with the fall of the iron curtain, a no-less-global conflict has proliferated in relation to terror—prosecuted by terrorists themselves online and through the bombing, kidnapping, enslavement, and execution of civilians, and by nations fighting terrorism through enhanced surveillance, regional military campaigns, extraordinary rendition, and drone strikes. At the same time, significant developments have taken place in both parliamentary and extra-parliamentary contexts with respect to rejection of armed intervention in different theatres of the "war on terror"—from mass marches against the second war on Iraq in 2003 to the British MPs' vote against sending forces to fight the Syrian regime of Bashar al-Assad in 2013.

Theologically, there have been various direct attempts to engage with these shifting, latter-day manifestations of, and responses to, violence by Christian ethicists, and by political and social theologians. More tangentially, however, developing theological approaches to violence have also been manifest in the way Christian scholars have approached the doctrine of the atonement.

On the one hand, theologians such as J. Denny Weaver, Joel Green, Tim Gorringe, Christopher Marshall, and Rita Nakishima Brock have suggested variously baleful connections between penal substitutionary and satisfaction-based models of atonement and retributive and/or martial approaches to justice-making—approaches that are presented as fostering, rather than resisting or mitigating, violence. On the other hand, theologians from mainly conservative evangelical constituencies like Don Carson, Wayne Grudem, J. I Packer, I. Howard Marshall, and David Wells have defended penal substitution in particular as central to understanding how God deals with sin and evil, and have either implicitly or explicitly linked this to the retributive use of violence as a legitimate means of resisting sin and evil. This study, however, suggests a somewhat different approach.

Smith argues strongly here that attempts at "non-violent" doctrines of God and atonement are unfeasibly disconnected from Scripture, tradition, and majority Christian experience. At the same time, however, he insists that while satisfaction and penal substitution address the forensic and juridical dimensions of redemption, in and of themselves they underplay the palpable, ontological threat represented by Satan and his angels—a threat periodically expressed through both Old and New Testaments in violent attacks on the people of God, and met in both Testaments with resistance, which might at times be non-violent, but which is often plainly violent. Hence, whereas Denny Weaver sees the Christus Victor model construed by Gustav Aulen from patristic and Reformation sources in the 1930s as adaptable to a modern "non-violent" approach, Smith contends that this is only possible by an expunging, symbolizing, or demythologizing of the demonic—and of demonic violence in particular—that betrays exegetical anachronism, hermeneutical "Marcionism," and cultural chauvinism.

With specific regard to the doctrine of God, Smith argues that while God must be defined ontologically and intrinsically as Love, Scripture and experience compel the conclusion that he is also both able and willing to use violence "extrinsically," as a function of his will to effect justice, redemption, and salvation. While proponents of "non-violent" theologies often set divine love over against violence as something innately evil, Smith develops Miroslav Volf's notion of violence as a facet of the "might," "force," and "power" that God harnessed constructively in the creation of an ordered and "good" cosmos from a chaotic void. When the orderliness and goodness of God's thus-created world is assailed by sin and evil, Smith follows Hans Boersma in proposing that violence can, in fact, be a positive outworking of God's hospitality—and, indeed, of God's love. When such sin and evil are as frequently and as violently associated as they are in the Bible with "an actual, evil enemy opposed to both God and his purposes"—that is, with the devil and his legions—Smith submits that it is understandable that the God of the Bible should be seen so often intentionally to harness actual violence to combat that actual enemy. Smith offers impressive exegetical evidence to support this point, importantly adducing "violent" New Testament texts like the temple incident (Matt 21:12–13, par.), Romans 13, and Revelation

13–14, as well as more frequently-invoked Old Testament examples like the Genesis flood, the destruction of Sodom and Gomorrah, and the "ban" on Canaan. Thus, Smith also challenges the tendency to Testamental dualism (or "Marcionism") of Anabaptist, pacifist, and other apologists for a "non-violent" God, who risk unduly cleaving apart "law" and "gospel" in their quest to dissociate Jesus from the martial history of his own people, Israel.

Relating all of this more specifically to the cross, Smith emphasises that although Jesus is clearly a victim rather than a perpetrator of violence, he is nonetheless a *willing participant* in the drama of salvation which has his execution at its heart: setting his face towards it in order to see the "greater life-good" of his Father's loving and redemptive will accomplished—a greater life-good that Christus Victor underlines more powerfully than satisfaction or penal substitution alone, by linking the resurrection more overtly to the crucifixion in its dramatic theodicy. Smith engages in a rewarding dialogue with the Reformed theologian Nicholas Wolterstorff on this point, preferring Wolterstorff's account of a God "irresistibly" disposed to vanquish evil to René Girard's better-known theory of "mimetic violence," which Smith finds ontologically deficient, and insufficiently heedful of the qualitative distinction that must always be maintained between God's appropriation of violence *as God* and our application of it as creatures marred by sin (cf. Deut 32:35; Rom 12:19). As Smith puts in his Conclusion, the fact that violence has been "the bane of human history" does not mean that God cannot "endorse or even utilise extrinsic violence as a means of accomplishing *his* goals."

I started with various praxeological reflections on the timeliness of this book as it relates to contexts of violence in today's world. At the *viva voce* examination that approved the original text for a PhD, I suggested that both the author and his future readers might fruitfully regard the fine foundational work done here as a basis for more concentrated exploration of specific instances of violent conflict that have proved especially challenging for Christians, as well as for others. For example, certain of those who supported the German Confessing Church against Hitler in the 1930s, or who backed the Kairos Document's opposition to apartheid in 1980s South Africa, justified armed resistance against each regime on the basis that they represented the Antichrist, Satan, or some other embodiment of evil. Indeed, as chief drafter of the former text, Karl Barth would later suggest that some governments or political leaders might become in effect one of the Beasts of Revelation 13 rather than the benign emperor wielding the sword of justice in Romans 13—and that those who do so might deserve violent overthrow rather than obedience. Given that Smith's apologetic for divinely-appropriated and divinely-sanctioned violence here rests on a substantive ontology of evil personified in Satan and his hordes, these examples might prove persuasive. Yet they nonetheless raise a crucial point about the reliability of *ascription*—or what Paul more specifically calls the "discernment of spirits" (1 Cor 12:10). If "rulers, authorities and powers" in this world *can* so thoroughly manifest the "spiritual forces of evil in the heavenly realms" (Eph 6:12) that they warrant violent opposition, and if God *does* use humans as agents in such violent opposition, what criteria can we apply in any instance to ensure that violence is justified—or more justified than, say, continued negotiation or sanctions? These, of course, are questions that cross over into moral and political theology, and I realise that this is essentially a book about the doctrine of God. Yet Smith's very stress on the *extrinsic* quality of divine violence means that it can only be *contingently* instantiated, as God deals with the world, and with human agents and institutions in the world—that is, in real life situations of conflict.

So as we "ground" this study we will need to consider why not all in the Confessing Church followed Dietrich Bonhoeffer in supporting the plot to assassinate Hitler in 1944. We will need to note that not all signatories to the Kairos Document supported all aspects of the ANC's insurrection. We will need to examine the significance of the fact that both Ronald Reagan and the Ayatollah Khomeni characterised each other's regimes as "Satanic" in the 1980s, yet did not ultimately go to war. And will we need to note, by contrast, that George W. Bush termed Iran, North Korea, and Iraq the "Axis of Evil" in 2002 before invading Iraq a year later. Martyn Smith has done the theological academy and the church a very valuable service in clarifying the terms by which we might coherently and constructively articulate the relationship of God to violence. His work will significantly enhance our scrutiny of particular cases like those I have described—even as those cases continue to test our discernment, and drive us to prayer. For these reasons I very much hope that this book enjoys a healthy readership, and stimulates lively debate, not only among systematic theologians, but also among ethicists, political theologians, and biblical scholars.

Revd. Dr. David Hilborn

Principal, St. John's School of Mission, Nottingham

Prolegomena[1]

THIS THESIS IS ABOUT God, atonement, divine violence and the demytholo-gization of Christian views of the Satan and the demonic realm. On the latter, Girard notes that in the period when the German theologian Rudolf Bultmann had such great influence, all the theologians who were up to date "demythologized" the Scriptures with all their might but, he adds, they did not even do the prince of this world the honor of demythologizing him.[2] On the contrary, this desire to demythologize is not so prevalent today with other previously dark entities instead subsumed into the modern consciousness via their adaptation from mysterious and evil to scientific. Hjelm takes the concept of "vampire" and examines its new and old paradigms in film observing that the move of the vampire away from the demonic and towards the scientific—a worldview ironically rejected only by the most hardcore fundamentalists of any religion—can be seen as an outcome of the sensitivity that a religiously and spiritually pluralistic culture engenders.[3]

The vampire presented as an evil, demonic being, only to be confronted and defeated by the forces of good manifest in either the cross or a religious representative is now perceived as one suffering from various explicable conditions and faced with a nemesis armed with technological devices. Evil not demythologized, but rather re-presented and enculturated in postmodern forms. The conjoining of evil and postmodernity often causes

---

1. Pannenberg asserts, "In the presentation of a theme there is nothing unusual about postponing the actual treatment in favor of a few preliminary remarks on the theme itself and the mode of presentation." Pannenberg, *Systematic Theology*, 1:26–27. He cites various presentations of Christian doctrine which begin with introductory observations, including the prologue of Lombard's *Sentences*, the first *quaestio* of the theological *Summa* of Aquinas, and Melanchthon's introductions to his *Loci communes* and his *Loci praecipui theologici*. We will do likewise.

2. Girard, *Satan Fall*, 32.

3. Hjelm, "Celluloid Vampires," 119.

societal and theological consternation; indeed, in his speculation upon what postmodern society might exclude from conversation, for example, Wink concludes:

> Certainly not sex; at least in the more "sophisticated" circles accounts of sexual exploits scarcely raise an eyebrow. But if you want to bring all talk to a halt in shocked embarrassment, every eye riveted on you, try mentioning angels, or demons, or the devil. You will be quickly appraised for signs of pathological violence and then quietly shunned.[4]

In case Wink's observations appear dated it should be noted that in more recent times various invisible and visible forces, or monsters have become part of the postmodern vista and its parlance. In an article entitled "Monsters: The Theology of Frankenstein, Werewolves, Vampires and Zombies," Beck notes the various ways in which these monsters have taken on new meaning and content as a way of engaging with existential fears as well as confronting and understanding the world at large.[5]

Moving back to the primary focus of this thesis, however, in terms of concerns about divine violence, particularly in the atonement –in both ancient and contemporary contexts– these too are acknowledged as potentially controversial areas of study and yet ones that should not and must not be ignored.[6] The endeavor to engage with and expound these thorny themes requires explicit theological parameters, namely that dogmatics has the presupposition, a *petitio principii*, that there *is* a God revealed through a Word—spoken, written and incarnated. Indeed, "God" is the key-word in theological vocabulary; a theology without God would be like Hamlet without the Prince of Denmark.[7]

Yet, in regard to the quest to remain aloof from a priori perspectives in the face of contentious issues, the illusory nature of theological objectivity must be acknowledged; the search for "unconditional certainty"[8] is now

---

4. Wink, *Unmasking the Powers*, 1.

5. Beck, *Experimental Theology* (blog), October 26, 2010, http://experimentaltheology.blogspot.co.uk/2010/10/monsters-theology-of-frankenstein.html.

6. Boersma, *Violence, Hospitality and the Cross*, 42. He further postulates that "the sheer number of articles and books in the last few decades implicating traditional models of the atonement in brutality and abuse make it necessary for us to reflect carefully on the issue." Ibid., 42.

7. Macquarrie, *God-Talk*, 99.

8. Arguing that scientific endeavor is subjective and prone to aesthetic prejudice and interests, Polanyi notes, "Theories of the scientific method which try to explain the establishment of scientific truth by any purely objective formal procedure are doomed to failure. Any process of enquiry unguided by intellectual passions would inevitably

deemed an epistemic fallacy falling victim to its own desire for objectivity. Indeed, in his assessment of the word "hermeneutics" Davis notes that it takes its name from Hermes, a richly ambivalent deity who is both the messenger of heaven and the one who blinds those whom he leads into the realm of the dead! The metaphorical root of the term should, he warns, "alert us to the possibility that unconscious, archetypal structures may both positively and negatively influence the direction of our search for understanding." He concludes that there is a universal assumption that a so-called "right hermeneutic" could unlock all the mysteries of revelation in unambiguous terms; this is, he says, "a fact that blinds us to the dark side of every hermeneutic."[9]

Again, in a chapter entitled "Certainty as the Way to Nihilism," Newbigin charts the rise and fall of the Western concept of "certainty" from the seventeenth and eighteenth centuries and the mathematical physics of Isaac Newton to the individualism and multi-culturalism espoused today. He concludes that there is an irony in human history which has sought absolute certainty and yet this quest for indubitable certainty has led to what seems to be an abandonment of the claim to be able to know the truth.[10] "Detached observers," reporting reality from a safe distance therefore find themselves at the center of their observation, necessarily affecting perceptions and findings, making themselves the "locus of absolute truth."[11] Thus, in undertaking potentially provocative theological explorations, instead of claiming to work outside such constrictions, it is prudent to admit inevitable agenda and involvement, simply making sure that this is not disruptive or intrusive to overall objectivity.

When examining divine predicates and knowability, including potentially unpalatable findings such as the presence of violence, parameters must be set and criteria of understanding applied. Those involved in apologetics, dogmatics, or theology, of course, aspire to operate in the "right way"; the difficulty is to find a universally agreeable understanding of this "way." Those advocating biblical theology rightly give primacy to Scripture as their yardstick for adjudicating on theological issues, particularly contentious ones; this pre-eminence is such that possibilities other than those indicated by the Word of God will not come into consideration at all.[12]

Even for those upholding this position there remains a clear and present danger in every theological era of "letting go" doctrines which do not

---

spread out into a desert of trivialities." Polanyi, *Personal Knowledge*, 135.

9. Davis, "Seeds of Violence," 35.

10. Newbigin, *Pluralist Society*, 36.

11. Pannenberg, *Systematic Theology*, 1:47.

12. Barth, *Church Dogmatics (CD)*, 2/1:9.

appeal to or, in fact, scandalize a contemporary audience; such is the case today with divine violence.[13] For the Christian Gospel and its proclamation, however, the danger is not solely one of letting go—but rather of seeking a redefinition for a post-modern secular and religious audience—this, however, is a potentially disingenuous activity. Finlan, for example, reinterprets what he sees as the salient features of the Gospel message in response to his concern that modern proponents have overemphasized certain elements at the expense of others.

> The Incarnation is an essential Christian idea: the Atonement— at least one that entails God as Sacrifice Demander and Jesus as punishment-bearer—is not. It is a mistake to identify atonement as the central Christian doctrine, although it is central to the Pauline tradition, to First Peter, Hebrews, First John, and Revelation. But these books, in their entirety, compose only 39 percent of the NT. The main positive function of atonement doctrine has been to help transmit information about the Incarnation of the divine Son. But that information can be transmitted just as well without atonement, as is seen in the Gospels and Acts of the Apostles.[14]

Theological endeavor should and must therefore always have the freedom to arrive at potentially difficult findings, even if these contradict previously held views or unsettle contemporary audiences.[15] Theology must be careful not to borrow from elsewhere a fundamental outlook or account of society or history and then to see what theological insights might cohere with it. No such fundamental account, in the sense of something neutral, rational or universal is, however, available and instead theology has to provide its own account of the final causes at work in human history on the basis of its own particular and historically specific faith.[16]

---

13. In his assessment of humanity's perceived irreducible progress, Volf notes that from the Enlightenment onwards the optimistic vision of society is that "all irrational and anti-social drives will be progressively suppressed and violence increasingly eliminated from social life." Volf, *Exclusion and Embrace*, 279. It has followed, as we shall see, that in such a social milieu violence will also be perceived as negative and thereby removed from theological speculation.

14. Finlan, *Problems with Atonement*, 120.

15. In delineating the pitfalls of the theological task, Macquarrie warns that sometimes, "in a pathetic desire to be 'contemporary' and 'relevant,' [the theologian] reduces the Christian faith to a pale reflection of whatever happens to be the currently popular philosophy." Macquarrie, *Christian Theology*, xi.

16. Milbank, *Theology and Social Theory*, 382.

Whatever perspectives are chosen and whatever issues prioritized, an agenda is de facto taken. So instead of being stultified by myriad options limiting objective reasoning a position is chosen, worked with and *within*, acknowledging its associated weaknesses and celebrating its strengths. What cannot be upheld is the illusion of transcending individual particularity, exchanging "the view from here" for "the view from nowhere" instead of a "view from somewhere else."[17] Everyone seeking answers, in whatever field of enquiry, cannot achieve "objectivity" because it does not exist—the only option is to accept and work within inevitable subjectivity.

Acknowledgement of these limitations and the futility of the fabled "view from nowhere," as Nagel called it, are thus essential theological prerequisites, especially when engaging with topics, like divine violence, which engender division and diversity.[18] This concession does not necessitate marginalization, but acceptance of natural and inherent human shortcomings, thereby ultimately producing a stronger theological and epistemological position.

The utilization of this model requires academic humility and an awareness that the chief tools of theology have always been words and their related concepts with the proviso that words are finite, drawn from the pool of language and experience and presented by humans making no more claim to have transcended their finitude and sinfulness than can their readers.[19] There are, of course, inevitable human problems in trying to understand an infinite, spiritual, eternal "being" whose transcendent nature is de facto resistant to definition, let alone one who may be manifesting predicates, such as violence, that can be construed as both controversial and contradictory.

In his appeal to personal knowledge Polanyi thus argues against belief in "scientific detachment" in which the observer claims impartial objectivity. He proposes, rather, that the enquirer acknowledges involvement in their investigation without having to defend against subjectivity.[20] The mistaken aspiration is the belief that one's subjectivity may be replaced by pure

17. Hart, *Faith Thinking* , 64.

18. Ibid., 48.

19. Hart, *Regarding Karl Barth*, 174–75.

20. Polanyi posits, "Such is the *personal participation* of the knower in all acts of understanding. But this does not make our understanding *subjective*. Comprehension is neither an arbitrary act nor a passive experience, but a responsible act claiming universal validity. Such knowing is indeed *objective* in the sense of establishing contact with a hidden reality; a contact that is defined as the condition for anticipating an indeterminate range of yet unknown (and perhaps yet inconceivable) true implications." Polanyi, *Personal Knowledge*, vii–vii.

objective observation—a position which does not exist.[21] Consequently, rather than eschewing preconceived viewpoints, a commitment must be made to what is perceived to be the most effective place from which to work.[22]

Barth pre-empts Polanyi, stating that the a priori possibility of knowledge of God presupposes a place *beyond* such knowledge from where it can be judged. Acceptance of such a neutral "place" of observation also presupposes a theory of knowledge as a hinterland where consideration of the truth, worth and competence of the Word of God, on which knowledge of God is grounded, can for a time be suspended.[23] Blumenthal questions the viability of such a "hinterland":

> To be a theologian is to be on the boundary. To be a theologian is to be a voice for the tradition. It is to speak its words, to teach its message, and to embody its authority. However, there is no single entity one can call the tradition. There is no one message, no sole authoritative voice. Rather, the tradition is multivocal, multifaceted; and some of it has been repressed. Hence, no one can speak for the tradition in its entirety.[24]

That which has been "repressed," in relation to divine violence and the demythologization of the Satan, are primary issues in this thesis and the arguments presented will accept the contentious nature of even attempting to ascribe violence to an ontologically loving God and of the potential re-personification and re-spiritualization of the Satan—both issues that are generating scholarly interest.[25]

The theologian must, therefore, accept the position of speaking from within a tradition or some part of it, garnering whatever authority, epistemic reasoning and evidence is possible whilst acknowledging inevitable

---

21. Vahhoozer warns that those seeking to define "postmodernity" do so at their own peril because whilst definitions may appear to "bask in the glow of impartiality" they instead invariably exclude something and are therefore complicit in politics. A definition of postmodernity, therefore, "is as likely to say more about the person offering the definition than it is of 'the postmodern.'" Vanhoozer, "Condition of Postmodernity," 3. So too with theological endeavor and expression.

22. Hart, *Faith Thinking*, 65.

23. Barth, *CD* 2/1:5.

24. Blumenthal, *Facing the Abusing God*, 3.

25. Amongst contemporary theologians attempting to address these issues are Boersma, *Violence, Hospitality and the Cross*; Boyd, *God at War*; Girard, *Violence and the Sacred*; Gunton, *Actuality of Atonement*; Hamerton-Kelly, *Sacred Violence*; Heim, *Saved from Sacrifice*; Darby-Ray, *Deceiving the Devil*; Weaver, *Nonviolent Atonement*; Wink, *Engaging the Powers*.

and necessary limitations and listening to the inner resonances of the tradition in order to measure their own music against the inner tones of the tradition to the best of their ability, recognizing the scale of the task and its endemic dangers and pitfalls.[26] On God, his character and predicates, including divine violence, and of that or whom he is contending against and how he might counter and overcome, it is patently not possible to say everything; *something*, however, can be said. That is enough.

Definition alone cannot, however, be the primary task of theology, but is instead subsidiary to trying out the new metaphors and models drawn from general experience in order to express aspects of the God-world relation as experienced by people today.[27] The theologian is not merely a processor of abstract, objective facts but one who incorporates elements of poetry, interpretation and artistic creativity. Additionally theology includes an inherently heuristic element as theologian and theological community explore, grow, experiment and change, maintaining an attitude of provisionality in order to facilitate openness to the possibility of error, ancient and modern, and the hope of potential break-throughs in the endeavor to better know, understand and engage with the living, eternal, God—his purposes and plans and his chosen means of achieving them.[28]

These problems and limitations, however, suggest the potential failure of theological endeavor before it begins, relegating it to a finite, subjective, philosophical and linguistic exercise steeped in futility.[29] This is not the case at all. Progress can be made, even with such contentious issues as divine violence and God's battle against evil, by proceeding with humility and dili-

26. Blumenthal, *Facing the Abusing God*, 3.

27. Hart, *Regarding Karl Barth*, 181.

28. Commenting on the Patristic era Kelly notes that, "Modern students are sometimes surprised at the diversity of treatment accorded by even the later fathers to such a mystery as the Atonement; and it is a commonplace that certain fathers (Origen is the classic example) who were later adjudged heretics counted for orthodox in their lifetimes. The explanation is not that the early Church was indifferent to the distinction between orthodoxy and heresy. Rather it is that, while from the beginning the broad outline of revealed truth was respected as a sacrosanct inheritance from the apostles, its theological explication was to a large extent left unfettered. Only gradually, and even then in regard to relatively few doctrines which became subjects of debate, did the tendency to insist upon precise definition and rigid uniformity assert itself." Kelly, *Early Christian Doctrines*, 4.

29. "In the public mind statements about God are mere assertions which are ascribed to the subjectivity of the speaker and the truth claim of which not only needs to be generally tested before it can be accepted but is for the most part set aside in advance, the belief being that the testing will lead nowhere and that the truth claims of statements about God are not even worth discussing publicly." Pannenberg, *Systematic Theology*, 1:64.

gence whilst concurrently acknowledging the scale and parameters of the issues and with the application of due provisionality to theological propositions. God-talk can, of course, occur but always mindful that language, necessarily and by definition, is a limited medium; if human speech is problematic then human speech about God is all the more so.[30] There is certainly more to the truth than words can convey; this does not mean, however, that nothing should be said, but rather to say little, carefully and provisionally.

30. Hart, *Regarding Karl Barth*, 173.

1

God & Violence

The Problem

RESEARCH IN RECENT DECADES that implicates traditional models of the atonement in brutality, abuse and violence suggests careful reflection be made on the issue.[1] Whilst each generation views and understands itself within the broader context of theological development it also does so in relation to previous doctrines and creeds. As thought and human history develops the temptation can be to jettison unpalatable ideas due to their impact on current sensibilities.[2] Instead, options should remain open until there is substantive evidence to believe otherwise at least in order to challenge the affiliated belief that there has historically and theologically been a de facto positive and progressive evolution of human morality, understanding and practice.[3]

The central issue to be addressed in this thesis, therefore, is whether God has, however minimally, an intrinsic part of his character that is violent and whether this violence is essential in terms of how God both chooses to deal with and reveal himself to humanity. Further, it will be considered if such violence is necessary as God's chosen means of overcoming an actual, ontological enemy, the Satan and a demonic, evil realm. Finally, the Christus Victor atonement model will be explored as potentially the best, perhaps the only, means of understanding and presenting these features and purposes of God. It will then be considered whether divine violence is

---

1. Boersma, *Violence, Hospitality and the Cross*, 42.

2. Boersma notes that "the concerns about divine violence in the atonement—both ancient and contemporary—are significant and should not be ignored." Ibid.

3. As posited in Pinker, *The Better Angels*.

ontological and soteriologically asserted as the essential and only means of The Satan's demise.

These issues call into question the very nature of the Christian Gospel and how it should be framed; not only in terms of what it *is* but for *whom* it is and on what *basis*. The question whether humans are well disposed to embrace a Divine Message that includes violence because of problems of palatability is, however, theologically irrelevant to how the Gospel is understood and presented. Walker notes that the Gospel is not only the central message of the Christian faith: it is both the story and its telling that makes the message become gospel.[4] Specifically it is a Gospel detailing a macro-narrative, a salvation history that presents God as One who urgently desires to be known, perhaps at any cost and by any means, but who has an enemy to himself, his message and its recipients.

Most of the New Testament uses of εὐαγγέλιον are in Paul and in almost half of the passages where he uses the term he speaks of it in the absolute, not using nouns or adjectives to define it, such was the extant familiarity with the term; it remains, however, a somewhat elusive word, not compliant to expression in a brief formula. Predominantly it is a *nomen actionis* describing the act of proclamation, praise at the preaching of the Gospel and the beginning of activity as an evangelist. This "Gospel," therefore, does not bear witness to merely an historical event for the concepts it recounts, namely resurrection and exaltation, are beyond the scope of historical judgment, thereby transcending history. Nor is "Gospel" a set of narratives and sayings concerning Jesus to be believed and learnt by Christians; on the contrary, it is a word and a concept related to human reality and to be perceived as living power.[5] In contrast to its usage in the Old Testament and in Jewish and secular Greek literature, where it meant "news of victory" or "recompense for a good report" εὐαγγέλιον in the New Testament denotes news concerning or coming from God.[6] The biblical noun "gospel" is beheld in the notion of *euangelion,* the *evangel,* or message and is perceived as a positive, living message from God that must be treated and relayed with urgency and import.

A key paradox of these gospel propositions and of atonement doctrine in particular is that they present an unusual marriage of primitive concepts of a violent god and the revealed teaching of a loving God.[7] These seemingly mutually exclusive and apparently contradictory theological elements being

4. Walker, *Telling the Story,* 12.

5. Friedrich, "εὐαγγέλιον," 729, 731.

6. Strecker, "εὐαγγέλιον," 70.

7. Finlan, *Problems with Atonement,* 98.

conjoined and in this instance being expressed as "good news" represent another key subject receiving attention in this thesis. These difficult issues can be framed in terms of whether the marriage of an ancient idea, in this instance atonement and a newer one of God's love, can nonetheless endure or whether they are mismatched from the start, incorporating a pouring of new wine into old wineskins.[8] Certainly these are thorny and controversial issues that at best appear to represent a conflicted message and at worst a conflicted God. Nonetheless a resolution will be explored in order to avert the accusation that in atonement models little more is being done than to provide mere restatements of the happening and not explanations.[9]

Rather than setting up an interpretative and perceptual dichotomy between a message of peace and violence it might be asserted that religion is nothing other than an immense effort to keep the peace and that *the sacred is violence,* but that if religious man worships violence it is only insofar as the worship of violence is supposed to bring peace; religion is entirely concerned with peace, but the means it has of bringing it about are never free of sacrificial violence.[10] This linking of violence and peace as necessary corollaries within the sacred and the religious is suggestive and will be at the forefront of this thesis.

It will be argued that the desire to disassociate God with violence has caused the revision of significant elements of many theological propositions. This is perhaps particularly true of the main atonement models—particularly in regard to God making a deal with or deceiving the Devil, or of sacrificing his innocent Son on the cross; indeed, God can only be shielded from the violence of the cross at the cost of parting ways with the tradition of the Church.[11] There may be times where such a parting is legitimate, or even necessary; but only after careful consideration and because of concern over explicitly non-biblical doctrine or unsubstantiated theological perspectives. It should be with great caution that such a parting ever occurred and especially if it is in order to match a priori desires that require the delivery of doctrines that "sit well" with particular personal, doctrinal or historical preconceptions of God. Rather than changing theology to match a view of God it is instead apposite to consider how biblical theology might change to fit the revealed nature of God, perhaps including his use of, association with, endorsement or predicate of violence. Whether the resulting theology is palatable or likeable is secondary.

8. Ibid.

9. Winter, *The Atonement,* 35.

10. Girard, *Things Hidden,* 32.

11. Boersma, *Violence, Hospitality and the Cross,* 43.

The atonement is, of course, essential to Christianity and any doctrine deemed to have such primacy must, of course, be thoroughly explored. When a doctrine includes potentially problematic ramifications, notably in associating God with violence, then such exploration must be undertaken with extreme caution. It must not, however, waver from its findings, however unpalatable, unfashionable and shocking they might be.

Religious Use and Understanding of Violence

Before considering violence and divine predicates, it is necessary to construct a definition of violence as it will be used and understood in this thesis. The definition is our own: *violence is a potentially irresistible force (whether physical, mental, spiritual or verbal) exerted to achieve a desired end.*[12]

Exertion can be positive or negative depending on various factors: the context of the exertion; the reason for it; who is exerting and upon whom the exertion is occurring. There is also a difference between exertion being manifest as either persuasion or force. It is incorrect to correlate these two concepts, perceiving them to have the same meaning, because persuasion is not simply force, a point illustrated by the frequency with which people are able to resist persuasion. This, in fact, is what makes force force and violence violence: potential irresistibility.[13]

Conversely, whilst violence manifested as persuasion *can* usually be resisted, this is not always the case. Likewise, even violence of the most vociferous and torturous force can still be endured, resisted and, in some cases, overcome and redeemed by those subjected to it. An outstanding example of such fortitude and overcoming in the face of extreme violence is the life and experiences of Primo Levi, the Italian Jew who survived imprisonment in Auschwitz. He details numerous stories of individuals and the ways in which they resisted and overcame their circumstances in the concentration camp in *Moments of Reprieve*; Ignatieff notes of Levi's observations that "in showing us that it was possible to remain a human being in conditions of extremity and horror, the author shows us what it *is* to be a human being."[14] Such distinctions highlight the difficulty in proffering a definitive

---

12. Acknowledgement is given to the works that helped the construction of this definition, most notably Cavanaugh, *The Myth of Religious Violence*; Chase, "Introduction," 9–19; and in particular, Lawrence, "General Introduction." Lawrence concludes that "there is no general theory of violence apart from its practices. In other words, theories of violence must be as varied as the practices within which they occur; shadows abound, but rays of light also glimmer, and they, too, must be noted." Ibid., 7.

13. Jacobs, "Afterword," 234.

14. Ignatieff, preface to Levi, *Moments of Reprieve*, 3.

classification on violence; what is offered instead is a broad schema that best represents the usual understanding of violence, its purpose and parameters.

Persuasion and Coercion

The feature, in terms of the means of violence and human response, is developed by Foucault who argues that there is both a blurred line and a possible nuance between persuasion and coercion.[15] He idealizes a violent past that inflicted the worst kind of government-sanctioned, torturous violence in order to discipline and punish the individual, warning society against perpetrating anti-social activities.[16] By inference Foucault concedes the appalling nature of such public violence, nonetheless preferring this to his feared alternative of a modern world which instead punishes and subdues its subjects using modern controlling techniques such as psychological therapy with its concomitant *self*-disciplining and *self*-policing.[17] At least in the "good old days," he argues, the violence was not secret and therefore not illusionary or insidious, but rather clear, blatant and intelligible. People therefore knew where they stood in regard to violence and punishment and were under no illusions as to either the reasons for it or the need for its public implementation.[18]

The "Violence" of Conversion

A strict construction of Foucault's argument leads to the conclusion that modern, proselytizing religions such as Christianity and in particular its "seeker services," offering the non-believer opportunity to hear its message, pose a more dangerously coercive ideological model than the Spanish Inquisition's *auto-da-fé*.[19] The thin ideological line dividing these two means of "persuasion" is particularly apparent in a religious context, with its complicated set of agendas, methods and expectations. Not least amongst these agendas is the desire to convert and thereby change those currently outside its scope and parameters.[20]

15. Foucault, *Discipline and Punish*, 1991.

16. For a particularly disturbing description of an officially sanctioned, violent public punishment from history, see ibid., 3–6.

17. Jacobs, "Afterword," 232.

18. See Pinker for his thesis that, conversely, violence has subsided historically. Pinker, *The Better Angels*, 2011.

19. Jacobs, "Afterword," 233.

20. Walker argues that the Christian gospel is not a grand narrative to "shore up"

This desire is not seen as being negative, much less violent, by those seeking such change; instead, this agenda is by definition at the very center of any proselytizing religion's mandate. Conversely, Blumenthal notes that those proclaiming a message of love that necessitates conversion do not understand the nature of the love they profess. Instead, he asserts, love is the acceptance of the other, not the desire or attempt to change them and especially not through emotional and spiritual violence.[21] This raises perplexing issues for those who disavow God of violence whilst concurrently upholding the importance of personal transformation of outlook in order to facilitate the embracing of a relational model of engagement between God and humanity.[22]

This idea of the violent nature of mission and evangelism presents a further problem for any religion advocating expansion and conversion. After all, in regard to the *auto-da-fé* it sought to burn the body, whilst the stratagems of religious evangelism go further, seeking to capture the will.[23] Foucault's point initially seems like a *reductio ad absurdum* when the blatant differences between literal torture and death and an act of emotional or spiritual persuasion are compared. Conceptually, however, there is much in common between two methods that in their respective, but ultimately coercive and forceful ways, both seek the same goal of change and conversion. In other words, both are exerting a potentially irresistible force in order to achieve a desired end—or rather, they are both violent.

The charge leveled against certain elements, historical and doctrinal, of the Christian Church and the God it claims to represent is that throughout history outright violence and violent coercion have been used against people in order to convert or restrain, physically, emotionally, theologically or praxeologically. Dawkins recounts instances, both modern and biblical, in which believers and their God have committed acts that can only reasonably be described as flagrantly violent.[24] Such observations are not so much

western civilization—"the purpose of the story is not to improve the world but to turn people away from its false hopes and self-delusions." It is not there to functionally change a person's outlook and perspectives but to initiate ontological change, a conversion. Christianity, he concludes, "is in effect a rescue mission for humankind, for through the telling of the story, people find themselves enabled to indwell it, make the story their own, and discover in it ultimate concern—their true end." Walker, *Telling the Story*, 8.

21. Pfau and Blumenthal, "The Violence of God," 192.

22. Theologians in this camp include Boersma, *Violence, Hospitality and the Cross*; Holmes, *Wondrous Cross*; Marshall, *Aspects of Atonement*; Stott, *Cross of Christ*; and Weaver, *Nonviolent Atonement*.

23. Jacobs, "Afterword," 234.

24. In a chapter entitled "The 'Good Book' and the Changing Moral Zeitgeist,"

accusations but a simple recounting of biblical stories requiring honest engagement and response rather than denial or avoidance.[25] The charges they
represent are leveled at the Church and the One who instituted it and upon
whom it is based.

The further accusation following from these charges is that a Christian
reading about God's passion towards the "lost" might then engage in pros-
elytization that violates the integrity and conscience of those being sought
in much the same way as God and his ancient followers have done.[26] This
could either be in consciously or subliminally and unconsciously chosen efforts. The charge nonetheless remains that God and Christians are, to some
degree, caught up de facto in an endeavor that will always, by its nature, be
at least coercive and at worst cross the line into outright, explicit violence.

Jesus as a Model

Another means of understanding the character and violence of God is to
reflect on Jesus of Nazareth as the physical, historical and human manifestation of God; the plans and purposes of Jesus are given priority as a means
to explicate the place and priority of violence within Christianity.[27] Such
engagement with Jesus facilitates understanding of his outlook, teaching,
praxis and methodology in order to express God's perspectives and goals.
His actions, outlook and beliefs are analyzed so that when Jesus is cited as
a model for those presenting theologies of violence it is done within the
context of his being God's incarnate revelation to humanity.

For example, Jesus was active within the Jewish tradition, in which it
was decisive for all powers hostile to God to be overcome. Faith in the Jewish deity Yahweh knew two primary ways of achieving this: the destruction
of enemies and/or their conversion.[28] This model for Jesus' mission presents

Dawkins delineates a range of actions and events ascribed to God and his followers
throughout the Old Testament, the New Testament, and within modern western Christianity. Dawkins, *God Delusion*, 268–316.

25. Dawkins is not alone in highlighting perceived inconsistencies in the Bible and
its claim to represent a loving God who nonetheless appears to endorse and utilize often
extreme forms of violence and actions that are "just plain weird . . ." (Ibid., 268). Other
writers addressing similar issues include Mills, *Atheist Universe*; Stenger, *God the Failed
Hypothesis*; Harris, *End of Faith*; and Hitchens, *God Is not Great*.

26. Chase, "Introduction," 10.

27. For a thorough-going analysis of Jesus as the physical manifestation of God's
saving activity from Israel to Christ, see Schmiechen, "Christ the Goal of Creation,"
222–52.

28. Schwager, "Religion as the Foundation," 122. Schwager cites Zeph 3:9f; Mal 1:11
and Isa 60:1–5 as key examples of this destruction/conversion model.

him as a new paradigm through which God manifests and reveals his so-teriological purposes.[29] This would be accomplished with less emphasis on overt, tangible violence through literal, historical destruction and opposition to various human power-constructs and more by overcoming God's enemies manifest in the spiritual sphere of the Satan and the demonic realm. Wright highlights this change of focus in Jesus' life and ministry arguing that it is a theme that looms large in the Gospels. Instead of Jesus helping Jews and others to fight Rome or the Gentiles, he rather encourages those wanting to inherit his coming Kingdom to battle against the Satan and evil powers. Wright notes that stories of the kingdom of Yahweh were essentially stories of conflict; summarizing this conflict by claiming,

> The true god was not at the moment ruling the world in the way that he intended to do. Evil powers had usurped his authority, and they would have to be defeated if he was to regain his rightful throne.[30]

It was to the defeat of these evil powers that God, in Jesus, would now turn his attention.

Jesus & Confrontation

This does not mean that human constructs are free from being a means of demonic influence. Macquarrie notes that it was the original sin of idolatry that caused humans to turn from worship of the Being to the beings, causing an ontological rift between God and humanity. The practice of humans putting some*thing* before some*one* in regard to their response to God has meant, he argues, that anything other than God which becomes of ultimate concern is "demonic" in the sense that it dominates humans, their lives and their relationship with their Maker.[31] In perceiving the demonic and sin as individual and structural social forms, the way is open for ancient images of salvation as victory over hostile powers to take on fresh significance and meaning.[32]

---

29. Fiddes notes, "in ancient Israel the critical act was the ritual of sacrifice, and for Christian believers atonement happens because of the death of Jesus in a Roman execution one Friday afternoon." Fiddes, *Past Event*, 4.

30. Wright, *Jesus and the Victory*, 448.

31. See Macquarrie, *Principles of Christian Theology*, 260–63.

32. Fiddes, "Salvation," 177–78.

Whilst this cosmological context may be a primary way of understanding Jesus' priorities in fulfilling God's soteriological mission,[33] it does not follow that there is a lack of evidence for him addressing injustice and unrighteousness when he encountered it in tangible form. For example, on the basis of his understanding of the biblical terminology surrounding "power" and "structure" Yoder argues that in modern social analysis these concepts can only reasonably be understood in social and political terms and that, therefore, Jesus was engaging both cosmologically and *politically* throughout his ministry and mission.[34] Further, those reading Jesus' denunciation of hypocrisy and his concomitant physical disruption of the temple market[35] may be forgiven for seeing some acts of violence as being advocated by Jesus himself and perhaps, therefore, as necessary acts of righteous indignation against a wayward religion and culture.[36]

Such instances could allow the Christian to cite precedence from Jesus for their own acts of violence against whatever regime, structure or person they find unrighteous or counter to their perception of Christian purposes. In discussing this phenomenon Niebuhr illustrates such an outlook in Frank's consideration of the Spanish conquistadors who invaded and subdued the indigenous population in South America in the fifteenth and sixteenth centuries. After committing acts of the most grotesque and violent kind Frank alludes to the Christian faith that sustained and justified such outrages because for the conquistador, "Within his cruelties is the intuition of his destiny as an agent of the divine."[37] This idea of working on God's behalf and within a modus operandi he is believed to have utilized and endorsed has continued to fuel, motivate and justify acts of violence by those aligning themselves with Christianity.[38]

---

33. Yoder notes that that it has been argued (the classic expression being Bultmann, *Theology of the New Testament*) that in the centuries following Jesus' death, when Christians found themselves in positions of social responsibility, they had to seek out sources other than Jesus for their own ethical insight and response. It is difficult to draw a specific ethical/political message from the Gospels because "Jesus had nothing much to say on the subject." Yoder, *Politics of Jesus*, 136.

34. Ibid., 136–38.

35. This will be explored in "The Temple Incident" below.

36. Chase, "Introduction," 10.

37. Waldo, *America Hispana*, 49; quoted in Niebuhr, *Moral Man*, 65.

38. For contemporary illustrations of this, see Juergensmeyer, *Terror in the Mind of God*.

The Possibility of Divine Violence

The following chapters delineate methods of interpreting language and bringing meaning to concepts via symbol and metaphor; first is the question of whether violence is connected with a God biblically revealed as potentially being ontologically love. For biblical reference to this concept from the New Testament, see 1 John 4: 7–21; of particular note is the ontological nature of the verse, "Whoever does not love does not know God, because God is love." (v8). Smalley observes that John does not merely say that "God loves," but rather that God is love which means that God is not only the source of love, but is love itself. Thus the assertion "God is love" means not simply, asserts Smalley, that love is *one* of his activities, but that *all* his activity is loving.[39] Further St. John states, "And so we know and rely on the love God has for us. God is love. Whoever lives in love lives in God, and God in him." (v16 NIV). Smalley concludes that the sentiments this verse portrays form the high point of the Johannine contemplation of God.[40] Conversely, Tracy argues for a metaphorical understanding of the Johannine understanding of God's nature in his letters. For him, John's statement that "God is love" does not say literally what God is but instead *produces* a metaphorical meaning for what God is like and in this re-descriptive sense, the statement defines, for Tracy, who for the Christian, God *is*.[41]

In the quest to understand the purpose and use of violence from such a God of love a conceptual duality, or antagonistic *dichotomy*, has developed in regard to violence and the created order. This is seen in chapter sub-headings such as "The Goodness of Creation Versus an Ontology of Violence."[42] Creation is presented as existing in a state in which original, implicit goodness came about because of the inherent love of the Creator; not because it had to exist and certainly not because of a battle that God engaged in with evil.[43]

Ancient Near Eastern Context

Ancient creation stories, in particular the Babylonian myth, make it possible to consider the pre-eminence of violence in the chronological revelation of the created world. Delineating the full story of the Babylonian Creation

39. Smalley, *John*, 228.

40. Ibid., 243.

41. Tracy, "Metaphor and Religion," 103.

42. Middleton and Walsh, *Truth is Stranger*, 152.

43. Ibid., 153.

Epic, Unger notes that in the primitive age when only living uncreated matter existed the mythical god-figures present gave birth to many offspring who were so annoying in their conduct that their father, Apsu, made up his mind to do away with them.[44] This violent behavior was only a pre-cursor to what would follow as another god, Ea, found out about this plan, foiled it and gave birth to Marduk—the great Babylonian hero-god of the Epic. The ensuing battles and destruction of enemies are presented as a violent suppression of anyone and anything that stood in the way of the gods who created this world. It is a bloody and violent story of war, intrigue, obsession and decimation; evil and violence are pre-eminent and remain central to understanding the Babylonian gods, how they created the world and the way they would rule and sustain it.

The question as to the chronological appearance of goodness or violence in the creation process is addressed in the Babylonian creation story *Enuma Elish,* a text that was likely to have been known by the ancient people of Israel.[45] In this account, the god Marduk has to subdue the chaos monster Tiamat before going on to create the world out of Tiamat's dead body.[46] The key issue is that the world's elements of evil emanate inevitably out of the evil from which it was originally made. Other Ancient Near Eastern (ANE) creation myths also observe that good is not always prior to evil in the chronology of creation, leading to the proposition that violence might be considered as an element in the godhead, or at least a means of divine revelation and the unfolding of a Deity's purposes.[47]

When these perspectives are contrasted with the Judeo-Christian creation stories it has led to the observation that the two positions are diametrically opposed.[48] Brueggemann acknowledges that the opening verses of the Genesis creation account suggest that God is at work on an already present chaotic reality and that the mood of this rhetoric shows God as serenely and supremely in charge without the presence of struggle, anxiety, or risk.[49] In contrast to other ANE creation myths this suggests that the biblical

44. Unger, "Babylonian and Biblical Accounts," 305–6.

45. See Heidel, *Babylonian Genesis,* 228–77 for the full text of this story and a commentary on it.

46. Placher, "Is God in Charge?," 94.

47. Dalley, "Epic of Gilgamesh," 228–77.

48. Wink contests that in the biblical account of creation, "a good God creates a good creation. Chaos does not resist order. Good is ontologically prior to evil." Wink, *Engaging the Powers,* 15.

49. Brueggemann, *Theology of the Old Testament,* 153.

God of creation is in providential control such that nothing outside of him can impede or influence his being, creation, or purposes.[50]

Conversely, a broad approach to themes common within ANE creation stories detects many shared macro-ideas. The Gilgamesh epic and the biblical account, for instance, agree on the existence of an invisible, supernatural world and a God or gods that are personal and can think, speak and have a desire and ability to communicate with humans and seek to control human affairs.[51] From the perspective of the biblical God with an ontology of love, creation comes about by divine choice and power as an inherently perfect and good thing for the fulfillment of a good God's purposes. This leads to the conclusion that a biblical worldview would not grant ontological pre-eminence to either evil or violence.[52] In fact, God is seen to be both fully in control of creation and at the helm of an ongoing plan of love to redeem people from evil and the consequences of their choices and actions.[53] A good God creates a good world and has a good plan for it and its inhabitants.[54]

The Chronology of Evil

This being the case, whether in God or creation, it follows that evil, as ontological source, and violence, as functional manifestation, are not necessarily synonymous or even conceptually conjoined. The world is sharply separated in its nature from the God who made it since it did not *emanate* from him but was called into being by a pronouncement of his will.[55] Notwithstanding this "separation," a world called into being at the behest of God and by his free will is by its nature his possession and he its creator, owner and Lord.[56]

50. By providence, Barth asserts, "is meant the superior dealings of the Creator with His creation, the wisdom, omnipotence and goodness with which he maintains and governs in time this distinct reality according to the counsel of His own will." Barth, *Church Dogmatics (CD)* 3/3:3.

51. Wenham, *Genesis 1–15*, xlviii.

52. Middleton and Walsh, *Truth Is Stranger*, 153.

53. Goldingay observes, "In creation God reaches out in grace to all people, and in living in an ordered, created universe humanity has the prior contact with God and his ways upon which conversation about the possibility of redemption can build." Goldingay, *Theological Diversity*, 220.

54. Gunton notes that "there is a history of relations between God and the world, so that the world which *was* created can be understood now to take shape in constant interaction with its creator and to be in dynamic process towards its completion." Gunton, *Christ and Creation*, 77–78.

55. Rad, *Old Testament Theology*, 142.

56. Ibid., 143.

Conversely, God's relationship to the world should not be seen in terms of his being a Creator who merely makes a Creation as just another act amongst many others. Such a view suggests the possibility of a gap and therefore the potential for an inherent difference between God and the world he has made. Rather than suggesting, therefore, that a creator God makes a creation as something distinct and separate from himself it is more apposite to project a closer, *integral* link.[57]

The link, whilst not necessarily ontological per se, is at least one of extreme proximity and identity, such that it would be difficult to argue for an evil world being made by a non-evil God. This scenario exacerbates the existence of a clear differential between evil and violence, because whilst violence *can* be borne out of an ontology of evil, this need not always be the case. Additionally, the idea of God having evil as an ontological trait is strongly refuted, as is the notion that God could ever functionally express evil.[58] Boersma observes:

> When theologians express fear of "implicating" God in violence, such implication is clearly understood as a negative thing. It seems unthinkable—perhaps particularly in our late modern context—to associate God with violence. The problem of God and violence appears to us analogous to the problem of God and evil. We find it impossible to worship a God who is implicated in violence as to worship a God who is the author of evil. The underlying assumption in many discussions of divine violence appears to be that violence is inherently evil and immoral . . .[59]

So, whilst God being perceived as ontologically evil is rigorously denied, equal vigor should be applied to the divine right for God to functionally choose to express himself and his purposes via violent means; this proposition can be held without having to concede that he must have an ontological base of evil.[60] This is not a semantic exercise but a foundational

---

57. McFague notes that the world should be seen as "within God," and that rather than distancing God and his creation, the world should be perceived as "God's 'body'— rather than externally related as an artist is to his or her production." McFague, "Is God in Charge?," 102.

58. There are a plethora of biblical verses pointing to God as the source and being of goodness and love and in which evil is seen as the diametric opposite of all that God is, all that he stands for and all that he wants to achieve (for example, see 3 John 1:11; Amos 5:14–15; 1 John 4:16).

59. Boersma, *Violence, Hospitality and the Cross*, 43.

60. For a thorough exploration of this assertion, see Pfau and Blumenthal, "Violence and God," 177–200.

assertion in the setting of biblical and theological parameters for God's possible relation to and use of violence.

The Divine, Evil, & Ontology

In microcosm this is one of the positions this research is exploring, namely that Christian understanding of God does not have to accede to ontological divine violence, let alone evil. It also does not follow de facto that the "charge" against God of using violence has no grounds, or that God requires humans to justify his seemingly difficult-to-explain-actions.[61]

Terminology that charges or accuses God can be seen, therefore, as unnecessarily perjurious, juridical and bound by cultural and historic forms and contexts. It is evident, for example, that how the cross "speaks" to a particular people at a particular time is partly dependent on how and what they are capable of hearing and understanding within their historical epoch. It follows that those communicating their understanding of the Christian gospel must be adept at interpreting and translating its message via new conceptual forms in each generation and to each group of people they are addressing.[62] This process might necessitate the Christian theologian and apologist repackaging, retranslating and re-presenting *old* forms to establish whether they retain meaning and relevance for a modern audience.[63]

Within such reappraisal and reinterpretation positive terminology might be utilized in describing God's willingness to utilize violence for purposeful and soteriological means—this in *spite* of the reality of ontological goodness and love that would ordinarily be understood to curtail such activity. God's desire to draw errant humanity back into the fold of his plans is such that perhaps he is willing to act *outside the expectations* of One who is ontologically love. He is also willing to enter into the experience and suffering of humanity in a way far outside the reasonable expectations that humans have of Divine Beings. Moltmann speaks of this willingness and engagement when, in a chapter entitled Beyond Obedience and Rebellion, he notes that God is, if one is prepared to put it into inadequate imagery,

61. "God seems to resist exoneration. The whole enterprise of theodicy—of justifying God's ways to man, or rewriting the definition of God such that God can be justified—failed long ago . . . God refuses to fit the mold of perfection." Madsen, "Notes on God's Violence," 232.

62. Green and Baker, *Recovering the Scandal*, 171.

63. Williams proposes a method by which postmodern evangelical Christians can rediscover their indebtedness to the theological foundation laid by post-apostolic Christian theologians. See Williams, *Retrieving the Tradition*.

transcendent as Father, immanent as Son and opens up the future of history as the Spirit.[64]

This view of the triune God, revealing and dealing with humanity in the past, present, and future as transcendent, immanent, and eschatological presents a God who is not only profoundly un-deistic but supremely involved with the world, going beyond what might be reasonably imagined, expected, or hoped for in order to engage with and save a lost humanity.

Such action and choice does not defame the Christian God or accredit him with negative predicates. On the contrary, it presents a sacrificial theology of the highest order, not merely of a creature, which though belonging to God can nonetheless be sacrificed for divine purposes, but rather the ultimate sacrifice available—of a human being, Jesus Christ, provided by God for this reason and ontologically linked in his being to both humanity and deity. Jenson observes, for example, about animals and particularly their use for food and sacrifice that all meals, in fact, are intrinsically religious occasions, indeed sacrifices, and were so understood especially in Israel; for all life belongs intimately to God, so that the killing involved in eating—which is, he contends, not at all avoided by eating vegetables—is an intrusion into God's domain.[65] This is an intrusion that God not only allows but actively encourages; it remains an intrusion nonetheless into the sphere of divinely-ordained animal sacrifice for human pleasure and benefit.

This demonstration of the created order and its concomitant hierarchy of beings exhibits the inalienable realization that whilst animals undoubtedly hold an essential place in God's creation, humans are nonetheless not merely pivotal, but are primary and the very reason for the creation existing in its current form.[66] Willingness on God's part to make this ultimate sacrifice expresses his all-encompassing purpose to do all that it takes soteriologically, even when the costs infringe upon his own Being and sensibilities.[67]

---

64. Moltmann, *Crucified God*, 256.

65. Jenson, *Systematic Theology*, 2:185.

66. Gunton points out that even though humans should be seen as "the chief ministers of creation . . . ," this should not "blind us to the fact that the difference between human and non-human creatures is relative, not absolute." Before a manifesto of equality between beings is attributed to Gunton, however, even after further extolling a creaturely "capacity to generate beauty and truth," he ascribes to non-human life-forms the moniker of "lesser creatures." Gunton, *Christian Faith*, 8.

67. "If we understand God in this way, we can understand our own history, the history of suffering and the history of hope, in the history of God. Beyond theistic submissiveness and atheistic protest this is the history of life, because it is the history of love." Moltmann, *Crucified God*, 256. Moltmann's contention is that the triune Christian God acts towards humanity not merely on the basis of covenant, or of commandments or religious indebtedness, but rather out of love—a love ontologically sourced

The paradox of divine violence linked to a God of love apparently leaves little room for theological maneuver and yet further investigation reveals a more textured and multi-layered view of the personality, purposes and character of God. Theologians have long sought to understand and delineate what they consider to be appropriate divine attributes, traits deemed to be mutually exclusive can, however, too easily be balked at or ignored.

Concerning these supposed contradictions within Godself Pannenberg states that he is concurrently the God of covenant righteousness, but also the eternal, almighty and holy God before whose wrath the ungodly and sinners are destroyed.[68] This wide-ranging affirmation of seemingly opposing elements is intrinsic to describing the spectrum of divine attributes and although Pannenberg does not explicitly use the word violence its inference is inescapable when reading of a "holy God before whose *wrath the ungodly and sinners are destroyed*" (italics mine). Linking wrath and destruction in this way leads to the possibility of God manifesting an attitude of powerful anger, potentially leading to the destruction of those standing counter to his purposes and plans.[69]

Assertions and biblical depictions of God utilizing blatant aggression imbue him with at least the potential of having an extrinsic and perhaps even *intrinsic* attitude, acceptance or endorsement of violence. They suggest a Being who might choose to act in ways that can only be properly understood as being violent. Various biblical instances in which God exerts aggression, violence, or destruction against humans can be presented; in Exodus 12:29, for example, it describes how God "strikes down" ("smote" KJV,) the firstborn in the land of Egypt during the plagues. Whilst the root of this verb can be used in a variety of contexts, here it demonstrates God killing people to fulfill his purposes; the verb most ordinarily translated as meaning, "smite, strike, hit, beat, slay, kill."[70]

It has been seen as at least a *possibility* that violence could be considered within the praxis of this Judeo-Christian God. Such a possibility is an appropriate starting point and it is now important to consider the various

---

and functionally presented.

68. Pannenberg, *Systematic Theology,* 1:360.

69. As will be seen, few are willing to consider even the possibility of such a link. For instance, whilst considering various divine adjectives Macquarrie is unable to accept the notion of "wrath" in anything like its usual meaning, noting that "these expressions do not mean that God conforms to a code of laws any more than his 'wrath' indicates anger." Instead of wrath being construed as a negative or difficult ascription for God, Macquarrie states that such terms are "not really different from his righteousness and justice, for ultimately they are all rooted in his 'letting be.'" Macquarrie, *Principles of Christian Theology,* 209.

70. Harris, *Theological Wordbook of the Old Testament,* 2:1364.

means by which violence and atonement is presented as a concept via metaphor, symbol, language and story.

Knowing God

All the models and metaphors historically used to explain the atonement acknowledge, at least tacitly, violence[71] raising the theological issue of interpretation and whether God's connection with violence should be addressed directly or obliquely. The former explains the importance of violence whilst acknowledging the difficulty in correlating it to an ontologically loving God. The latter interprets divine violence in terms that distance violence both from God and its normative use as a word and concept. Either way, violence in the atonement and the character and attributes of God is a contentious issue.

The opening sentence of the Geneva Catechism states that the primary goal of human life is to know God.[72] This proposition is not an archaic vision of human life, but an allusion to the theological mystery interwoven with Christian belief: living has something to do with knowing God.[73] This core tenet of faith and theology expresses the human desire to know God in a manner which encompasses frank engagement with the biblical revelation,[74] including any unfavorable or unpalatable elements; a priori preclusion of anything perceived as negative cannot be countenanced.[75] Amongst these unpalatable elements in theology is, according to McFague, uneasiness with the relational and passionate language inferred in creedal statements. She

71. "Atonement is all about violence and how we perceive God's relation to violence." Hardin, "Out of the Fog," 76.

72. Given in response to the first question, "What is the chief end of human life?" and the reason for humans doing so is, "Because he created us and placed us in this world to be glorified in us. And it is indeed right that our life, of which himself is the beginning, should be devoted to his glory." Calvin, *Tracts and Treatises*, 37.

73. Kooi, *As in a Mirror*, 1.

74. On basing theology within Scripture, Barth notes that "true knowledge of God is not and cannot be attacked; it is without anxiety and without doubt. But only that which is fulfilled under the constraint of God's Word is such a true knowledge of God. Any escape out of the constraint of the Word of God means crossing over to the false gods and no-gods. And this will shew itself by leading inevitably to uncertainty in the knowledge of God, and therefore to doubt." Barth, *CD* 2/1:7.

75. It is acknowledged of Marcionism that "the psychological appeal of ditheism, as a resolution to the ambivalences inherent in monotheism, is obvious. The Good God, the God of Jesus, becomes a relatively uncomplicated character, full of unmitigated goodness and love. The pain, suffering, and evils of life can be systematically shifted to the second, Malevolent God." Beck and Taylor, "Emotional Burden of Monotheism," 152.

notes that from Augustine through Thomas and to the Westminster Confession the "end of man" was to "know" and "enjoy" God forever; beyond fear of judgment and punishment for sins, she observes, and beyond relief and gratitude for forgiveness, lies loving God for God's own sake—because God is God, attractive, valuable, lovely beyond all knowing and all imagining.[76]

Theology, of course, begins and ends within the human realm, so insofar as humans claim to know God they do so because God comes to be with humanity in their sphere—not because he lifts them out of it.[77] The "problem" of engagement with God is not a philosophical conundrum, it is a realization that finite humans are acknowledging, responding to and speaking about a God who has made himself known and wants to *be* known.[78] For those seeking to express something of this knowable Being, the doctrine of God is a principal topic of Christian theology.[79] Its special concern is God's nature and the character of his dealings with the world revealed in the history of Israel and articulated in the life and witness of the Church.[80]

Relationship With God

In the description of God in Genesis and Exodus, for example, words like "omniscient," or "omnipresent" are not found and Pannenberg argues that infinity is, in fact, not a biblical term for God. It is however implied, he concedes, in many biblical descriptions of God, and especially clearly in the attributes of eternity, omnipotence, and omnipresence that are ascribed to him.[81] Further, Macquarrie considers the grouping of these concepts to be centered in the notion of *overwhelmingness*, discussion of them not primarily being in terms of their explicit biblical references, but rather of their philosophical cogence and how they enable the theologian to preserve, what he calls, the existential dimension in our interpretation, for this word

76. McFague, *Models of God*, 128.

77. Hart, *Regarding Karl Barth*, 178.

78. "No matter how the Bible speaks of God—mythically or unmythically, imaginatively or conceptually, prosaically or poetically—the relationship to God as to one who faces us and can be addressed, as to a thou who may be called person and personal or even suprapersonal and transpersonal, or what you will, is a basic constant factor of the biblical faith in God that can never be abandoned, but always needs to be interpreted afresh." Küng, *Does God Exist?*, 634–35.

79. "So God's relation to the world is conceived on the pattern of the speculative intellect's ascent to divinity. God, as the first, cannot be said to be conceived directly in the image of human intellect, yet the way to God certainly is." Burrell, *Unknowable God*, 74.

80. Kaiser, *Doctrine of God*, vii.

81. Pannenberg, *Systematic Theology*, 1:397.

[*overwhelmingness*] describes God as he relates to man, God being manifest as the *tremendum*.[82]

The prevalent biblical concepts instead identify God in terms of his relationship to individuals and his deeds on their behalf.[83] Fiddes highlights the relationality of God in describing those who stood against Arius and Arianism in their desire to reduce Jesus to a semi-divine and perfectly created being. Instead, he argues, the Church re-asserted its position that the story of salvation tells us that God always goes out from God's self in love, sharing the divine being in a communion of life, concluding that the God of salvation lives eternally in relationship.[84] Fiddes places God's actions in the context of the doctrine of a God whose life and reality consists in relationships; moreover, he argues that these "relationships are not static links between individuals, but are love in movement, making an interweaving dance of 'perichoresis' in which we are summoned to be involved. God happens, moves and comes."[85]

God is therefore not concerned with either convincing people of his reality or of providing a theological lexicon[86] and instead extends *relationship* towards humanity providing a basis of *knowing* One who is knowable, loving and loveable.[87] Biblical theology must, therefore, acknowledge the Old Testament's troubling images and these must be reconciled with the revelation of God in the New Testament, particularly in Jesus Christ. This will enable a theology which does not deny or ignore polarities, but rather

---

82. Macquarrie, *Principles of Christian Theology*, 204.

83. Kaiser, *Doctrine of God*, 3.

84. Fiddes, *Participating in God*, 7.

85. Ibid., 115–16.

86. Williams notes that the unity of theology, both systematic and mystical, could be taken for granted in Augustine's time and laments that, at present, "academic theology has been reduced to a set of propositions about God that are at least by intention free from the supposed subjectivity and irrationality of spirituality, and spirituality has been reduced to a set of sentiments that are likewise intentionally free from the supposed aridity and narrowness of academic theology." Williams, "Contemplation," 124.

87. Macquarrie does not decry the importance of theology as opposed to spirituality and yet argues that each leads to the goal of interacting with and knowing God, stating that "the subject matter of Christian theology, God in Christ, is not a passive object laid out for our scrutiny, not even another human reality to be met in terms of reciprocity, but the transcendent reality which already encompasses us." Macquarrie, *Paths in Spirituality*, 70. He concludes, "Knowledge of God, like knowledge of our friends, must finally be based on communing. The knowledge of God merges with the love of God." Ibid., 72. Conversely, Williams notes that "knowing God means having a personal relationship from which mastery of information is virtually excluded; it is apparently possible to love God without knowing much about him." Williams, "Contemplation," 124.

incorporates them into an intra-testamental schema to better explicate, understand and facilitate relationship with God as a multi-layered Being, replete with nuance, difficulty and complication.[88]

Divine Attributes

This "chasm" is keenly felt in regard to establishing God's attributes, with an emphasis upon where, if at all, violence might be situated. Barth warns against the arrogance and anthropocentrism that can be at the heart of such endeavors; in delineating the Old Testament meaning of truth he notes that it indicates the propriety of a process or state, and therefore its solidity, force and permanence, and therefore its authenticity, validity, necessity and impregnability.[89] For Barth God-talk is possible because it is sourced not in humans, but in God; he argues that ontological truth can only be seen as the predicate and prerogative of God as the Lord who speaks and acts in Israel.[90]

Aposiopesis

When speaking of this God of Israel all statements must be held lightly; conclusions and propositions being made with the incorporation of appropriate humility and provisionality. Rorty posits the contingency of language and truth, claiming that the one cannot properly be understood, or even exist, without the other:

> Truth cannot be out there—cannot exist independently of the human mind—because sentences cannot so exist, or be out there. The world is out there, but descriptions of the world are not. Only descriptions of the world can be true or false. The world on its own—unaided by the describing activities of human beings—cannot.[91]

88. Young warns, "Some would even say that such a task is impossible." Young, *Violence of God*, 33.

89. Barth, *CD* 2/1:207.

90. "But this very reality, which makes possible and establishes not only human knowing and speaking, but in the long run human life as a whole, does not have its original place and therefore its source in man, so that to know and declare the truth, to establish the truth as such, to live by the truth and in the truth, does not lie in man's capacity and existence. But properly and decisively, and therefore in truth, the truth is seen throughout as a predicate of the prerogative of God as the Lord who speaks and acts in Israel." Ibid., 207.

91. Rorty, *Contingency, Irony and Solidarity*, 5. He goes on to conclude that "the world does not speak. Only we do. The world can, once we have programmed ourselves

God can only live in the grammar of religious talk when that talk
expresses God's freedom from it. We have something to say to human reli-
giousness, our own included, Williams argues, but we are not in the business of winning arguments for good and all. He concludes that what the
world, religious and secular, does with the news of Jesus crucified and risen
is beyond our control, and if it were otherwise we should have lost what our
own "news" is news of.[92]

Another example of aposiopetic theology came in the Middle Ages
when thinkers were debating whether God has qualities that are crucial to
human understanding of him—that are a part of his ontology. Maimonides
taught that God is so unlike anything that can be thought about God that he
cannot be said to have any attributes at all; at its most coherent it can only be
said that God is not a member of the class of beings that possess any given
trait or its contrary—this is "negative theology."[93]

The Deeper Essence

Conversely, Otto claims that it is essential to the Christian conception of
God that it designates and precisely characterizes deity by the attributes
spirit, reason, purpose, good will, supreme power, unity and selfhood.[94]
These attributes, he argues, are definite concepts that can be grasped by the
intellect and analyzed by thought and are to be deemed rational, so that
belief in such a God is possible as opposed to having mere *feelings*.[95]

Otto warns against the danger of believing that any supposedly ex-
haustive list of "rational" attributions can represent the full nature of God.[96]

with a language, cause us to hold beliefs. But it cannot propose a language for us to
speak. Only other human beings can do that." Ibid., 6.

92. Williams, *On Christian Theology*, 106.

93. Maimonides, *Guide of the Perplexed*, 1:50–58, quoted in Blumenthal, *Facing the
Abusing God*, 6.

94. Otto, *Idea of the Holy*, 1. The Orthodox tradition, on the contrary, is wary of
lists of attributes, instead focusing on a Trinitarian foundation to its understanding of
the divine essence. So, "unlike the scholastic notion of divine attributes, which deals
with them under the rubric of one God (*de Deo uno*), Orthodox tradition, represented
by St Gregory Palamas, states that the divine energies are completely trinitarian: all of
them issue from the Father and rest in fullness on the Son through the Holy Spirit."
Bobrinskoy, "God in Trinity," 55.

95. Otto, *Idea of the Holy*, 1.

96. Otto finds congruence with Orthodox tradition, which likewise emphasizes
provisionality regarding God's attributes or his explicability as Trinity. This is highlighted in the Orthodox reluctance to speak forensically of the Holy Spirit, preferring
to admit to "the utter human inability to discern the mystery of the Spirit." Bobrinsky,

He acknowledges that such attempts are worthy and necessary and yet that they can also inadvertently shroud a fuller and more holistic understanding of God by means of highlighting "synthetic essential attributes" to the detriment of the "deeper essence" of deity and the "profounder religion" that the inclusion of mysticism can facilitate.[97] Otto, therefore, introduces an element of alterity into his theology, a theme that will be returned to shortly.[98]

Without ascertaining divine attributes it would be difficult to engage in affirmative God-talk, hence the proposition of qualities perceived to be of God's essence, "essential attributes," or words used to relate to God, or "accidental attributes."[99] On whether divine violence might be integrated into God's attributes, reflection upon both elements will be undertaken to ascertain whether, if to be included at all, it might be an ontological or functional divine attribute.

God's Personhood

The question arises as to what God-talk is appropriate in terms of divine character, personality and relationality, whilst acknowledging that the ascription of personhood to God is fraught with difficulties.[100] The God of the Bible is never called "person" or "personal," the term is exclusive to Greek theatre of the time referring to the actor's mask.[101] This "mask" as "persona" nevertheless presents a potential predicate of God in that whatever can be "seen" of God is only that which he chooses to show, in terms which humans can engage with and understand.[102] It is another example of God perform-

"God in Trinity," 56. Otto would concur.

97. Otto, *Idea of the Holy*, 1–3.

98. See the section on Rudolf Otto in chapter 4, "Scholars on Violence," below ([x-ref]).

99. Blumenthal, *Facing the Abusing God*, 6.

100. "In many of the classical sacred texts of the tradition, God walks and talks. God feels anger, despair, and joy. God exercises moral judgment. God even laughs. 'Personality' is the quality that best conveys the person-ness of the subject who engages us. It is that congery of emotion, intellect, moral judgment, and personal presence that identifies each of us to ourselves and to others. God, too, has personality, according to the texts of the tradition; or, to phrase it more systematically, personality is integral for the understanding of God, according to several major streams of the tradition." Blumenthal, *Facing the Abusing God*, 6–7.

101. Küng notes, "Nor did this term play any part even in Greek philosophy. The Greek word for person, prosopon (Latin *persona*), comes from the language of the theater. It means the mask worn by the actor in ancient drama, the role he played, and later, more generally, the countenance." Küng, *Does God Exist?*, 631.

102. "When we call the Father, Son, and Spirit three forms of the existence of

ing or revealing to accommodate human limitations—again similar to the mother talking baby-language to her children.

In the history of theology this is how concepts of God have been framed. Macquarrie notes that even though ideas of God have undergone huge change in the interests of transcendence since the earlier mythological level of understanding in which God was conceived anthropomorphically, there nonetheless remains the idea in traditional theism that "God was still thought of as a person, but a strange metaphysical kind of person without a body."[103]

A *via media* has also been observed, that

> it is part of the completely incommensurable nature of God that he is neither personal nor nonpersonal, since he is both at once and therefore transpersonal. The decisive thing is that God is not below our level. Which means that, even though we can speak of God only in analogical terms, metaphors, images, ciphers and symbols, we can nevertheless *speak to* him meaningfully with human words. This much should be clear to us from the Bible. We need not try to think out in precise terms the reality of God, but we should squarely face that reality. Man should not lose his power of speech at this point, but should stand up and speak out in a genuinely human way. From the first to the last page of the Bible, the talk is not only of and about God but continually also to and with God, praising and lamenting, praying and protesting. From the first page to the last—here Feuerbach was undoubtedly right—God in the Bible is subject and not predicate: it is not that love is God, but that God is love.[104]

God—in the world, yet also, transcending the world, in eternity—we give a first close definition of their personality. The essence has its existence in the person just as the self is manifested in the I." Pannenberg, *Systematic Theology,* 1:358–59.

103. Macquarrie, *Principles of Christian Theology,* 116.

104. Küng, *Does God Exist?,* 634. The theology of the Orthodox Church has always run counter to these perspectives, arguing for a resolutely personal view of the triune God; historically framed in the earliest theology of the Fathers. Gregory of Nazianzus, for example, in introducing Orthodox Trinitarian theology speaks of divine personhood, stating that "no sooner do I conceive of the One than I am illumined by the splendour of the Three; no sooner do I distinguish *them* than I am carried back to the One. When I think of any One of the Three I think of *him* as a whole . . ." Gregory of Nazianzus, *Oration 40,* 41 (italics mine). Contemporary Orthodox theology expresses the personal nature of God as supremely revealed in the Trinity; there is a commitment to avoid any theological demarcation that might see the persons of the Trinity de-personalised or only each active in separate ways, such as the Father in the old covenant, the Son bringing redemption and the Holy Spirit giving life to the Church. Instead, it is argued that "in reality, these three 'stages' or 'epochs' of the history of salvation are all characterised by the common action of the three divine persons . . ." Bobrinskoy, "God

There are two offences to Modernity[105] in the Old Testament here: firstly, God is presented as a *person* to whom humans can only relate personally; secondly, he is *transcendent*, extending beyond the deepest penetration of human religious understanding—moreover, he is both of these together.[106] Using the language of medieval thinkers, God has, according to Blumenthal, at least two essential attributes: holiness and personality; God is incarnate in personality and holiness; so is humanity, God becomes through personality and holiness; so does humanity, holiness and personality are attributes (Hebrew *yĕḥāsîm*); they are relation and relatedness (Hebrew *yaḥas*).[107]

Elsewhere, Blumenthal exegetes seeming contradictions in the attributes and character of God; considering the *Zohar*, a medieval theosophical work, he notes that it is sometimes presented in the classical midrashic style of showing a contradiction between two verses which would otherwise seem to eradicate each other. According to the *Zohar*, he argues, God is made up of ten dimensions, called *sefirot* (singular, *sefira*) and these sefirot are not extradeical hypostases, nor are they intramental attributes; rather, he contends, they are extramental, intradeical dimensions of God's very being; that is, they are real, external to our minds, but also they are inside God's very being.[108]

Feuerbach argues that this understanding of God is prone to error and that such theology is simply anthropology as there is no distinction between the predicates of the divine and the human nature in the mind of the theologian and thus no distinction between the divine and the human *subject*.[109] The classic expression of Feuerbach's concept does not believe

---

in Trinity," 49–50.

105. Taking what he calls the "longest view," modernism for Norris is philosophy starting out with Descartes's quest for self-evident knowledge confirmed by reason and secured from the "demons of sceptical doubt." He notes that the term invokes those currents of thought emerging from Kant's critical revolution in the spheres of epistemology, ethics, and aesthetic judgment, concluding that "modernity" and "enlightenment" tend to be used interchangeably. Norris, "Modernism," *Oxford Companion to Philosophy*, 583.

106. Kaiser, *Doctrine of God*, 2.

107. Blumenthal, *Facing the Abusing God*, 7.

108. Blumenthal, "Confronting the Character," 42–43. Or as Tirosh-Rothschild puts it, "The mode of signification of the *sefirot* is that of analogical terms, formed in our religious discourse, the reference of which is one: God's infinite, perfect, reality." Tirosh-Rothschild, "Essence of God," 420.

109. Feuerbach, *Essence of Christianity*, x. Pannenberg acknowledges that "the anthropological interpretation of the proofs of God, or of the concept of God in general, might also become the basis of an atheistic argument that presents the thought of God as the expression of purely subjective needs or as the product of the projection of earthly human ideas into thought of the infinite," adding that "Ludwig Feuerbach

that theologians are dragging divine predicates into the realm of humanity but that they are projecting the very best of human accomplishments and attributes onto an ultimate, aspirational being who is the greatest thing they can conceive of and more.[110] Theology, in this sense, can only exist as the human-bound reflection of religion upon itself in its use and endorsement of both anthropopathy and anthropomorphism.

Schleiermacher likewise notes that religion is finite and therefore subject to imperfections[111] whilst Macquarrie observes, in his attempt to encapsulate the essence of theology, that it "may be defined as the study which, through participation in and reflection upon a religious faith, seeks to express the content of this faith in the clearest and most coherent language available."[112] The adjunct to his definition is that anthropopathy and anthropomorphism are therefore, by definition, the very clearest, most accessible and coherent concepts available for finite humans seeking to explicate and engage with an infinite, ethereal being in a manner which they can relate to.

Thinking & Speaking

Contrary to anthropocentric theology Hilary of Poitiers claimed, whilst speaking about God as Father,[113] that it is more prudent to think of these things than speak of them, admitting the inherent limitations of language as expressions of what might be said about God. Moreover, Hilary observed, that in regard to what he is in himself he is incomprehensible, invisible and immortal and that in these words there is already an encomium of his

---

was not the first to develop this line of argument." Pannenberg, *Systematic Theology*, 1:92. He cites Fichte as a forerunner of Feuerbach in the latter's attempt, as part of the atheism controversy, to show that ideas concerning God as substance and person are de facto contradictory because they are incompatible with the concept of the infinite. See Fichte, "Über den Grund," 1–20, esp. 15–20.

110. Feuerbach, *Essence of Christianity*, 12. Assessing the starting-point of theological discourse and expression, Barth is critical that this endeavor might start with man rather than emanating from God, especially *post Christum* in the incarnation of the Word. He contends that the first to challenge this theo-centric model was Schleiermacher, "and then, with malicious intent, Feuerbach." Barth, *CD* 1/1:128.

111. Schleiermacher, *On Religion*, 59.

112. Macquarrie, *Principles of Christian Theology*, 1.

113. Kaiser notes that "Tertullian (early third century) was perhaps the first to appreciate the significance of the names Father and Son. Like all terms, he recognised, these are used analogically; but, whereas other analogical terms like Lord and Judge indicate a merely functional relation to the world, the names Father and Son point to an ontological relation of distinct persons within the godhead itself." Kaiser, *Doctrine of God*, 52.

majesty and an intimation of human thoughts and thereby a sort of definition of human meaning.[114] As noted, speech as a result will necessarily
surrender to the nature and words do not and cannot portray the subject
as it actually is.[115]

A modern proponent of this outlook, Riddell, challenges the "propositional nature" of much modern Christianity which has, he argues, embraced
the post-Reformation creedal nature of Christianity to the detriment of an
open-ended and relational understanding of God. On speaking authorita-
tively about God and his nature he warns that God will not be contained
and that the attempt to construct boxes for the divine presence is doomed
to tragedy; concluding, "It is no denial of the centrality of Christ to say that
we are still finding out who God will be. Christian faith is not a deposit of
information, but a relationship with a partner who is constantly luring and
dancing in the direction of the horizon."[116]

This nevertheless does not defer the conclusion that attributes can and
should be ascribed to God; because, indeed, without such ascriptions it is
difficult to engage in any God-talk at all. The difficulty arises in the category
differences that exist between finite, tangible creatures and an infinite, intangible God. Macquarrie argues that there is

> justification for talking of God in personal language, and for
> regarding him as personal. But this adjective "personal" is predi-
> cated of God symbolically, not literally. This fact seems to dis-
> tress some people, but it need not. We can certainly assert that
> God is not less than personal, and that the dynamic diversity-
> in-unity of personal life affords our best symbol of the mystery
> of God. But it cannot exhaustively comprehend this mystery. In
> general, the discussion of the attributes in relation to the mys-
> tery of God points us to the paradoxical, or dialectical, charac-
> ter that belongs to every adjective applied to the incomparable,
> which nonetheless draws near in revelation and presence. God
> is both hidden and manifest, our highest attributes fall short, yet
> in so far as they make God unhidden, they are true.[117]

---

114. Hanson notes of Hilary's theological perspective that "God cannot be understood (i.e., fully grasped or comprehended), but he can be believed in (and therefore, of
course, known)." Hanson, *Christian Doctrine*, 476.

115. Hilary, *The Trinity*, 41.

116. Riddell, *Threshold of the Future*, 174.

117. Macquarrie, *Principles of Christian Theology*, 204.

With these provisos in mind the exploration and explanation of the nature of God, and whether this nature incorporates violence at some level, continues.

Disturbing Divine Behavior

A critical juncture has been reached with the issue as to what degree of violence, if any, should be ascribed to God, either ontologically or functionally. Seibert presents an analysis of "disturbing divine behavior"[118] addressing how such manifestations of God's character might prove "particularly troubling to some people" and of the kind of questions which might be raised by "thoughtful readers of Scripture" and of "the potentially problematic dimensions of these portrayals of God."[119] In an a priori manner he decides what reactions and responses would be made by post-modern readers approaching scriptural descriptions of God that might be interpreted as unpalatable.

In this regard Barth asserts:

> Our undertaking to view and conceive God will not, then, involve self-deception, and our attempt to speak of God will not involve the deception of others. We shall not want to speak of more than an undertaking and attempt, and therefore not of an undertaking that has "succeeded." Our viewing and conceiving of God and our speaking of Him will never be a completed work showing definitive results: and therefore we can never view what we do as something which has already "succeeded." In this respect the hiddenness of God as the point of departure of this activity of ours defines at the outset the limit which will not be infringed even at its finishing point. The perfect work of truth will always be God's own work and not ours.[120]

A Priori Agendas

Barth's emphasis is upon God and his purposes, regardless of theological agenda, consequences and preset parameters.[121] It would therefore

118. This phrase is utilized whenever he refers to "God's troubling conduct in the Old Testament." Seibert, *Disturbing Divine Behavior*, 2.

119. Ibid., 16–17.

120. Barth, *CD* 2/1:208.

121. Reflecting on why Barth is, for him, an important theologian who stands apart from other, more apologetic practitioners, Hart concludes that Barth is one who, "rather than prioritising 'relevance' and seeking it through the abandonment or total

be anachronistic to preclude certain traits and characteristics that, whilst difficult to understand in a contemporary context, might have been both explicable and necessary in another cultural and historical context.

The same charge might be brought against those in a contemporary context who are condemning religion and God in similar fashion; Dawkins, for instance, is scathing of the Deity represented in the Old Testament without once acknowledging that the biblical narratives occurred in a culture and at a time entirely alien to our own.[122] In like manner he might also criticize the scientists of that era for being ignorant of quantum mechanics. Römer too asserts that it is inappropriate to obfuscate ancient texts without acknowledging their original context. He notes that those editing an anthology of theological discourses across a wide historical period "would attempt to understand these various writings as products of specific periods and circumstances in which writers spoke about God in certain ways."[123]

The need to let the text speak on its own terms is nowhere more urgently required, in fact, than in a situation where a bloodless present might de facto inaccurately understand and thereby misinterpret a bloody past. The task of interpretation always operates out of a personal framework and both the interpreter's presuppositions and their personal or professional interests specify that framework. These issues inevitably determine the questions and methods that the individual interpreter deems appropriate for the text as well as the explanations they will accept or allow.[124]

An example of a "personal framework" of interpretation comes in the a priori agenda and associated theological parameters exhibited by Macquarrie in his search for God's character. When considering potential interpretative models for atonement he starts by "clearing the ground"; setting aside theologies of atonement he acknowledges as influential but nonetheless presupposes ideas of God which, from his perspective, are questionable.[125] He is no different to any other scholar in terms of working from within a

reconstruction of Christian identity, or making a show of having stepped outside the Christian tradition in order to consider it 'critically', was actually convinced that it was necessary to pursue the critical dialogue and hence to rejuvenate that same tradition unashamedly *from within*, and doing so precisely in order to address the wider intellectual, social, political and ethical concerns and challenges of his day." Hart, *Regarding Karl Barth*, x.

122. Dawkins, *God Delusion*, 269–83.

123. Römer, *Dark God*, 6.

124. In a section entitled, "Presuppositions about the Nature of the Interpreter," it is noted that "interpretation always derives from the interests or concerns of the interpreter. People interpret the Bible for a reason and with some agenda." Klein et al., *Introduction to Biblical Interpretation*, 93.

125. Macquarrie, *Jesus Christ*, 401.

particular position and outlook; what is different is his admittance of the
fact. He decides the parameters of divine possibility in terms of character
and purpose and then sets these as the borders to his understanding and
theological construction. 2

This method de facto inhibits and limits any conclusions reached
thereby hampering the broader search for metaphors and analogies to
explicate deity and divine purposes. The purpose of analogy, metaphor or
theology is to make meaningful that which would otherwise remain beyond
understanding. If divine reality were already explicable there would be no
need of expressive, interpretative tools and methods; the caveat being that
all such attempts retain the limitation of human language and conceptual
understanding. It is therefore unwise to exacerbate further these limitations
with a new set of self-imposed parameters before the theological quest has
begun.

Feuerbach's Projections

To do this is to fall, once again, into the scenario delineated by Feuerbach,
who suggests that the human quest for the divine is no more than humans
projecting their ideals for the perfect Super-Human onto the canvas of an
aspirational, "deity."[126] In fact, Feuerbach goes further, charging Christianity
of being afraid of its own theological pronouncements, choosing to limit
itself to self-imposed parameters of perception and description. He argues
that the one who earnestly believes in the divine existence would not be
shocked at attributing even the most grossly sensuous qualities to God.[127] It
is ironic that an atheist engaged in a polemic against philosophical Christianity is nonetheless forthright in defending an open-ended view of divine
predicates.[128] Feuerbach contends that believers ascribe attributes to God on
the basis of their own subjective experience of the very best human traits,
amplified and projected onto the divine.[129] Wisdom, for example, is thus

126. "Religion is the disuniting of man from himself; he sets God before him as the
antithesis of himself. God is not what man is—man is not what God is." Feuerbach,
Essence of Christianity, 29.

127. Ibid., 13.

128. His atheism is demonstrated in the notion that "in assessing God as a mere
projection and mirror image of the human, he did not see God as having any enduring
power to disclose the depths of human experience. Ultimately, God talk must be seen
as an irrelevance." Sabatino, "Projection as Symbol," 184.

129. Reflecting upon the excellence of character he perceived in his father, Ellens
confirms, "I easily project upon God the image and metaphor that my father has become in my conscious and unconscious mind, and so to me God is the epitome of

presented as a divine attribute because humans seek wisdom as an aspirational and positive trait.

Likewise benevolence and goodness are projected, culminating in the ultimate human goal of love being predicated onto this divine being.[130] All that is best and most positive in humans is projected onto God in whom these traits find their absolute completion.[131] It follows that the opposite is also true and that humans, or indeed theology, is keen to distance God from any attribute that would be unpalatable or undesirable in itself; this, of course, causes distinct problems in even potentially ascribing violence to God.

Commenting on Feuerbach's model Pannenberg notes that the critical description of this procedure as projection gained force once the resultant concept of God was seen as a unified but contradictory model, since the qualities ascribed to God still bear traces of finitude (in opposition to God's infinity) along with anthropomorphic features.[132] Psychological motivation was all that was needed, he adds, for the human imagination to project ideas of God which would ascribe to the divine essence qualities analogous to those of human and finite things.[133] This is all that humans can hope for in their desire to describe God and his supposed attributes; the difficulty being that given human limitations and an inherent inability to acknowledge and accept negative ascriptions coupled with the transcendent nature of God, language is at best limiting and at worst ineffectual in its attempt to describe the indescribable and to ascribe the unpalatable.[134]

---

grace, patience, and decency. There is much in the Bible to illumine and certify this. I could never know or believe in any other kind of God." Ellens, "Religious Metaphors," 264.

130. Feuerbach, *Essence of Christianity*, 15.

131. "Therefore, God is an existent, real being, on the very same ground that he is a particular, definite being; for the qualities of God are nothing else than the essential qualities of man himself, and a particular man is what he is, has his existence, his reality, only in his particular conditions." Ibid., 16.

132. Sabatino acknowledges this anthropomorphism, observing that "Feuerbach claims that God, as the one who eternally loves and understands, represents the human imagination's re-working of the phenomena of human love and reason which are raised up as absolute and ultimate realities. Thus, the divine being is human nature in its highest attributes, purified of its limits, made objective, and experienced as an infinite and distinct being. God represents an acknowledgment by humanity of the divine quality of those attributes most associated with God (e.g., love)." Sabatino, "Projection as Symbol," 180.

133. Pannenberg, *Systematic Theology*, 1:363–64.

134. "The most troubling and alienating character of this religious projection of God for Feuerbach is that through this mirror of God humanity sought to deny and escape the finite condition of its nature which was now found to be negative. The projection of the divine personality existing in absolute transcendence represented the

Wisdom's Parable

In regard to linguistic terms, the choice between the utilization of equivocal or univocal language means that the theologian is caught between the proverbial rock and a hard place, a point examined by Flew in his adaptation of Wisdom's Parable of the Gardener.[135] In the parable two explorers, on finding a clearing in a jungle, speculate how it may have got there; they decide to test the hypothesis that a gardener must have created the plot. They await the gardener's arrival to no avail and then wonder whether he is being consciously illusive and so construct a barbed wire perimeter around the garden, set up trip wires and post guard dogs. After another fruitless wait one of the explorers becomes cynical as to whether there is, in fact, no gardener at all. The other explorer maintains his faith that a gardener exists and provides provisos and caveats to explain the gardener's inability to meet their "existence criteria." "But what remains of your original assertion?" the cynical explorer questions, "Just how does what you call an invisible, intangible, eternally elusive gardener differ from an imaginary gardener or even from no gardener at all?"[136] The "believer" remains staunch in his assertion that the gardener remains real, despite seemingly compelling evidence to the contrary.

Flew uses this parable to illustrate the point that once an assertion is challenged and defended in such a manner it loses its credibility and thereby, what is otherwise a fine brash hypothesis may thus be killed by inches, what Flew describes as death by a thousand qualifications.[137] This parable is useful in two ways. On the one hand, it can be used to verify the belief that God should in no way be associated in any manner with violence. If he were to be linked in this way then the problem is raised as to what would be meant by God's "love" if when such a love is qualified it comes to represent a love that can punish, commit violence, seek revenge, that is wrathful and exhibits favoritism.[138] It would have come to mean a love that is difficult for

---

desire of persons to be released from the limits of their own natural existence; and their personal dependency upon God acted as a substitute for their dependency upon one another." Sabatino, "Projection as Symbol," 181.

135. Flew, "Theology and Falsification," 48–49.

136. Ibid., 48.

137. Ibid.

138. Or, put into the context of specific biblical accounts, what does the "love of God" mean in the face of God's punishment of offenders (Lev 26:14–17); violent acts (Gen 6:6–7); revenge (Deut 32:35); wrath (Num 16:46); and favoritism (Deut 14:2).

anyone to understand in normative usage and, therefore, be a love "killed" by a thousand qualifications.[139]

Conversely, all of these qualifications are *human* qualifications projecting human finite and limited, sensibilities and understandings onto a transcendent being. The issue becomes, once again, the difference between a theo-centric and anthropo-centric theology of God's attributes. We choose to use the parable as a means of confirming the limitations of human endeavor to understand that which is outside its comprehension, thus opening the way for a theology that is predominantly biblical rather than cultural and theological rather than merely anthropological.

Hart acknowledges that, indeed, all human communities have a story told to themselves and others expressing their distinctive origins and *raison d'être*; the Christian community likewise uses the Bible as "scripture" formalizing its role as primary text and basis of meaning and identity to fulfill a similar aim and to accomplish a similar task. This story, which the Church is based upon and which it offers to the wider community, "is founded decisively upon the text of the Bible and the "story" which it in turn tells with its classic themes of creation, sin, covenant, redemption and hope . . ."[140]

Responding to Violent Accusations

Hanson provides an example of this perspective when he considers the epistemological paucity of his perceived three most-used responses to the Old Testament God represented as a warmongering, warrior Deity. Response one is to emit an ominous silence; response two is to accept Yahweh as warrior; whilst response three is to conclude that the God of the Old Testament is in some manner a lesser deity than the God portrayed in the New Testament.[141] If these three ways of interpreting God's biblical activity as One who at least endorses war fall short Hanson proposes a further option of a biblical theology in which Old and New Testaments bear witness to one universal redemptive drama.[142] In the confessions of Israel and the

---

139. The originator of this parable, Wisdom, whilst enormously appreciative and yet critical of anti-metaphysical arguments, nonetheless acknowledged that the extraordinary, paradoxical-sounding claims of poets and scientists, theologians, and metaphysicians can be illuminating as well as misleading, and are in fact often both. Lyon, "John Wisdom," 912.

140. Hart, *Faith Thinking*, 107.

141. Hanson, "War and Peace," 342.

142. In regard to this theme running throughout both Testaments Schmiechen observes that as early as the Apostolic Fathers it had been acknowledged, noting that "for Irenaeus, Christ recapitulates the history of the race and is the beginning of the

early church this theology discerns the efforts of God to gather an obedient community around acknowledgement of its sole origin in divine grace and its sole vocation in worshipping God and becoming an instrument in his creative, redemptive plan for the world.[143]

Marshall, too, acknowledges the necessity to move away from endorsing any one response to presenting God's soteriological plan; he appeals to the various metaphors and analogies that together represent Christ's accomplishments in his incarnation, obedient life, death and resurrection and heavenly reign which are all, he argues, to be treated seriously.[144] Unfortunately, Marshall does not elucidate what "treated seriously" means; he is comfortable to engage concurrently with metaphors that express palatable aspects of God's character whilst questioning those which represent perspectives out of line with his own outlook and sensibilities.

For example, he considers the metaphors of "destruction and death," noting various New Testament references where God incontrovertibly promises the dispensing of physical, ultimate death and destruction for those found in sin and for the Devil and his agents.[145] Having assessed this imagery he then balks at the theological ramifications in regard to God's character, attributes and purpose.[146] He therefore inadvertently debunks his own translation of the metaphors, concluding that he believes it would be wrong to take the imagery to imply that God behaves in a way that would arouse the criticism of a cosmic equivalent of Amnesty International or similar agencies.[147]

What Marshall means by "wrong" is the apparent potentially negative ethical implications for God in dispensing death and destruction, thereby admitting that what had previously seemed to be a straightforward hermeneutic and application of the metaphors is, in fact, not accurate. What transpires is that many divergent and difficult aspersions are aimed towards

---

new humanity in the Spirit. He sums up all that has gone before, but in his obedience and victory, overcomes all that was destructive of God's plan for creation." Schmiechen, *Saving Power*, 125.

143. Hanson, "War and Peace," 344.

144. Marshall, *Aspects of the Atonement*, 10.

145. Ibid., 18.

146. "Each and every interpretation of the Atonement is most closely connected with some conception of the essential meaning of Christianity, and reflects some conception of the Divine nature." Aulén, *Christus Victor*, 12–13. If this is the case, it might be supposed that the link between God's perceived functions and his character will be even more pronounced in regard to his eschatological activities.

147. Marshall, *Aspects of the Atonement*, 18.

God when considering his biblical responses to sin, the Satan and his dealing therewith.

The danger theologically is, once again, the avoidance of a position
which then facilitates subjective "cherry-picking" of favorite metaphors or
biblical passages thus enabling the theologian to acknowledge and engage
with some issues whilst explaining others away.[148] Our position is that it is
more consistent and honest and thereby yielding of more accurate results,
albeit potentially unpalatable ones, to decide on an interpretative methodology and then apply it in an objective manner, regardless of potential pit-falls
for a particular view of God, his attributes and his purposes.

Unacceptable Ascriptions

Such an anachronistic attitude does not have to apply only to biblical perspectives, however, as Macquarrie demonstrates when he decides in advance, having considered Anselm and Calvin in regard to their views of
God's character, that such harsh, even tyrannical, pictures of God are unacceptable.[149] Such ascriptions say more, however, about Macquarrie, his own
character and outlook than they do about the attributes of God; such will be
the case for all anthropocentric theology.

A priori dispositions against presenting God in an "unfavorable light"
lead to the pre-exclusion of attributes construed as malicious or capricious
on God's part.[150] This pre-ordained desire to be entirely "positive" to God,
his attributes and purposes de facto causes theologians to eradicate factors they find negative or "unhelpful." The theological fear of "implicating"
God in violence understands such a process as negative and unthinkable,
analogous to the perception that it is just as impossible to worship a God
implicated in violence as it is to worship One who is the author of evil.[151]

---

148. On biblical hermeneutics Stott concedes, on behalf of the evangelical church,
that "we must therefore acknowledge with deep shame that our treatment of Scripture
seldom coincides with our view of it. We are much better at asserting its authority than
at wrestling with its interpretation. We are sometimes slovenly, sometimes simplistic,
sometimes highly selective and sometimes downright dishonest." Stott, *Obeying Christ*,
21.

149. Macquarrie, *Jesus Christ*, 401.

150. Borchert, "Wrath, Destruction," 991.

151. Boersma, *Violence, Hospitality and the Cross*, 43. Milbank notes that "traditionally, in Greek, Christian and Jewish thought evil has been denied any positive foothold
in being. It has not been seen as a real force or quality, but as the absence of force and
quality, and as the privation of being itself. It has not been regarded as glamorous, but
as sterile; never as more, always as less." Milbank, *Being Reconciled*, 1.

That said, the distinction, demarcation and status between these elements is essential to a theology of God and his relationship with violence. Anger, for instance, is normally understood as a sinister, malignant passion, an evil force, which must under all circumstances be suppressed; its association with God, however, is altogether more difficult to pin down in a definitive manner.[152] According to Heschel such features are accretions and exuberances—functions, rather than ontological; he admits that anger comes dangerously close to evil and yet concludes that it is ultimately wrong to identify the two together; it may be evil by association, but not in essence.[153]

God's Wrath

Another ontology and function issue comes in the Old Testament where God's wrath is viewed not as an essential attribute but an expression of his will in his engagement with rebellious humankind.[154] This understanding is based within various philosophical presuppositions originating in classical Greek thought which have left Jewish and Christian theologians wrestling with frequent biblical references to God "becoming angry."[155] Amongst these presuppositions is the idea that every emotion, especially anger, is aroused by "evil spirits" dwelling in the soul so that every act undertaken because of emotion or anger is a sign of weakness or sickness. Other presuppositions are based upon the Platonic distinction between reason and emotion whilst subsequent Hellenistic notions about God emphasized divine mind and thought, transcending joy and sorrow.[156]

Countering the potential unpredictability of God and the emotional or dangerous exercise of his anger or wrath, these elements have been framed

152. "Words for anger are connected with God three times as often as they are connected with man in the OT." Johnson, "Divine Anger," 356. Further, "The OT does not consider divine anger to be merely a negative thing. It can also be an indication of the unlimited greatness and sovereignty of God." Ibid., 359.

153. Heschel, *The Prophets*, 360. Additionally, "There is no divine anger for anger's sake. Its meaning is . . . instrumental: to bring about repentance; its purpose and consummation is its own disappearance." Ibid., 367.

154. Borchert, "Wrath, Destruction," 991. Herion notes various contexts in which God reveals his wrath in the Old Testament, grouping them in the overarching categories of inexplicable caprice, human sinfulness, covenant trespass, pagan arrogance, and the day of God's wrath. Herion, "Wrath of God," 993–94.

155. Herion, "Wrath of God," 989.

156. Ibid. Philo, for example, contemplating the wrath of God in Scripture, noted that "some people who hear these words suppose that the Existent feels wrath and anger, whereas He is not susceptible to passion of any kind." Philo, *Quod Deus Immutabilis Est, XI*, 52–54, quoted in Heschel, *The Prophets*, 359 n*.

in a more palatable context. Schroeder, for example, argues that God's wrath is not expressed as divine arbitrariness but is manifest when social cohesion and solidarity break apart.[157] It is thereby presented as being both purposeful and positive. Likewise, Heschel provides a positive context and genesis for divine wrath arguing that God's concern is the prerequisite and source of his anger and it is because he cares for man that his anger may be kindled against man.[158]

Paul takes up similar use and understanding of wrath to describe the effect of human unrighteousness on the world, though God's wrath is not something for which he is merely responsible, neither is it merely an attitude of God, far less a vengeful or negative attitude, but instead simply something he does.[159] The Pauline conception of God's wrath is framed in the debate of whether he understands it as emotional in nature (affective) or the necessary consequence of a holy God encountering sin (effective).[160] Borchert notes that any ultimate solution to this problem must factor in both the judgment and the love of God in his dealings with Israel and humanity in general and must exclude either malicious or capricious anger on God's part.[161] Either way, in the Old and New Testaments the idea of violence and its subsidiary elements and manifestations as they relate to God are exhibited and yet it seems that in both the motif is primarily interpreted and perceived to be one of expression or function.[162]

The attempt to distance God from violence is real and if downgrading it to a function is considered to be falling short of acceptable detachment then the causes for God's exercise of wrath, for example, can be removed from him entirely. Fiddes equates God's wrath with human sin and its consequences, taking the onus away from God and placing it with humans in regard to any potential violence God might be exhibiting. In the context of Israel, he states that God's wrath is his active consent to the working out of

---

157. Schroeder, "Standing in the Breach," 20.

158. Heschel, *The Prophets*, 363–64.

159. Dunn, *Romans 1–8*, 54–55. Further, "Paul never uses the verb, 'to be angry,' with God as subject," so that *wrath* ascribed to God is "curiously impersonal." Dodd, *Epistle to the Romans*, 21–22. It is something God does because of and for humanity, so for Paul, in the crucifixion, "Jesus takes upon himself not the wrath of God but the sinful existence and acts of all human beings." Schroeder, "Standing in the Breach," 21.

160. Borchert, "Wrath, Destruction," 991.

161. Ibid.

162. Young goes further, stating, "In my opinion, the violence of God in both Testaments in the Bible must be accepted as an irreducible part of the overall biblical picture of the divinity." Young, *The Violence of God*, 7.

Israel's sin into its inevitable results.[163] This linking of God's "wrath" with human actions is, for Fiddes, an interpretation that saves Christianity from the need to identify supposed divine punishments that have been inflicted upon them, including earthquakes, famine, sickness or bankruptcy.[164]

McCabe takes a similar stance explicating how evil might be associated with and founded in God; his threefold defense of God in relation to evil and his potential guilt in initiating it firstly suggests that everything good in the world is brought about by God. He suggests that some kinds of evil—such as suffering—are necessary concomitants of certain types of good, thus God can only have brought them about in the sense that he had initially brought about good. He acquits God of the final kind of evil—sin— as this is brought about by humans exercising their choice in God's neutral material world. He concludes that "since there is no good at all, except incidentally, in a morally evil act, in evil done, there is nothing created there, hence no action of God."[165]

In such instances the ramifications of an outlook are being considered in a pre-determinative manner to their original biblical context; or rather, given the possible negative outcomes and difficult associations that such opinions incur, current sensibilities are read back into the text to find answers consistent with extant perspectives and ideologies. If this is not done, according to Fiddes, there would have to be admission that the views held promote an unhealthy sense of human guilt and the image of a tyrant God;[166] neither of which, apparently, are acceptable options.

Anthropocentric Outlooks

A similarly anthropocentric and consequential view of sin, God's wrath and violence is presented by Green who argues that it is wrong to hold God responsible for his exertion of wrath against wayward humans. He posits that humanity's sinful acts do not invite God's wrath but rather that they prove that God's wrath is already active.[167] What is required for Green is not

163. Fiddes, *Past Event*, 92.

164. He concludes, "It hardly needs a fable like Albert Camus's *The Plague* to realise that such a view promotes an unhealthy sense of human guilt and an image of a tyrant God." Ibid., 93.

165. McCabe, *God Matters*, 27, 36.

166. Fiddes, *Past Event*, 93.

167. In terms of humans stepping into the breach on God's behalf and risking their lives sacrificially, Schroeder considers if this levels the charge of violence at God or whether humans are implicated in God's violence through their punishment, concluding, "But this has nothing to do with punishment by God. In wanting human beings to

a transformation of God's disposition toward the unrighteous and ungodly but a transformation on the human side.[168] The onus is again taken away from seeing God as one storing up and unleashing his wrathful judgment on a recalcitrant humanity or on God in some way needing to be appeased because of the wanton, chosen sinfulness of disobedient humans. This is a similar defense to those who might claim that they did not want to steal but the prohibitive price of the item made their illegal acquisition of it both necessary and inevitable.

Again, divine judgment, for Green, is not something to fear eschatologically but is an anthropocentric fulfilling and outworking of human choice and consequence; it is not God requiring justification or defense but humans—culpable for their own misdemeanors. If God's "wrath" is exhibited, therefore, it is no more than they deserve as a consequence of voluntarily-chosen actions; if God unequivocally demonstrates violence by means of his wrath it is not his fault—humans have driven him to it, contrary to his best intentions and purposes.[169]

An alternative to these anthropocentric models is that the text should be freed from a modernist agenda and allowed to present its own perspective and theology regardless of postmodern sensibilities and cultural mores. Goldingay, for instance, uses an interpretation of Psalm 94 which calls upon the "God of vengeance" to give the arrogant and the wicked their "just desserts" as a model to pursue the *more natural translation* of the Hebrew text (italics ours).[170] He avoids taking a biblical passage's supposed "natural" meaning, however, instead choosing to understand it as having a diametrically opposite explanation. Such a method does not resolve the subjectivist issue as to who would be ultimately responsible for defining what a "more natural" translation is.

Necessary Violence

Conversely, Boersma seeks an agenda-free understanding of "God's violence" by seeking to define what violence is per se.[171] He acknowledges that some violence might, at the least, be considered necessary and at most essential in a fallen world and yet baulks at equating violence with God in

---

put their lives at risk on behalf of others, God does not commit violence. God uses these humans as God's instruments and servants." Schroeder, "Standing in the Breach," 20.

168. Green, "Kaleidoscopic Response," 113.

169. Ibid.

170. Goldingay, *Old Testament Theology*, 144.

171. Boersma, *Violence, Hospitality and the Cross*, 43–51.

anything but the most minimalistic and perfunctory functional manner. He presents a counter-balance argument in which God's positive attributes can only be meaningful when placed in the context of their necessary corollaries:

> God's hospitality requires violence, just as his love necessitates wrath.[172] This is not to say, of course, that God's violence and wrath are his essential attributes. God *is* love, not wrath; he *is* a God of hospitality, not a God of violence. There is an absolute primacy, therefore, of hospitality over violence. Hospitality bespeaks the very essence of God, while violence is merely one of the ways to safeguard or ensure the future of his hospitality when dealing with the humps and bumps of our lives. Divine violence, in other words, is a way in which God strives toward an eschatological situation of pure hospitality.[173]

Boersma's contention is that however bad the picture looks in terms of linking violence with God, there is no cause for concern because ultimately the end justifies the means. If he is correct the issue remains as to whether a functional and purposeful violence of this kind stems from or is separate to an ontology or essence of God that includes, incorporates and endorses violence.

Linking ontology and function in this manner and in answer to those who argue that the one does not have to be conjoined to the other, Pannenberg states that it will be different if attributes are viewed as external to things themselves; as merely a means by which humans might grasp these things. The thing as the thing in itself is behind the attributes that we ascribe to it and yet we may not arbitrarily ascribe such and such attributes to this thing or that. The attributes are those of the thing itself and they belong to its essence.[174] Only then are they its attributes, and only then can the essence

---

172. Heschel notes the "complimentary" nature between otherwise seemingly contradictory elements, stating that "the stormy violence of the manifestations of God in the Bible cannot be reconciled with an apathetic-harmonious divinity. These outbursts must be seen as an aspect of pathos which is characterized by the correlation of love and anger, mercy and justice." Heschel, *The Prophets*, 391.

173. Boersma, *Violence, Hospitality and the Cross*, 49. In Levinas's and Derrida's perceptions of hospitality, the centrality of "fear" in a desire for God should be noted, hospitality being described as "a welcoming of the other as (the) totally Other, as the other in whose trace, transcendence, and dimension of height we find the sole access to—indeed, the very desire for and fear of—God." Vries, *Religion and Violence*, 301. The intrinsic linking of desire and fear is a useful caveat to employ in the utilization of this concept.

174. On this dialectic in the relation of essence and attributes cf. Hegel, *Science of Logic*, 484–89.

manifest itself in them.[175] We endorse Pannenberg's observations whilst acknowledging that it would be extremely difficult to affirm God's *attribute* of violence without concurrently predicating to God an *ontological violence* from whence this function might proceed and be made known.

Orthodox Perspectives

This perspective should be compared with Orthodox theology which differentiates between God's essence and energies. The essence or inner-reality of God is that which is totally transcendent, unreachable, incommunicable, unknowable, whilst the energies of God are perceived as the reality of God which exists outside the essence (τα περί τήν ούσίαν), in which God exists outside his inner-reality. In this sense the energies have no real value or meaning unless they are traced back and related to the essence from which they emanate; rather like the distinction and corollary between God's ontology and function framed here. For the Orthodox, God is "present" to himself in his "essence" whilst being present to his creation in his "energies," in which he really "exists," or rather in which he makes his reality present to the creation without communicating his "essence."[176]

In Orthodox theology, whilst God may not communicate his essence to humanity, the expression of his energies is nonetheless dependent upon his essence as its ontological source.[177] Or rather, whilst humans cannot know God ontologically in Godself, they can still engage with and know God functionally through his actions, or energies, in creation and recreation.

This ties in with the ideas expressed in our Prolegomena, in which the difficulties of "knowing God" in a definitive, ontological way were acknowledged, thus abrogating the claim to "unconditional certainty." Rather, an attitude of provisionality was commended which accepts that whilst *all* may not necessarily be known, at least something, *enough*, can be experienced to maintain knowledge, engagement and faith.

---

175. Pannenberg, *Systematic Theology,* 1:360.

176. Aghiororgoussis, "Christian Existentialism," 16–17. For further discussion of the genesis and development of the Orthodox idea of essence and energies, see Chryssavgis, "Origins of the Essence-Energies," 15–31.

177. It was on Mount Athos in the thirteenth and fourteenth centuries that St. Gregory Palamas became immersed in the Hesychast tradition of contemplative prayer. "His experience of divine light through prayer led him to develop the ancient distinction between the essence and energies of God: whereas the divine essence remains unknowable, the uncreated energies permeate all things." Cunningham and Theokritoff, "Orthodox Christians," 6.

This is a useful position to maintain whilst addressing claims of divine violence in the biblical canon; facilitating acceptance that whilst it may not be possible to ascribe ontological violence to God it need not mean that such violence does not exist, but is rather manifest functionally through divine *acts*.[178] In such manner God's essences remain veiled and impenetrable to analysis and yet his energies give glimpse to their source thereby revealing, at the very least, a potential endorsement of violence.

178. Such a position is paralleled by the pneumatology of St. Gregory Palamas in his Trinitarian understanding of the divine energies. He argues, in line with Orthodox theology, that the Holy Spirit proceeds from the Father alone and rests eternally on the Son, but is at the same time activated by an energy that belongs to the Holy Trinity as a whole, illumining and sanctifying the world. He argues that "this distinction is valuable because it underlines the utter human inability to discern the mystery of the Spirit, on the levels both of the eternal trinitarian life (trinitarian doctrine) and of trinitarian grace (trinitarian economy), which affects the human being in his most profoundly inward state." Bobrinskoy, "God in Trinity," 56.

2

Biblical Violence

Old Testament Violence

TO CONSIDER GOD'S ATTRIBUTES, reflection must be made on God's character as revealed through both the Old and New Testaments of the Judeo-
Christian Scriptures; it has been noted that God's violence is so much a part
of this tradition that most Christians today barely even notice it.[1] Schwager
adds that many Old Testament texts, in fact, confirm that bloody and violent
divine actions were particular signs by which Israel recognized the might
and glory of its God.[2]

Such ascriptions lead to the atheist Dawkins's observation that

> the God of the Old Testament is arguably the most unpleasant
> character in all fiction: jealous and proud of it; a petty, unjust,
> unforgiving control-freak; a vindictive, bloodthirsty ethnic
> cleanser; a misogynistic, homophobic, racist, infanticidal, geno-
> cidal, filicidal, pestilential, megalomaniacal, sado-masochistic,
> capriciously malevolent bully.[3]

Whilst in a chapter entitled, "Distorting the Character of God," the
theist Seibert concedes that, indeed,

> within the pages of the Old Testament, one meets a God who
> instantly annihilates individuals, massacres large numbers of
> people, and commands genocide. God frequently behaves vio-
> lently in the Old Testament and many readers are troubled by
> it. The "God of the Old Testament" often seems to be an angry,

1. Young, *Violence of God*, 8.
2. Schwager, *Violence and Redemption*, 53.
3. Dawkins, *God*, 51.

vindictive deity determined to punish sinners and evildoers severely. Many Old Testament portrayals of God are unflattering, to say the least, and do not inspire worship.[4]

What is to be done, therefore, with all the violence and bloody war perpetrated in the Old Testament? Brueggemann suggests that this question acknowledges that such "texts of violence" are at the very least an embarrassment, morally repulsive and cause theological problems in the Bible; not so much because they are violent per se, but because this is a violence perpetrated in the name of, or at the hand of Yahweh.[5]

Römer observes that, indeed, after the end of the Second World War the image of the God of the Old Testament improves considerably amongst Christians, most notably in certain Protestant circles that feel close to Judaism. Here, he argues, the pendulum swings in an interpretative direction which erases or assimilates into apologetic and harmonious readings all that might appear forbidding or incomprehensible in the Old Testament texts.[6]

In appraising the Old Testament as a whole, however, Schwager notes that the theme of God's bloody vengeance occurs more frequently than the problem of human violence. He points to approximately one thousand passages speaking of Yahweh's blazing anger, his punishments by death and destruction and how, like a consuming fire, he passes judgment, takes revenge, and threatens annihilation, concluding that there is no other topic as often mentioned as God's bloody works.[7] Or expressed another way, by any normative standard of measure, Old Testament narratives assign, as Seibert puts it, an enormous amount of killing to God.[8]

In regard to these passages of Scripture that represent God in difficult ways, Israel's counter-testimony, Brueggemann posits that it has been made clear that Yahweh is a God capable of violence and that further, the texture of the Old Testament is deeply marked by violence.[9] In the end, he

---

4. Seibert, *Violence of Scripture*, 23–24.

5. Brueggemann, *Divine Presence*, 11.

6. Römer, *Dark God*, 5.

7. Schwager, *Violence and Redemption*, 55.

8. Seibert, *Disturbing Divine Behavior*, 146.

9. Castelo remarks that this "countertestimony" is both helpful and underdeveloped by Brueggemann—helpful in that it illuminates a level of diversity that many are not willing to acknowledge within the biblical text, while the "difficulty in this reading . . . is that Brueggemann promotes the tension in a short section of his book without taking the next *theological* (as opposed to *hermeneutical)* step of making that tension do theological work." Castelo, *Apathetic God*, 26–27.

concludes, "a student of the Old Testament cannot answer for or justify the violence, but must concede that it belongs to the very fabric of this faith."[10]

Types of Violence

In a broad overview of the various ways in which violent divine retribution is wrought, Schwager notes that there are four series of biblical texts in evidence. In the first, God appears as an irrational being, killing or wanting to kill without apparent reason.[11] Secondly, there are those texts in which he reacts to evil deeds perpetrated by humans, and he himself takes revenge. Thirdly, are those where the wicked are punished by their deeds recoiling on themselves.[12] Finally, there is the series in which God punishes evildoers by delivering them in his anger to other (cruel) human beings.[13] These four types of divine violent retribution forcibly illustrate the point that there are not only a small sample of violent acts and activities associated with God in the Old Testament, but rather a whole schema of them.[14]

Whilst reflecting upon biblical passages that apparently point to wrath being a trait of God, Hershel demonstrates the issue facing those seeking to acknowledge, understand and then potentially associate violence with the biblical God. He notes that some have remained open to the message of the anger of God, to which the Bible, and particularly the prophetic writing, refers again and again whilst acknowledging that some others have recoiled;

10. Brueggemann, *Old Testament Theology*, 381.

11. Schwager notes that throughout the Old Testament, and particularly in the prophets, "Yahweh's violent activity is totally tied up with the concept of judgment. As judge God does not present himself as the calm and superior lord. Many texts describe how he reacts in hurt and anger. Quite often it even seems as if he agitates himself into a bloody rage." Schwager, *Violence and Redemption*, 53. On the "wrath of Yahweh" Otto notes that "in the first place, it is patent from many passages of the Old Testament that this 'wrath' has no concern whatever with moral qualities. There is something very baffling in the way in which it 'is kindled' and manifested. It is 'incalculable' and 'arbitrary.' Anyone who is accustomed to think of deity only by its rational attributes must see in this 'wrath' mere caprice and wilful passion." Otto, *Idea of the Holy*, 18.

12. "In fact when the prophets and psalmists think more personally about the relationship between God and His people, they speak of the divine judgment upon human beings in another way, in terms of His 'giving up' people to the natural consequences of their own sin. It is characteristic of Hebrew thought to depict God as 'hiding His face' from His disobedient people, or 'letting them go.'" Fiddes, *Past Event*, 92.

13. Schwager, *Violence and Redemption*, 61–63.

14. As Schwager notes, "We have not chosen isolated texts; we could add almost any number of further statements about Yahweh's violent anger. Wherever judgment is mentioned, Yahweh is portrayed as an aroused and passionate lord." Ibid., 55. For a full discussion of this issue see, Koch, "Doctrine of Retribution," 57–87.

others have treated it allegorically; while still others have been repelled by it.[15] Hershel concludes, however, that it is impossible to close one's eyes concerning the words of the wrath of God in Scripture.[16]

The extensive, far-reaching and overarching Old Testament evidence as to the centrality of the Divine Warrior theme, of God's wrath and of holy, violent war and genocide against Israel's enemies and of judgment and violent punishment upon Israel itself leads to other, difficult conclusions. Extensive and widespread violence has throughout history been perpetrated against people generally in indirect ways, covertly and explicitly, in what is called "institutional" or "structural violence"; war and other systematic corporate actions of killing and destruction are only the most overt examples of this institutionalized violence.[17] This being the case, we will demonstrate that God could be said, in some manner, either intrinsically or extrinsically, to be "institutionally violent" in the context of his character, actions and purposes as revealed in his violence in the Old Testament.

Abrahamic Violence

In terms of the Abrahamic religions Jacobs argues that they are, in fact, all intrinsically violent and violent from their origins; Abraham himself, after all, is most vividly associated with his willingness to perform the ultimate act of violence upon his own son, at God's behest.[18] Dawkins opines on this story that

> a modern moralist cannot help but wonder how a child could ever recover from such psychological trauma. By the standards of modern morality, this disgraceful story is an example simultaneously of child abuse, bullying in two asymmetrical power relationships, and the first recorded use of the Nuremberg

15. Those suffering at God's hands often offer what Westermann calls "The Complaint Against God"—not a vengeful or adversarial complaint, but, he observes, "In the complaint against God, the sufferers cling to the one who causes suffering, as God is the only one who can turn aside their suffering." Westermann, "Complaint Against God," 239.

16. Heschel, *The Prophets*, 359. Miller goes further, claiming that "the divine warrior imagery speaks theologically about some very significant dimensions in the understanding of God from the Old Testament perspective . . ." Miller, *Divine Warrior*, 172. He elucidates key themes, such as salvation, judgment and kingship, which he argues are integrally linked to the theme of God's wrath, violence, and divine warrior status. Ibid., 173–75.

17. Horsley, *Spiral of Violence*, 21.

18. Jacobs, "Afterword," 225.

defence: "I was only obeying orders." Yet the legend is one of the great foundational myths of all three monotheistic religions.[19]

As if this were not enough, there is cause to wonder at a God who not merely asks such a thing of Abraham—but to wonder even more at One who would but *appear* to ask such a thing, but then further *trick* or mislead Abraham.[20] Kierkegaard agonizes over this story, using it as the basis for his *Fear and Trembling,* in which he grapples with the ethical and religious conundrums faced by those who believe in a God requiring so much from a person such as Abraham.

This one biblical story exists for Kierkegaard as the frame into which he centers his understanding of what faith in God is. He interprets and reinterprets the story of Abraham in *Fear and Trembling* concluding that religious faith is faith in the absurd, arrived at not through reasoning and thought but by a leap into absurdity, perhaps at the behest of God—just as in the Abraham story.[21] He states in his exploration of the themes inherent in God's request to sacrifice Isaac that he would extract from the story its dialectical element in the form of *problemata,* or various issues raised by a faith such as Abraham's. He did this in order to see how monstrous a paradox faith is, a paradox capable of making a murder into a holy act well pleasing to God and a paradox which gives Isaac back to Abraham and which no thought can grasp because faith begins precisely where thinking leaves off.[22]

As in the story of Abraham, God and Isaac, there are any number of foundational moments in the interaction and establishment of relations between God and humans in which there is at least the specter, if not the

---

19. Dawkins, *God Delusion,* 274–75.

20. Hitchens wonders at any religion that takes such a story at face value and can "praise Abraham for being willing to hear voices and then to take his son Isaac for a long and rather mad and gloomy walk. And then the caprice by which his murderous hand is finally stayed is written down as divine mercy." Hitchens, *God Is not Great,* 53.

21. On the contrary, in his assessment of The Human Person as Yahweh's Partner, Brueggemann highlights "Primal Trust" which he presents as the juxtaposition of obedience and discernment, together giving a warrant for accountability and venturesome initiative, thus leading to *trust.* He likens this trust to the most elemental confidence a baby begins to have in its mother—trusting that the mother is reliably concerned and attentive even when not visibly present. Rather than a "leap into absurdity," therefore, Brueggemann contests that "to be fully human, so Israel testifies, is to have a profound, unshakable, elemental trust in Yahweh as reliable, present, strong, concerned, engaged for; and [like the parallel with the baby] to live and act on the basis of that confidence, even when Yahweh is not visible and circumstance attests to the contrary." Brueggemann, *Old Testament Theology,* 466–67. Such was the faith of Abraham.

22. Kierkegaard, *Fear and Trembling,* 61.

full-blown actuality, of violence.[23] The potential for divine violence is built into the Covenant through which God chose the Hebrews as his people.[24] According to its terms (Genesis 17; Exodus 24; Deuteronomy 29), he undertakes to be the God of the Hebrews and, in return, they undertake to obey his Law. The various benefits of this transaction for the Hebrews include the gift of the Promised Land, whilst the means by which God brings it about is violence—through violence he rescues Israel from Egypt, overturning the forces of Pharaoh,[25] and through violence God enables the Hebrew tribes to conquer and annihilate the Canaanite peoples and to settle the Promised Land.[26]

In this context early Jewish theology and understanding of God were wrought; by relating to Ancient Near Eastern cosmology the experiences as slaves delivered by the righteous, compassionate God Yahweh, the early Israelites developed a unique, dynamic notion of chaos and shalom.[27] Shalom was a state of harmony given to the community acknowledging God's sovereignty and embodying his righteousness and compassion in its communal life, whilst chaos was the intrusion into the community of anything that might disrupt this covenant of peace.[28]

---

23. Indeed, Rahner argues that "force would not have existed in the original, sinless order of things willed by God, and at the same time we declare that it is natural in itself, created by God." Rahner, *Theological Investigations*, 4:397.

24. Jantzen notes that there are technologies of power implicit in the ideology of covenant and that covenant has "multiple investment in violence and saturation in blood." Jantzen, *Violence to Eternity*, 87.

25. Epitomizing salvation for the Israelites, but something altogether different for Egyptians; as Dozeman observes, "The literary problems of character and causality are anchored in a theological problem concerning the nature of divine power, since they raise the troubling question of whether the God of the exodus is, in the end, a despot, who manipulates others through events that are already predetermined." Dozeman, *God at War*, 5.

26. Young, *Violence of God*, 4.

27. On whether wrath, anger, and passibility are to be ascribed to God, Hershel asks, "Are we to suppose that the ancient Hebrew excluded passions from the divine Being and yet pictured to himself divine indignation as a real fact—and felt that he was delivered over to it to the very roots of his existence? No. To experience divine anger 'as if' God were provoked is a subterfuge alien to the biblical mind. Both in predictions of things to come and in descriptions of things that came to pass, the word about the divine anger points to a stark reality, to the power behind the facts, not to a figure of speech." Heschel, *The Prophets*, 359–60.

28. Hanson, "War and Peace," 361. Brueggemann notes of Joshua 11 that its theological outcome "concerns the will and capacity of Yahweh to overturn the present historical arrangements of society that are judged to be inequitable and against the purposes of Yahweh. Yahweh is here revealed as the true governor of the historical-political process, armed alternatives notwithstanding." Brueggemann, *Divine Presence*, 61. The

The Divine Warrior

One of the primary means by which this disruption could occur was the outside influence of other nations, their cultures, their religions and their desire to expand; in such a manner, the theme of God as Divine Warrior was established.[29] This theme has long evoked problems in biblical interpretation, for example in the move from biblical exegesis to theology and preaching and thereby to the proclamation of God and Jesus Christ.[30] This picture of God as warrior therefore forms the *skandalon* of the Old Testament for modern people, including Christians.[31]

It would have been difficult enough if such a motif had occurred only occasionally in the Old Testament. The real problem is that this image of God, one which portrays him as being, at the very least, responsible for the killing of large groups of people through his role as Divine Warrior, is one of the most pervasive and unsettling in the Old Testament.[32] It has, therefore, to be addressed and considered and for this thesis it provides a lens through which to view the character and activities of God during the whole Old Testament period.

The theme of Divine Warrior does not stand alone as a discrete issue; instead, closely allied with this imagery, is the ancient institution of Holy War in Israel.[33] War was regarded as a highly sacral affair in which the

---

key issue, of course, remains to what degree he is willing to go in order to accomplish this "overturning."

29. "The study of warfare in the Old Testament reveals that Yahweh is a God of war. Yahweh is depicted as warrior both at the beginnings of Israel's history, as early poetry and prose testify, and also at the end of the Old Testament period, as stated in prophetic and apocalyptic writings." Lind, *Yahweh Is a Warrior*, 23.

30. In his overview of the way the Church has dealt with "the prevalence of violence in the Bible, including a violent Yahweh . . . ," Daly observes that "one becomes aware that, despite the great progress made in modern biblical interpretation, we have, with regard to the theme of violence in the Bible, not moved significantly beyond the position of the fathers. Indeed, as far as faithfulness to the Bible is concerned, we probably lag considerably behind them because they at least were reading, albeit typologically and allegorically, parts of the Bible that we tend to bracket out because of our difficulty in reconciling them with our image of a loving God." Daly, foreword to Schwager, *Violence and Redemption*, vi.

31. Miller, "God the Warrior," 40.

32. Young, *Violence of God*, 22. Miller states that "one of the central Old Testament images for the nature and activity of God is that of the divine warrior." Miller, "God the Warrior," 39.

33. Kang observes that the epithet of Yahweh as warrior-king occurs in Psalm 24:10 where it says he is "YHWH Almighty." This special term, he notes, has been translated into various forms including, "YHWH the mighty one," "YHWH hosts of the celestial army," "YHWH militant," "YHWH (God) of armies (Israel's)," "He who brings armies

people assembled, made sacrifices, purified themselves, and sought God's aid and counsel, generally by some oracle device.[34] Numbers and weapons were relatively unimportant, as far as Israel was concerned; what mattered was that they were not to fear, but to trust God to deliver them.[35] A strong correlation and understanding was thus built between the people of Israel and their God in terms of salvation—inherent in the promise and expectation of divine deliverance by whatever methods were required.[36]

The history of the Israelites throughout the Old Testament regularly demonstrates in various eras and contexts that the primary means of such deliverance involved the explicit and often brutal exercise of God's violent intervention. Indeed, according to Brueggemann, Israel's counter-testimony to God makes it clear not only that Yahweh is a God capable of violence but that, in fact, the Old Testament itself is deeply marked by violence.[37] Lind challenges this, arguing that Yahweh, as Israel's God of war, fought for them by miracle and not by sword and spear. His position is an exercise in semantics, however, as whilst upholding that Yahweh's miracles are his primary means of defeating Israel's enemies, he nonetheless concedes (as he must) that

> Israel's fighting, while at times a sequel to the act of Yahweh, was regarded as ineffective; faith meant that Israel should rely upon Yahweh's miracle for her defense, rather than upon soldiers and weapons.[38]

The primary point is that fighting *still happened* and was sanctioned by Yahweh, or at the least was not condemned by him. In other words, if it were true that Yahweh wanted Israel to be entirely dependent on their faith in him for deliverance then there would never have been any need for them to take up arms at times of threat—whether as a prequel or a sequel to God's miraculous intervention. Indeed, in terms of God expressing his

---

into existence," "He who sustains armies," "He who overthrows armies (of Israel's enemy)," or "Creator of the heavenly armies." Kang, *Divine War*, 198–99.

34. "If the endless ritual slaughter of the sacrificial system is the preoccupation with death turned inwards, the holy warfare against the indigenous people of the land turns the violence outwards." Jantzen, *Violence to Eternity*, 73–74.

35. Miller, "God the Warrior," 40.

36. Miller concludes, "If one wished to know concretely what salvation meant in the early period—and indeed in later times also—it was simply: Yahweh fought for us and saved us." Miller, *Divine Warrior*, 173.

37. Brueggemann, *Old Testament Theology*, 381.

38. Lind, *Yahweh Is a Warrior*, 23.

frustration and punishment of Israel, this was in fact sometimes manifest by those outside the national borders.[39]

On this perception of God as warrior and the manifestation of his hostility, Juergensmeyer notes:

> Behind this arresting image is an interesting idea—that God is intimately tied to human relationships, including hostile encounters. God is someone, or something, that can become engaged in human affairs and take sides, favoring one group or another. The divine warrior image suggests a certain theology, but it also implies a theory of religious violence, for this theological image indicates that real acts of violence can have sacred significance. Violence is undertaken by no less a figure than God.[40]

The idea of Yahweh as Divine Warrior was not limited, however, to his dealings with those outside Israel. After citing Leviticus 26:14–17 with its lists of promised curses and punishments for those who violate God's commandments Young notes that in confirmation of God's domineering attitude towards Israel, the Hebrew Scriptures also contain numerous examples of a wrathful God punishing his chosen people, as well as other nations and specific individuals, for their transgressions.[41]

Further, in verse 18 of this passage in Leviticus it is promised, "I shall discipline you seven times more . . . ," causing Wenham to observe that throughout the Bible divine discipline is referred to and that God punishes his people not merely because they deserve it, but because he loves them and he wants to correct their foolish ways.[42] Wenham makes no attempt to explain or describe God's apparently violent ways, but neither does he deny them as a means of God achieving his purposes; in this instance, to demonstrate his love and to facilitate correction.

In acknowledging the double-edged nature of the Divine Warrior theme[43] it is essential to reiterate that the motif is ultimately soteriological;

---

39. Johnson notes that "hostile nations are the weapons of Yahweh, the instruments of his anger, who carry out judgment against his people." Bergman and Johnson, "Πνάφ," 359.

40. Juergensmeyer, "Religious Justifications," 7.

41. Young, *Violence of God*, 5.

42. Wenham, *Book of Leviticus*, 330–31.

43. In other words, that it is exhibited and expressed both against the Israelites directly and perpetrated against them by those outside their boundaries; in describing God's judgment in the Old Testament, Miller, for example, observes that "as he (Yahweh) fought for Israel to deliver her, so he could and did fight against her to punish." Miller, *Divine Warrior*, 173–74.

the most compelling example being the destruction of the Egyptian army which existed and still exists for Israel as a primary salvation story, central to which is the portrait of God in combat.[44] So essential, in fact, is this image of divine power that the complete annihilation of the enemy by Yahweh marks the moment of salvation for Israel and prompts its victory hymn of celebration in Exodus 15:3, "Yahweh is a warrior!" This war cry underscores how, for the Jewish nation, salvation is an event of divine warfare in which the destruction of the enemy is victory for God and liberation for Israel.[45]

This theme of liberation and soteriological violence, sometimes seemingly gratuitous, is one that will be returned to both in consideration of the New Testament and also of atonement in the final chapter. In terms of the Divine Warrior theme, let it suffice in terms of the Old Testament to conclude that one of the principal epithets for God found there is "Yahweh of Hosts" which can hardly mean anything other than "Yahweh of the armies" whether heavenly, earthly, or both.[46]

Divine Genocide

Having reflected upon various manifestations of God's violent character and acts we will now consider another way in which divine violence is particularly explicit as a representation of his being, actions and purposes—biblical instances of divinely sanctioned mass destruction and genocide.

In his reflection upon the nature of various Old Testament texts in which God's "repentance" is extant, or rather, where God turns away from

44. After this unique experience of deliverance, "He who had been Israel's only warrior was now her only king." Lind, *Yahweh Is a Warrior*, 170. Miller asserts that "it is not possible to talk of God as king without talking of God as warrior." Miller, *Divine Warrior*, 174. On Psalm 118:7, which states that "YHWH is, for me, my great warrior" (NIV translates: "The LORD is with me; he is my helper"), Kang notes that "in this passage the warrior epithet parallels the epithet king. Like the function of an earthly king who goes out before the people and fights their battles (1 Sam 8:20), the warlike function of YHWH as king can be understood in the same way in that YHWH goes out before the soldiers and fights for them." Kang, *Divine War*, 197–98.

45. Dozeman, *God at War*, 3.

46. Miller, "God the Warrior," 39. Elsewhere he notes that when facing an enemy the Jewish people of the Old Testament believed that "heavenly armies" were marching with them into battle, concluding that "in a quite definite sense Israel conceived of victory as being primarily a divine one and indeed a cosmic one wrought by forces above and beyond any action on Israel's part, which, however, worked to Israel's benefit." Miller, *Divine Warrior*, 158–59. Lind corroborates this viewpoint, stating that "this basic conviction in Israel's thought—that human fighting was not efficacious in the winning of the battle—is therefore not a late theological development, but dates from the beginning of Israel's history." Lind, *Yahweh Is a Warrior*, 71.

promised good in response to human wrongdoing, Moberly cites Gen 6:5–8. The fundament presupposition, he argues, is that God's relationship with people is a genuine, because responsive, relationship. The nature of this relationship between God and people, he asserts, is that it is characterized by a dynamic analogous to that of relationships between people: they are necessarily mutual, and they either develop or wither away. How people respond to God *matters* to God, and *affects* how God responds to people.[47]

As will be demonstrated, this mutuality of relationship is positive when human beings respond in a manner proscribed by God. The problem comes, of course, when they disobey his orders and operate beyond his moral, religious and relational parameters. The people of Israel fully understood the nature of this relationship, its requirements and its potential ramifications should they be unfaithful to God or otherwise go astray. In fact, they seemed aware of and comfortable with their God of strong and far-reaching providence. Helm notes:

> For the idea of God's rule over them was a consciously operating principle in the lives of many Old Testament men and women. One of the distinctive features of Old Testament piety is the recognition, on the part of certain people, that the Lord has the right to do with their lives what he has done.[48]

More than Old Testament believers merely accepting God's expectations and the potential consequences of disobedience, however, it was clear that they also understood the characteristics and character behind these divine covenantal and relational demands. Therefore, having presented various biblical terms for God's anger and the proliferation of its expression Lorberbaum concludes that many sections of the Bible, and particularly of the Pentateuch, may thus be read as the history of the Divine fury and the means of restraining it.[49]

Even more explicitly, Schwager notes of God's occasional genocidal intent:

> Aside from the approximately one thousand verses in which Yahweh himself appears as the direct executioner of violent punishments, and the many texts in which the Lord delivers the criminal to the punisher's sword, on over one hundred other passages Yahweh expressly gives the command to kill people.

47. Moberly, "God Is not a Human," 114–115. Wenham notes of the same passage that "'regret' or 'repent' may suggest a mere change of attitude, but when God 'repents' he starts to act differently." Wenham, *Genesis 1–15*, 144.

48. Helm, *Providence of God*, 112.

49. Lorberbaum, "Rainbow in the Cloud," 499.

These passages do not have God himself do the killing; he keeps somewhat aloof. Yet it is he who gives the order to destroy human life, who delivers his people like sheep to the slaughter, and who incites human beings against one another.[50]

In order to explore and explicate these claims we will take two classic representative instances of divine genocide: the Flood and Sodom and Gomorrah. We will then conclude our reflection upon biblical violence in the Old Testament by looking at an overarching theme that runs through both accounts and is also explicitly manifest in various other violent biblical events, occurrences and stories—חֵרֶם (ḥērem), the *ban*.

The Flood

Firstly, we will examine perhaps the most striking and certainly most far-reaching illustration of divine violence in the form of mass-genocide in the Old Testament—the Flood narrative in Genesis (chapters 6–9). Each new element of the Creation is initially deemed by God to be "good" and therefore presumably pleasing to him, manifesting both his presence and creativity.[51] It did not take long, however, for this most hopeful and wondrous of biblical narratives to become abrogated into something more foreboding. As Jantzen notes,

> Whatever we say about the creation story itself, divine violence quickly asserts itself in the Genesis text. Even though God is portrayed at the outset as transforming chaos into paradise without struggle, before six chapters are complete, God is so frustrated with what he has made that he plans and carries out genocide.[52]

In terms of the general bias and focus of this salvation-history, as delineated in Genesis 1–11, it is shown that God's punishment and forgiveness is not restricted to Israel alone, but rather that it extends beyond these limits to the broader horizon of sin and revolt as part of the overall human condition.[53] It is this condition that provokes divine violence, making it always

50. Schwager, *Violence and Redemption*, 60.

51. Wenham notes that in the first instance of creation's goodness being affirmed (Gen 1: 10), after water was gathered into oceans, and these great acts of separation of land and sea were finished, "God's glory was again apparent: 'It was good.' In the flood, the bounds established at creation were overstepped, and death and chaos returned." Wenham, *Genesis 1–15*, 20.

52. Jantzen, *Violence to Eternity*, 4.

53. Westermann, *Genesis 1–11*, 67.

an immediate consequence of evil human deeds; Yahweh's anger, therefore, does not erupt because he takes pleasure in killing or is totally irrational—rather, humans are the cause of his anger.[54] Such pronouncements do not, of course, mitigate expressions of divine violence; rather, they provide insight into their manifestation and purpose.

In his overview of the Creation narrative as a whole Lorberbaum points to the profound divine disappointment

> due to humanity's corruption, causing God "sadness of heart" that rapidly turns into fierce, disproportionate anger; that wishes to destroy everything and to return the world to chaos; and that concludes with God accepting and bearing His violent and impaired images.[55]

The Flood text therefore has special biblical and therefore theological significance because it describes the sin of all humanity and the kind of divine response that this elicits. Schwager observes that the decisive statement in the narrative is: "Now the earth was corrupt in God's sight, and the earth was filled with violence" (Gen 6:11); noting that this sin of the earth is characterized with one single word: violence (*hamas*), referring both to the ruthless violation of fellow humans and ultimately to their murder and that it is a word which under the priestly codex sums up all human misdeeds.[56] Brueggemann concurs, stating that there is no doubt that Yahweh has caused the floodwaters, and likewise no doubt that it was disobedience in the form of corruption and violence that evoked him to act.[57] Schwager opines that "every sinful act against one's fellow human tends towards violence, for which God punishes the earth by leaving human beings to their own devices."[58]

The notable oversight here, of course, is that in the instance of the Flood Yahweh did not, in fact, leave human beings to their own devices. Instead, he pro-actively intervenes thus overcoming and overrunning "human devices" to the degree that he enacts the most far-reaching genocide against humanity ever recorded.

In fact, God's pronouncement upon humanity of a flood in Genesis 6:7 could hardly have been any *more* explicit or all-encompassing. "So the

---

54. Schwager, *Violence and Redemption*, 57.

55. Lorberbaum, "Rainbow in the Cloud," 499.

56. Schwager, *Violence and Redemption*, 48.

57. Brueggemann, *Old Testament Theology*, 538.

58. Schwager, *Violence and Redemption*, 48. Lohfink agrees, stating that "in the last analysis, the biblical Flood represents what violence, the essence of all our sins, does to the world." Lohfink, *Great Themes*, 231.

LORD said, "I will wipe mankind, whom I have created, from the face of
the earth—men and animals, and creatures that move along the ground,
and birds of the air—for I am grieved that I have made them."" (NIV) Westermann notes that the verb מחה, "to wipe out, obliterate" is also used in
Judges 21:17 in regard to obliterating a tribe from Israel; it is a severe way
of describing the destruction and anticipates what he calls the "utter horror
of the decision."[59]

So, when these "evil human deeds" reach endemic proportions, as is
suggested in the biblical text before the Flood narrative (Gen 6:5–6), then
it is expected that God would take measures commensurate with the scale
of the problem. Indeed, Wenham notes of verse 5 that few texts in the Old
Testament are so explicit and all-embracing in specifying the extent of human sinfulness and depravity.[60] It is in the face of such definitive divine
judgment that Brueggemann acknowledges the nature of this kind of trade-
off when discussing the covenant curses of Yahweh; arguing that it is commonly accepted that if Yahweh is disobeyed, affronted, or mocked, he enacts
penalties. He concludes that this much is reasonable and the severity of the
affront will match the severity of the sanction.[61] Ergo, in the instance of the
Flood, if the whole earth is evil, then the whole earth will have to be dealt
with.

Facing up to this stark assertion is rather difficult, however, leading
Seibert to observe:

> Understandably, most modern depictions of the story focus
> primarily on the survivors: Noah's family and the fortunate
> animals in the ark.[62] Yet, despite cute songs, child-friendly play
> sets, and colorful artistic renderings of the story, "Noah's Ark" is
> not a happy tale of giraffes and panda bears clambering aboard
> a floating zoo. It is a story of catastrophic death and destruction
> that, incidentally, results from a divine decree. Nearly the entire
> population perishes because God drowns them. It is a disaster of

59. Westermann, *Genesis 1–11*, 411.

60. Wenham, *Genesis 1–15*, 144.

61. Brueggemann, *Old Testament Theology*, 373.

62. Fish notes that particularly in children's versions of the Flood story a simplified
version is presented either in the leaving out of details or by changing the story itself.
Indeed, she argues that "in many books, it has become a story about animals. Some
books exclude everything else, even Noah. Some books leave Noah in, and leave out
his family. Some leave God out, or replace Him with a radio that tells Noah about the
coming Flood. Many books do not refer to a corrupt generation, and so offer no reason
for the Flood." Fish, "Literary Themes," 74.

such epic proportions that even some of Hollywood's doomsday scenarios pale in comparison.[63]

Sheriffs prefers not to linger over the destruction that the flood heralded, but rather focuses on the righteousness of Noah, noting that the sacrifice he made after the Flood is not specifically commanded but is rather as example of his piety which is well received by God. He further observes that the "soothing aroma" is so called because it appeases and pacifies God's anger, leading to the divine decision to never again repeat such a universal judgment and punishment, concluding, in fact, that "soothing" (Hebrew *nîḥōaḥ*) plays on Noah's name (*nōaḥ*).[64]

Likewise Murdoch focuses on the biblical notion of Noah as a good man, as found in the New Testament, for instance in 2 Peter 3, 5, where it states that "he voiced righteousness," and the Greek refers to him as κηρυκα, "a herald," the Authorized Version presenting him as a "preacher of righteousness." In narrative terms, Murdoch argues, the introduction of these descriptors can have several functions such as stressing Noah's relationship to God whilst highlighting that his comments otherwise fall upon deaf ears, underlining further the moral failure of the wicked generations and hence justifying God's solution.[65]

Even when violence is inextricably linked with God, such as in this story of the flooding of the world and the salvation of a few via the ark,[66] Christendom still tends to interpret it in such a way that it becomes a story of salvation for the lucky few rather than a violent, global devastation of the many.[67] Commenting on God "wiping out" humankind (Gen 6:7a) Wenham, for instance, upholds the interpretative juxtaposition that whilst "a more catastrophic sentence is hard to imagine," it is nonetheless "tinged with a glimmer of hope."[68] So yes, humankind will be destroyed in a universal genocide, but there is still reason for optimism because one man and his family will be "spared."

Likewise, in her consideration of how the Flood story is represented, particularly in children's literature, Fish notes that their accounts are not

63. Seibert, *Disturbing Divine Behavior,* 20–21.

64. Sheriffs, *Friendship of the Lord*, 35–36.

65. Murdoch, *Medieval Popular Bible*, 105.

66. Genesis chapters 6–10.

67. Having recounted this story, Jantzen concludes that God did not even try to correct the actions of those he was condemning, but rather "his immediate reaction was to decide to kill everyone and everything. Violence, the text implies, must be at the heart of the divine. God's actions are astonishing in their gratuitous cruelty." Jantzen, *Violence to Eternity*, 5.

68. Wenham, *Genesis 1–15*, 145.

true to life whereas the biblical tale is. She observes that in contrast to the myriad of interpretations, the story of Noah is actually not about how bad men are killed and good ones saved, or of animals or miracles. Instead, she concludes, it is a story about a man who learns to give and who finds out the "hard way" about the consequences of selfishness.[69] The hard way indeed.

According to Jantzen it is quite simply astonishing that universal acknowledgement of God's blatant violence is not made by Christendom in its interpretation of the Flood narrative. How, she speculates, can an account of divine mercy to the few in the ark be coaxed out of a text which is rather the story of horrific, divine brutality and genocide to the many that perished? She conjectures that such a reading is comparable to a situation in which

> someone today planned and carried out nuclear holocaust which exterminated all life on earth except for one family and their livestock: should the perpetrator of this deed be venerated for his great mercy?[70]

Rather than highlighting God's supposed "great mercy" Turner, in his commentary on Genesis 6:6 ("The LORD regretted that he had made man in the earth. He felt bitterly indignant about it"), does not elucidate beyond prosaic necessity when encountering God's announcement of his regret at having created humanity, and his resolve to blot out his entire creation. The pleasure God had previously taken in his creation, he observes, contrasts with his present grief and sorrow.[71] It would be difficult to countenance a greater expression of understatement.

On this same verse Goldingay remarks:

> God's feeling emotion suggests that possessing emotions is one of the respects in which God and humanity are fundamentally alike. God is not without passions, as Christian doctrine has sometimes reckoned. As the First Testament will go on to show, God has all the emotions human beings have, and has them in spades.[72]

It is unlikely that Goldingay would uphold this assertion without adding the caveat—God has all the *positive* emotions human beings have. Otherwise, his anthropomorphic and anthropopathic representation of God would confer on him, for instance, sloth, lust, avarice and any number of other human vices and sins that are readily and regularly manifested,

69. Fish, "Literary Themes," 74.

70. Jantzen, *Violence to Eternity*, 5.

71. Turner, *Genesis*, 45.

72. Goldingay, *Old Testament Theology*, 168.

perhaps especially, however, those of wrath, vengeance, violence and even evil. In regard to such theological assertions which seek to conjoin God's character and emotions to those of humans Castelo notes that differentiation is not initially emphasized between the divine and the created until a conceptual demarcation is later deemed necessary when the similarity is no longer helpful.[73]

The issue remains, however, that whether such a similarity is helpful or not, in the specific issue of divine violence the Flood narrative presents a God who is capable of exerting the most all-encompassing violence, nay genocide, in the pursuit of his goals and the implementation of his purposes.

As Wenham puts it,

> In other words, he felt the bitter rage of someone whose closest friend had been terribly wronged. This is the anger of someone who loves deeply. It spurs on to drastic action, in this case nothing less than God's destruction of his creatures "man, animals, creeping creatures and birds."[74]

Or rather, in the story of the Flood, God demonstrated a genocidal violence born of love, for the ultimate redemption of humankind; the divine love not lessening the divine violence, nor the divine violence undermining the divine love.[75]

Sodom & Gomorrah

Amongst the plethora of incidents of divine violence, including those of genocide in the Old Testament, the account in Genesis 19 nonetheless makes for bizarre reading. Not least in terms of the baying mob and their desire for gang-homosexual rape, the tone then lowered even further by Lot's bewildering offer of his innocent, virgin daughters by way of placating the potential rapists. In a moment of exquisite understatement Turner describes this latter act as "quite shocking,"[76] although perhaps not quite as shocking as the fact that in his commentary Turner is entirely silent about

73. Castelo, *Apathetic God*, 25.

74. Wenham, *Genesis 1–15*, 147.

75. In the aftermath of this divine violence, in Gen 9:12–17, Lind observes that "God sets in the cloud his unstrung bow as a sign of his new *shalom* to his enemy man. The war is over and man will not again suffer the violence of God's overwhelming wrath." Lind, *Yahweh Is a Warrior*, 128. The promise is that such an outpouring of universal divine violence will never occur again; not an apologetic for its manifestation or a denial of its reality.

76. Turner, *Genesis*, 87.

verses 24–26 of Genesis chapter 19 where God is said to rain down sulphur from heaven. This action kills every inhabitant of Sodom, destroying even the vegetation, the whole plain and its adjoining cities; it is difficult, therefore, in the face of such blatantly aggressive divine acts to countenance the scale of Turner's theological obfuscation of divine violence in this pericope.

Additionally, after recounting the sorry tale, following the destruction of Sodom and Gomorrah, of Lot's two daughters first inebriating and then copulating with their father, Dawkins notes that if a dysfunctional family of this kind was the best Sodom had to offer by way of morals, it might be possible to feel a certain sympathy with God and his judicial brimstone.[77] Of this "judicial brimstone," Seibert notes that Sodom and Gomorrah is one of many Old Testament stories which portray God as a mass murderer.[78]

The text itself also speaks of smoke ascending like the smoke in a furnace, using words for smoke and ascent usually connected with the making of burnt offerings.[79] This mixture of divine wrath and liturgical offering suggests an example of God's attributes and actions which, Lorberbaum notes, there are repeated biblical incidents of and that culminate in God's furious anger, followed by "futile attempts" to appease him; he offers this episode at Sodom as a particular case in point.[80]

To balance this interpretation of divine anger and implacability Seibert considers examples of "virtuous" violence, again citing Sodom and Gomorrah, noting that the narrative itself suggests that God's actions were fully justified because its inhabitants were terribly wicked.[81] Barth too, in his reflection on the heavenly dimension, its scope and the manifestation of God thereof, acknowledges, but does not dwell on, any events which might be perceived as negative. So, whilst acceding that "fire and brimstone are rained on Sodom and Gomorrah" (Gen 19:24) by God from heaven, he incorporates this occurrence into other moments of divine activity and concludes,

> But all these divine benefits and judgments are only the epiphenomena of what comes primarily and centrally from heaven to earth, namely, the Word which the God who is gracious in His

77. Dawkins, *God Delusion*, 272.

78. Seibert, *Disturbing Divine Behavior*, 21.

79. Kass, *Beginning*, 331.

80. Lorberbaum, "Rainbow in the Cloud," 498.

81. Seibert, *Violence of Scripture*, 33. Likewise Lüdemann notes of the texts in which the Canaanites were slaughtered that "truly, the degree of wickedness of the Canaanites is only legendary and has probably been invented to justify the extreme cruelty of the mass exterminations reported by the biblical text." Lüdemann, *Unholy in Holy Scripture*, 53.

holiness and holy in His grace addresses to man as the Lord of the covenant; the Son in whose person He Himself becomes man and therefore earthly for our salvation.[82]

The decimation of entire cities and their environs constitutes for Barth "epiphenomena" which should be put in the much later context of Jesus' incarnation. This interpretation of events constitutes an extreme form of delayed gratification for those observing what would otherwise be blatant acts of divine retribution and violence.

Conversely, these acts in which God annihilates "the entire Plain" including "the vegetation of the ground" (Gen 19:25), whether or not they would later be explicable in the light of Jesus' incarnation, nonetheless cause what Ludwig calls, "That fatal fertility" in a manner so like Eden, in which Sodom and Gomorrah are withered in the flames whilst the earth that bore it is scorched. In its place, he argues, is left the sterility of the salt of the Dead Sea and of the pillar into which Lot's wife is turned, leading him to conclude that the punishment fits the crime, since in the midst of such fecundity, Sodom had enjoyed only her sterile attachments, generating nothing.[83]

THE SPECTER OF INFANTICIDE

The implementation of genocide or other mass destruction leaving an area sterile will, of course, necessitate the death of all humans present. The often un-spoken element of these death-tolls is the inevitable corollary that all children, of whatever age, will also be lost. Seibert notes that in addition to the obvious examples of such child-death, like the flood narrative, other stories of mass destruction, including Sodom and Gomorrah, display

> a similar lack of interest in the fate of the children—or virtually any other victim, for that matter. Even though each of these stories assumes the utter annihilation of every single child, these children remain virtually invisible.[84]

According to one count, there are almost 200 texts about violence against children in the Hebrew Old Testament.[85] A search for theologi-

---

82. Barth, CD 3/3:435.

83. Ludwig, "What's Wrong with Sodom?," quoted in Kass, The Beginning of Wisdom, 330.

84. Seibert, Violence of Scripture, 83.

85. Michel, "Violence against Children," 51. Michel notes that there are additional texts like these—"another 50 from the deutero-canonical writings of the Old Testament, and a few from the New Testament." Ibid., 51.

cal perspective and insight into these texts meets a resounding silence, or
perhaps rather a massive denial or conscious obfuscation of an otherwise
unbearable truth. The truth that God is, whether primarily or secondarily,
involved in far-reaching acts of infanticide in the implementation of his
purposes and will. Phillips suggests that the only way that texts of this kind
must be read is non-violently; or rather,

> Readers of the Bible must read differently, deferentially, deliber-
> ately for the children, lest they contribute to the formation of a
> culture that makes the murder of the innocents natural, inevi-
> table, biblical.[86]

The voices of these voiceless victims, Phillips argues, must be allowed
to interrupt our reading of the story. Such "interruption" occurs when particular innocent children disrupt the power biblical texts exercise in shaping
our perceptions and informing our world. By attending to these children's
faces and other innocents whose deaths rupture our critical strategies and
our memory, he contends, we open ourselves to the possibility of saying
"No" to all texts, biblical or otherwise, that kill children.[87]

Again Seibert agrees, arguing,

> Violence against children is never appropriate, never justifi-
> able, and never virtuous. If we condone textual violence against
> children, we have been seduced by Scripture. We must resist all
> readings as inherently violent and as a violation of our obliga-
> tion to read critically and ethically. For the sake of the children,
> we must read these texts nonviolently, in ways that neither
> legitimate the violence in the text nor justify it in our present
> context.[88]

Whilst Seibert advocates reading postmodern sensibilities into the
scriptural text he falls short of delineating whether he agrees that the text,
in its original form and context, actually *contains* violence, indeed divine
violence, or whether postmodern readers should merely *reinterpret* it
non-violently. If such a hermeneutic were to be utilized then, in the case
of Sodom and Gomorrah for instance, the issue ceases to be one of what
the text describes and means. Instead, the postmodern reader places their
own limitations and expectations upon the text to dilute its explicit meaning and thereby in the case of explicating the event and meaning of Sodom
and Gomorrah, offering an a-priori, non-violent appropriation of their own

86. Phillips, "Killing Fields," 254.

87. Ibid., 264.

88. Seibert, *Violence of Scripture*, 84.

theological sensibilities and parameters. Or, more simply, the postmodern reader will set up moral parameters within which it is acceptable for God to operate.

GOD'S APPROPRIATE RESPONSE?

Conversely, rather than projecting postmodern mores onto ancient biblical texts it might be more apposite to let the texts speak for themselves, even if their message is difficult to digest for the modern reader. Under the subtitle, "Expecting a Severe God" Moser, for example, observes that, as God is a being perfectly active in gracious righteousness he would be duty-bound to oppose whatever obstructs perfect righteousness amongst agents. This opposition, however, would be wisely intentional rather than impulsive or irrational; it could also, nonetheless, be severe in human life.[89]

With this attitudinal imperative in place, Schwager argues that in the Old Testament God is never seen to appear as a cool judge who, with utter detachment, guides the people in the strict observance of laws. Rather, Yahweh turns out to be a God who is directly affected by the deeds of men and women and correspondingly reacts to them. If the people's conduct is good, Schwager states, he becomes their friend and benefactor; if they disappoint him, he repays them in kind.[90]

Kass argues that Sodom's true crime was manifest in its inherent disregard of outsiders and its insistence on its own self-sufficiency.[91] He concludes:

> The city thus blinds its inhabitants to the truth silently carried by all strangers and beggars (and explicitly taught by many ancient peoples): any stranger or beggar may be "a god in disguise"—which is a poetic way of saying that he, and by implication we, continue to survive only by some power of grace. For all these reasons, men in every city will commit injustice towards strangers—eventually also toward neighbors—unless the city is informed by teachings of hospitality, teachings that are in turn informed by fear-awe-reverence for God and the ability to discern the divine image equally present in all human beings.[92]

89. Moser, *Severity of God*, 36–37.

90. Schwager, *Violence and Redemption*, 57.

91. ". . . because of the city's quest for self-sufficiency, city dwellers are more likely to forget about human vulnerability and man's dependence on powers not under human control." Kass, *Beginnings*, 329.

92. Ibid.

In other words, God was punishing Sodom and its environs because it had set itself up in opposition to himself as the One upon whom its inhabitants should have been dependent, with the inevitable manifestation of many attendant social, cultural and behavioral iniquities. The City had become a "god" and the true God would demonstrate his own judgment and ascendancy in the most definitive manner—the total and irrevocable destruction and genocide of every living being, even vegetation; to humble this city-pretender and thus re-instate both divine status and authority in the most violent manner imaginable.

In conclusion to his assessment of various biblical descriptions of Yahweh, his character and activity, including the events at Sodom and Gomorrah, Brueggemann therefore notes,

> In all of these noun-metaphors we can notice, alongside a tender inclination on the part of Yahweh, a dimension of fierceness that tilts towards potential violence. Thus I propose that in the full utterance of Yahweh, the thematization of Yahweh is as the powerful governor and orderer of life who is capable of generous and gracious concern, but this same Yahweh has a potential for extraordinary destructiveness.[93]

The lesson of Sodom and Gomorrah could hardly be more explicit in this regard: whatever stands against or sets itself up as an alternative to God will risk falling victim to his implacable wrath and its violent and far-reaching consequences and ramifications. The size of the disobedience will inevitably be matched by the size of Yahweh's, almost invariably, violent judgment and response as demonstrated in Sodom and Gomorrah—nearly all the people had rebelled and so nearly all the people had to be punished and punished in the most violent and definitive manner imaginable.

חֵרֶם—The Ban

Finally, in our consideration of Old Testament violence we come to what Niditch observes to be the most chilling of biblical texts which, in the context of war, refer to ḥērem, the ban; a divine imposition under which all human beings among the defeated are "devoted to destruction."[94] She notes that this ban is frequently issued with a reason for annihilation provided and that sometimes it includes not just enemy combatants but also women, children and infants along with all creatures associated with those being

93. Brueggemann, *Old Testament Theology*, 275.
94. Niditch, *War in the Hebrew Bible*, 28.

destroyed. It could hardly be any more shocking, appalling and difficult to understand, not least in the context of it being commanded by an otherwise loving and relational God. In summing up God's conditions and parameters of the *ban* Niditch concludes, "Let no one escape the imposition of total destruction and spare or be spared, a sympathetic mother, a piteous baby. The very language forbids the emotions of mercy."[95]

Etymology of the Ban

The root of the Hebrew noun referring specifically to the *ban*, חָרַם (*ḥāram*), means both to devote and to destroy utterly; its basic meaning further denotes the exclusion of an object from the use or abuse of man and its irrevocable surrender to God.[96] A derivative of *ḥāram* is חֵרֶם (*ḥērem*) which likewise relates to a devoted thing or the ban itself.[97]

In the Old Testament the rendering of something or someone as *ḥērem* marks that thing or person as unalterably off-limits and with respect to Yahweh, signifies a permanent transference into his possession and removal from common use or contact.[98] This seemingly innocuous connotation nonetheless invokes its definitive and non-negotiable nature—what belongs to Yahweh is to be his in its entirety with no exceptions whatsoever. In the most extreme and violent interpretations this has led Steffen to observe that from a moral point of view *ḥērem* is a demonic religious notion whereby God directs a total obliteration of the enemy, sometimes with rationalization, sometimes without.[99] The *ban*, therefore, is both at Yahweh's behest and indeed his whim and contains something threatening, dark, or worse.

On this theme Frederiksson notes,

> The regulations for all war legislation, which are calculated also
> to underscore the significance of cultic purity, are all rooted in

95. Ibid., 28.

96. Wood, "חָרַם," 324. "Usually *haram* means a ban for utter destruction, the compulsory dedication of something which impedes or resists God's work, which is considered accursed before God." Ibid.

97. Ibid. It is a noun used 28 times in the Old Testament to refer either to the object devoted or to the ban itself. Ibid., 325.

98. Hawk, *Berit Olam*, 101.

99. Steffen, *Demonic Turn*, 184. Steffen leans upon Tillich for his definition of the demonic: "In the sphere of the Holy itself there arises the polarity of the divine and the demonic. The demonic is the Holy (or sacred) with a minus sign before it, the sacred antidivine." Tillich, *What Is Religion?*, 85. Further, Steffen notes, "[But] a God acting to defy goodness is a God unleashing the power of the demonic." Steffen, *Demonic Turn*, 216.

the idea that Yahweh the war god was a sacred and dangerous
god. Here holiness has in it something of the demonic.[100]

As Niditch and Steffen acknowledge there are two sets of *ban* texts, one
in which reasons and rationales are given for the impending total destruction and those where such matters are not discussed. The understanding
prevails in these latter texts, however, that God has demanded that all that
breathes be devoted to him in destruction.[101] That which is under the ban
is indeed Yahweh's, but the means of his "receiving" the item or person first
precipitates their ceasing to be in an earthly sense.

Such a definitive and brutally violent divine injunction has, of course,
caused scholars to seek means of lessening its apparent severity. Gopin, for
example, questions if *ḥērem* laws were actually carried out[102] and whether
they were, in fact, merely a means of frightening syncretistic Jews into
monotheism. His further assertion that *ḥērem* laws were later discontinued
by Rabbis nonetheless comes with the concession that they are nevertheless part of a sacred tradition, the text of which has never disappeared, thus
evoking the possibility of a new hermeneutic existing as well.[103]

Applications of the Ban

There is patently a daunting element to the *ban* which causes problematic
questions about Yahweh's purposes, modus operandi and character, especially in regard to divine violence. As Gopin notes, however, application of
the *ban* is open to the possibility of a new hermeneutic such that Deutero-
nomic writers, supporters of the Josianic reform, for instance, consider the
ban primarily as a means of rooting out what they believe to be impure in
regard to sinful forces damaging the solid and pure relationship between
Israel and God.[104] Whilst this might be a reasonable assertion, the *ban*
nonetheless represents an inordinately violent way of Yahweh accomplishing this goal.

An alternative non-violent description of the *ban* is offered by Boling
who presents it as a liturgical device, comparable to the practices of other
extant cultures. Thus, he argues that it is the biblical equivalent of an old

100. Frederiksson, *Jahwe als Krieger*, 114.

101. Niditch, *War in the Hebrew Bible*, 34.

102. "How often Israel actually practiced the חרם is questionable." Butler, *Joshua*,
71.

103. Gopin, *Between Eden and Armageddon*, 85.

104. Niditch, *War in the Hebrew Bible*, 56.

Amorite expression, "to eat the *asakkum*" of a god or king and consequently had to do with certain spoils of war marked for the treasury of the royal house or for sacrificial offering to the deity.[105] As such, by prioritizing extant cultic activity and the positive purposes of the *ban*, the focus is turned from violence and its shocking implications for Yahweh in terms of his character, attributes and purposes.

Similarly Niditch concedes, "One group of biblical writers, like many modern scholars, tries to make sense of the ban in terms of justice in a way that discloses their own discomfort with the sacrifice tradition."[106]

Another who interprets the *ban* in nonviolent terms is Yoder who, whilst acknowledging that the conquest of Canaan is "full of bloodshed" explains, nonetheless, that this must, once again, be understood in its original cultural context, i.e., cultically. In other words, before the battle the enemy army or city would be under the *ban* and therefore "devoted to the Lord" and consequently comparable to an animal on the altar. He grants that no booty, slaves or cattle were to be taken but concludes that such killing was not *instrumental*, contributing practically to a political goal, but was rather *sacrificial* and thereby, in his opinion, acceptable.[107] In this manner he presents a sacred and holy context to *ḥērem* rather than one containing merely the banality of violence, albeit divine violence.

Conversely, Niditch considers the ramifications of the *ban*, asking for whom it might be meaningful in terms of such sacrifice, whether sacred or not. She concludes that rather than being focused upon the destruction of the enemy the *ban* in fact validates them as human and valuable, not turning them into a monster worthy of destruction or a cancer to be rooted out. Rather, the enemy is not the unclean "other," but a mirror of the self, that which God desires for himself.[108] Such an explanation might yet prove "thin gruel" for those exterminated and those mourning this extermination by and for Yahweh in his apparent desire to uphold and validate their value and humanity in the *ban*.

---

105. Boling, *Joshua*, 207. Further, he proposes that there may, in fact, have been a practical reason for the execution of the *ban*, arguing that in biblical texts it is "frequently associated with destruction by fire, and the latter has been interpreted as a response to epidemic disease, especially bubonic plague." Ibid. Boling argues this irrespective of the fact that the biblical texts fail to mention such contamination and its erasure by *ḥērem*.

106. Niditch, *War in the Hebrew Bible*, 34.

107. Yoder, *Politics of Jesus*, 78.

108. Niditch, *War in the Hebrew Bible*, 49–50.

Holy War & the Ban

As demonstrated, there are a number of biblical uses of the *ban* in the overall context of *ḥērem*, principally in regard to it being seen as a "devoted (thing)" and something set apart as belonging to Yahweh and thereby forbidden for profane use.[109] Whilst acknowledging this range of usage and the various means of interpretation, understanding and application we are primarily focusing on the complementary use of *ḥērem* as it pertains to divine violence in the context of war.

Conrad affirms this complementary nature of the *ban*, noting that it is used both in accounts of early Israelite conflicts to refer to war booty whilst being concurrently linked to that which is devoted to Israel; concluding that in a victorious militaristic milieu nothing is to be spared and that Israel must therefore "utterly destroy" everything.[110] All those interpreting *ḥērem* agree that destruction is complete; the arena of controversy exists only in regard to who initiates the *ban* and for what purpose.

The idea of total destruction is taken forward by Mayes who defines *ḥērem* as that which is used for the extermination of the enemy in a holy war as well as for the exclusive reservation of certain things to Yahweh. The common factor is that the things so designated are not available for common use.[111]

Where the word *ḥērem* is used with its full religious force, however, and always in its nominal form, it means uncompromising consecration without the possibility of recall or redemption. It was not, therefore, applied merely to idolatrous objects, but to all things which could have been taken as plunder or people who could have been enslaved. It was never presented, according to Lilley, as the normal procedure of war, although the verb could be used in this definitive secondary sense to denote overwhelming destruction of the enemy.[112]

It is this notion of "overwhelming destruction" with all its moral and theological ramifications which commends the *ban* to our study and understanding of not just Old Testament violence but divine violence per se. In the biblical accounts it does not appear as an arbitrary expression of force but rather as part of Yahweh's overall modus operandi and, more crucially,

---

109. Conrad, "Ban," 73.

110. Ibid., 73.

111. Mayes, *Deuteronomy*, 141.

112. Lilley, "Understanding the Herem," 177. "It forbade the use of property, or relationships with people. It applied only occasionally to loot, and not to idolatrous objects; but in its application to enemies, it involved extermination, and thus the verb acquired its secondary sense of 'destroy.'" Ibid., 169.

as part of his character, especially in regard to his covenantal relationship with Israel.

As Hawk observes,

> The verb occurs frequently in connection with the conquest of cities and peoples, often with a qualifying phrase or note that reports the annihilation of a population . . . These campaigns of extermination are usually presented as a response to a divine decree and place the conduct of war within the context of the nation's relationship with YHWH. The massacres of populations are cast as acts of careful obedience to the divine decrees and enhance the sense of Israel's covenantal loyalty.[113]

The Ban at Jericho

There are a great many Old Testament texts in which the *ban* is proscribed; Niditch, for instance, cites numerous examples in this war-category, including Deut 2:34–35, the defeat of Sihon; Deut 3: 6–7, the defeat of Og; Josh 6: 17–21, the destruction of Jericho and Josh 8:2, 24–28, the destruction of Ai.[114] The common factor amongst them all is that on Yahweh's behest all humans, regardless of age, gender or military status, are destroyed, in some instances livestock is also included in the slaughter.

To take one example—Joshua chapter 6 delineates how Yahweh gives over Jericho to "irrevocable destruction." In the story Yahweh is seen to instruct Joshua in his requirements for the inevitable fall of this great, walled city including stark and startling commands for every living person and animal to forfeit their lives upon pain of the *ban* coming back upon Israel.[115]

These plans of Yahweh included specific and detailed instructions for the exact means of this conquest to be successful, including what should be carried, by whom and the number of circumnavigations of the city walls and the manner and timing of the final denouement. The fall of Jericho therefore stands as a case study of von Rad's theory of holy war which he asserts was an eminently cultic undertaking, in that it was prescribed and sanctioned by fixed, traditional, sacred rites and observances.[116]

---

113. Hawk, *Berit Olam*, 99.

114. Niditch, *War in the Hebrew Bible*, 34–35.

115. "חרם was not only a program for Israel to accomplish. It was a temptation in Israel's way. She could be placed under חרם if she violated the program of חרם set out for her by her leader. The danger was not only individual. The individual's act endangered the entire community." Butler, *Joshua*, 71.

116. Rad, *Holy War*, 51.

Jericho is thereby interpreted and understood as an instance of Yahweh's holy war and also representative of a model of divine violence. As Steffen notes, in the realm of action, *ḥērem* refers to a divinely sanctioned use of force and violence for ends willed by God, so that *ḥērem* satisfies the formal criteria for invoking generic holy war. It is clear from the text, he argues, that *ḥērem* is here divinely directed, and the Hebrew Scriptures also clearly set forth the details of Yahweh's expectations.[117]

The text of Joshua is explicit and the goals and benefits for the Israelites are minutely delineated; in their obliteration of the town, divine wrath would be turned aside and the Hebrew nation would once again be able to enjoy Yahweh's compassionate attention.[118] Even the most non-violent reading and interpretation of this text would struggle to explain the blatant violent over and under-tones inherent in Yahweh's means of re-establishing the otherwise broken harmony between himself and Israel.

Steffen notes that *ḥērem* presents one version of a divinely commanded "holy war" in ancient Israel and is manifest in obliteration bordering on omnicide and when this command is given by God the expectation is that the faithful were always to respond with absolute fealty. He concludes that God's involvement in the actual destruction and the divine desire for the annihilation of enemies is unambiguous.[119] The unavoidable reality of the story of Joshua at Jericho is therefore that the irrevocable and absolute destruction of an entire city puts him back on strong relational terms with his chosen people; a more violent manner of reconciliation could however hardly be imagined.[120] This is further coupled and extrapolated by his threat of the *ban* being transferred upon the Israelites should they ever demure in the execution of his commands. This constitutes, to say the very least, an entirely violent milieu.

This story of Joshua's enactment of the *ban* remains emblematic for Jews, both in terms of their understanding of Yahweh's character as well as their relationship and commitment to him. It is also serves as a reminder of their ongoing responsibilities and the consequences thereof should they fail to adhere strictly to Yahweh's vision of their mutual relationship, given

117. Steffen, *Demonic Turn*, 184.

118. Hawk, *Joshua*, 108.

119. Steffen, *Demonic Turn*, 184–85.

120. "The practice of devoting something to destruction is associated with warfare throughout biblical literature and is signified in Hebrew by the root *ḥrm*." Hawk, *Joshua*, 99. He then notes that in Joshua 6:17–27 the root occurs five times both as a noun (*ḥērem*) and as a verb (*heḥĕrîm*) concluding that this root "has no precise equivalent in English (although NRSV's 'devote to destruction' comes close)." Ibid., 99.

sometimes through ferocious commands and forged in the crucible of divine violence and manifest in violent human conflict.

As Butler notes,

> The story of Jericho entertained and instructed Israel for long generations. Each new historical situation added another dimension of meaning to the narrative. Throughout the long history of telling and interpretation, one message continued to ring out loud and clear: God fights for his people. The people of God testified repeatedly that what they possessed came from the hand of god, not the strength of men. Israelite audiences never lost the captivating awe and mystery of the lesson. The most ancient city of the land with its seemingly impregnable fortifications fell easily before Joshua and his God.[121]

Conclusion

Not all however have understood the *ban* in violent terms; Yoder, for example, suggests that *ḥērem* was unique in relation to the morality of the time not in its violence, but in ensuring that war would never become a source of immediate enrichment through plunder.[122] He does not deny the *ban* or that it was exercised, he instead plays down the otherwise explicit violence with an appeal to the ethics of war and extant morality.

Another who accepts the reality of the *ban* and its historical application is Soggin who takes a wider view of its practice, arguing that it represents the total destruction of the enemy and his goods at the conclusion of a campaign with the implication that looting was never allowed in any circumstances.[123]

Both Yoder and Soggin engage with and express their respective understandings of *ḥērem*, illustrating the broad spectrum of scholarly agreement on its historical veracity and application. Where agreement ceases is in a shared consensus on the otherwise blatant violence of the instruction and its implications for God's character and divine violence in particular.

Admittedly, such a consensus raises thorny theological issues, both for Godself and for human praxeology. In regard to the ongoing relevance and potential applicability of *ḥērem*, for example, Gopin notes that as long as such biblical words were and are considered to be expressive of something

---

121. Butler, *Joshua*, 72.
122. Yoder, "If Abraham Is Our Father," 96.
123. Soggin, *Joshua*, 97.

that God wills, or willed at one time, it will always be more difficult theologically to categorically reject the morality of a war that systematically
slaughters the innocent, if they are non-monotheists or not of one's faith.[124]

In their desire to explicate *ḥērem* less violently and thereby to absolve
God of divine violence, either in the past or the present, scholars continue
to interpret and re-interpret its meaning, substance and potential ramifications. Niditch attempts a non-violent volte-face in her observation that
the *ban* as sacrifice has a terrifying completeness and fairness about it and,
because all has been promised to God, there is no individual decision that
need be made about sparing this person or that, no guilt about tactical or
surgical strikes that go awry. Rather, in the *ban*, all people are condemned
and the matter is out of one's hands.[125]

Whilst this might appear to be rather a neat apology for the *ban*, the
fact remains that in taking the matter out of human hands responsibility
necessarily transfers into the hands of God. This being so, consideration
must be given as to what implications the *ban* has on the one authorizing
it. It is certainly terrifying and complete, as Niditch suggests, but the arguments provided to suggest that *ḥērem* is also non-violent, kind or loving are
far from straightforward and certainly not compelling. Indeed, it is very
difficult to imagine or construct a context in which the *ban*, as biblically
presented in the context of war, is anything less than an entirely violent divine action.

More than this, *ḥērem*, taken on its face-value as expressed in the Old
Testament Scriptures in the war-texts, provides compelling insight into the
character of Yahweh and also his relationship with Israel; it is represented
as a covenantal relationship and one steeped in violence, both divine and
human.

As Wellhausen summarizes, "The armed camp, the cradle of the nation, was also its most ancient holy of holies. There was Israel and there was
Yahweh."[126] Or rather, *ḥērem* indisputably demonstrates that divine violence
is at the heart of Yahweh's purposes and modus operandi, especially in regard to his covenantal engagement with his chosen people, Israel.

124. Gopin, *Between Eden and Armageddon*, 94.

125. Niditch, *War in the Hebrew Bible*, 50.

126. Wellhausen, *Israelitische und jüdische Geschichte*, 26. In his introduction to von
Rad's theory of holy war, Ollenburger observes of Wellhausen's perspective that for him,
"war was not just a feature of Israel's experience, or even of its religion. Ancient Israel as
the people of God was a military camp, and its God was a warrior. War was at the heart
of Israel's religion and thus of its identity." Ollenburger, "Introduction," 3.

New Testament Violence

The Old Testament has provided a number of motifs, models and narratives that associate God with violence, to varying degrees. The New Testament might usually be seen as a less fertile ground for such evidence and yet it too provides numerous examples of violence, whether sanctioned, tolerated, promised, accommodated or perpetrated by God. Indeed, despite what Young calls the common Christian claim that the "loving" God of the New Testament is different from the "angry" God of the Old, violence, he argues, is also central to the New Testament: through violence God inaugurates the Christian dispensation and the primary Christian symbol, the crucifixion, which is the ineradicable centerpiece of the Christian message of redemption is, he concludes, indubitably an act of extreme violence.[127]

Further, as a foundational New Testament concept, even the clear, over-arching delineation between believers and unbelievers, between those considered good and bad, creates a mind-set predisposed to conflict and violence. Avalos suggests that violence emerges when there is a scarcity of resources and the deliberate restricting of access.[128] This is coupled with the eschatological promise given to Christians that the final consummation of history will take place through a great outbreak of divine violence, where evil will be destroyed, before the revealing of a new heaven and a new earth and that God has the power to destroy both body and soul in hell.[129] It is therefore apparent that there is at least an undercurrent and at most a distinct theme of violence running throughout the entire New Testament.[130]

127. Young, *Violence of God*, 5.

128. See Avalos, *Fighting Words*. In response, Neufeld observes that "with respect to the New Testament, the restriction of salvation only to the elect, or only to believers, thus renders it violent at its very core." Neufeld, *Subversion of Violence*, 6. Kille notes, in "Group Identity Formation," that through a process of causing a member of a group to be paranoid of those outside it the group is able to sustain itself and consolidate a feeling of belonging in the adherent. By this process, "'We' become the Children of the Light; 'they' are the Children of Darkness." Kille, "Bible Made Me Do It," 61.

129. In the context of New Testament eschatology, Beale notes that it speaks of "the future consummation of the latter days," and that "many eschatological events will not be fulfilled until Christ returns, including the bodily resurrection of all people, the destruction of the present cosmos, the creation of a new heavens and earth, and the final judgment." Beale, "Eschatology," 331–32.

130. Having delineated God's purposes and plans in the New Testament Stählin notes that "wrath is an essential and inalienable trait in the biblical and NT view of God." Stählin, "Wrath of Man," 423. Houtart observes that "the struggle between good and evil is another source of violence very closely linked to religion. It is largely present in the Bible, in both the Old and New Testaments." Houtart, "Cult of Violence," 1.

The Violent Cross

In his preamble to a consideration of the cross, atonement, and nonviolence, Belousek states that the cross of Christ is more than nonviolence and that, in fact, it reveals the way that God does justice and makes peace through acts of costly faithfulness for the salvation of humanity.[131] He later acknowledges the danger of an a priori agenda and admits that no method of interpretation and understanding is completely bias-free[132] whilst remaining seemingly oblivious to his own pre-agenda in terms of a cross which, whether it comes before nonviolence in his reckoning or not, is in its most basic form nonetheless a patently violent medium by which humanity's salvation might be won. Even if that which the cross accomplishes is inherently non-violent, the means to this end could hardly have been any *more* violent. Moser notes the crucifixion of Jesus as a particularly memorable case of God's severity, concluding that aside from its theological significance the human treatment of Jesus before his death was remarkably severe.[133]

To "soften the blow" of this perceived New Testament violence Boersma posits that although God steps into a violent world, on the cross he performs an act of amazing hospitality, which he accepts is attended by violence, and yet in so doing God reaches the eschatological goal of pure, unconditional hospitality.[134] Whether the act is "justified" or not by its ac-

131. Belousek, *Atonement, Justice, and Peace*, 68. Moltmann gives further primacy to the crucifixion, stating that "the death of Jesus on the cross is the centre of all Christian theology. It is not the only theme of theology, but it is in effect the entry to its problems and answers on earth. All Christian statements about God, about creation, about sin and death have their focal point in the crucified Christ." Moltmann, *Crucified God*, 204.

132. Belousek, *Atonement, Justice and Peace*, 71.

133. Moser, *Severity of God*, 41. On whether this treatment should be assigned to God Moser observes, "Nonetheless, God's *allowing* the crucifixion of Jesus is severe by any ordinary standard of severe permission . . ." Ibid., 42. Stott concedes that crucifixion "is probably the cruellest method of execution ever practised, for it deliberately delayed death until maximum torture had been inflicted. The victim could suffer for days before dying." Stott, *Cross of Christ*, 31. Cicero, in his defence of Gaius Rabirus, condemned crucifixion as *crudelissimum taeterrimumque supplicium*, "a most cruel and disgusting punishment" and explained, in regard to crucifixion and the veil covering the condemned man's head, that "these are horrors which ought to be far removed not only from the person of a Roman citizen but even from his thoughts and his gaze and his hearing. It is utterly wrong that a Roman citizen, a free man, would ever be compelled to endure or tolerate such dreadful things." Cicero, "In Defence of Gaius Rabirius," 277.

134. Boersma, *Violence, Hospitality and the Cross*, 37–38. He further notes, "Our post-modern eyes are perhaps trained to see the violence of the cross more clearly than its hospitality." Ibid., 37–38.

complishments, it is hard to sanction an interpretative method that, in such an overtly violent scenario, nonetheless seeks to convolute an explanation that is entirely violence-free.[135]

Denials of this kind raise the question of how *any* process of interpretation might be approached if the interpreter has embraced such an a priori position in regard to an attitude and outlook of nonviolence.[136] Flew's analogy of the Invisible Gardener[137] is once again instructive, as by the time an explanation is given as to how non-negative "violence" is by means of a thousand qualifications, its use has been illegitimatized from normative usage and understanding. Further, an interpretation of the cross shaped by a presumption of nonviolence might also miss or dismiss, whether consciously, or unconsciously, the "violence" of God's own action through the cross.[138]

God's Hospitality

When seeking to accommodate violence in a doctrine of God and the atonement it is, therefore, possible to focus attention on his desire to deliver humanity back into "hospitality" with himself. With this primary focus the *means* by which it might be achieved can, however, be forgotten, underplayed or ignored. Those advocating a doctrine of non-violence find it difficult to conceptualize this endeavor in terms of an actual deliverance of human beings by the overcoming of an actual Satan and real demonic hordes, the defeat of sin and the resultant setting free of people from death. This war-like scenario, if it be the case, necessitates a victory being won in a far from non-violent manner.[139]

---

135. "By presuming nonviolence as the answer to violence in atonement theology, we may make the cross a stumbling block to ourselves, such that we fail to see how God-in-Christ acts redemptively in response to human violence, not despite the cross, but (as Paul says) *through the cross.*" Belousek, *Atonement, Justice and Peace,* 73.

136. Boersma acknowledges that "there is no denying that the cross is a place of violence." Boersma, *Violence, Hospitality and the Cross,* 38. He then questions, "When we say that hospitality is accompanied by violence, are we saying that it is accompanied by something negative or morally insidious?" Ibid., 38.

137. Flew, "Theology and Falsification," 48–49.

138. Belousek, *Atonement, Justice and Peace,* 73–74. He adds that "Paul depicts God's just act of forgiveness through the cross of Christ with a startling image that is explicitly violent: God crucifies both our transgressions and the legal demands against us (Col 2:13–14)." Ibid.

139. "Beginning from a 'presumption of nonviolence,' one might tend to neglect the potential significance of such [violent] imagery. While the violent imagery of the cross needs to be appropriated carefully to avoid abuse, it should not be ignored." Belousek, *Atonement, Justice and Peace,* 74.

Alternatively, this power-encounter can be framed as a *battle* to be won in order to pre-empt the end of an eternal war and it would, like any war, necessarily be bloody, messy and involve conflict, courage, sacrifice and, inevitably, violence. This does not necessitate the advocacy of violence per se but rather opens up awareness of its potential presence and the affiliated admission and realization that only God has the capacity and capability of waging and winning such a war—whatever his chosen means of doing so.[140] If God's accomplishment is viewed this way it is fitting to state that a non-violent God would not be *capable* of securing victory on behalf of a lost humanity and certainly not against such formidable foes.

The Temple Incident

Having acknowledged some of the expansive and over-arching violence prevalent in the New Testament, our chosen means of addressing the topic of New Testament violence will be to focus on one particular event as paradigmatic of the overall theme. Given the subject of this thesis it is particularly resonant that the issue chosen features the incarnated Jesus Christ in an historical activity. The event is one that has come to be known as The Cleansing of the Temple although Matson prefers Temple Incident to "cleansing" since the latter implies prior judgment of the meaning and interpretation of the event.[141] Ellens argues that to demystify the event further it should be ascribed by what he calls its right name: Jesus' violence in the temple;[142] because whatever Jesus' ulterior motives for acting this way in the temple, Ellens asserts that they were nonetheless essentially violent, abusive and sacrilegious.[143] It is, therefore, a compelling and important event in Jesus' life, offering unique theological insight into the character, purpose and actions of God, as manifest in Jesus Christ, in the context of a divine soteriological plan.

There are many similarities between the Johannine account of the Temple Incident and those portrayed in the Synoptic Gospels; Morris contests this, arguing that despite the assertions of some critics there are practically no resemblances between the two narratives, apart from the

---

140. "One important reason why God is so often depicted as violent in the Bible is that the myth of redemptive violence has been influential upon the biblical view of God." Young, *Violence*, 55. See Wink, *Engaging the Powers*, 28, for further discussion of this point.

141. Matson, "Temple Incident," 145.

142. Ellens, "Violent Jesus," 34–35.

143. Ibid, 25.

central act.[144] Besides that stating there are "practically no resemblances" far over-reaches the point, our area of focus is on what Morris calls the "central act"—the actions of Jesus in the Temple area during this incident; on this issue there is a great deal of convergence between the four gospel accounts.

We, however, will highlight the Fourth Gospel account[145] because of its greater attention to detail in regard to the historical occurrences of the event. Most notably, in the Fourth Gospel Matson notes that Jesus drives out not only the sellers of animals but also the sheep and oxen themselves and that in particular, to highlight this act, the Fourth Evangelist has Jesus making a whip of cords to help drive out the animals, thus underscoring their presence in the Temple court and emphasizing the dramatic nature of the action. In similar fashion, Matson concludes, this account has Jesus actually pouring out the coins of the money changers—again a dramatic emphasis of an action only implied in the other accounts.[146]

So, whilst almost no New Testament event receives unanimous affirmation as to its historicity, this one meets many of the main criteria. For instance, in regard to the multifarious difficulties in ascertaining historicity of a biblical story or incident Marshall asserts that it is clear that many factors enter into the historian's reconstruction of the past, thereby hindering the arrival at certainty. In fact, the sources are fragmentary and opaque too often and the original events are too complex, he states, for any source to reproduce them fully, whilst several reconstructions of what happened are often possible. He concludes that the historian is therefore frequently reduced to reasoned conjectures and assessments of comparative probabilities.[147] To clarify and counteract these issues Marshall suggests a list of seven historical criteria to be applied to biblical texts to ascertain historicity.[148]

Certainly, the passage is multiply attested, fulfills both dissimilarity and embarrassment criteria, does not go against the grain of naturalism and it coheres with the sort of prophetic work Jesus is thought to have performed—and the fact that it is presented differently in John when compared with the other synoptic accounts bolsters its historical plausibility.[149]

---

144. Morris, *Gospel According to John*, 167.

145. The passage has generated much scholarly literature. In addition to the commentaries, see the following representative essays and the literature they cite: Chilton, "[ὡς] φραγέλλιον ἐκ σχοινίων," 330–44; Evans, "Temple Action of Jesus," 634–37; Fredriksen, "Historical Jesus," 249–76; Matson, "Contribution to the Temple Cleansing," 489–506; and Moloney, "Reading John 2:13–22," 432–52.

146. Matson, "Temple Incident," 146.

147. Marshall, "Historical Criticism," 127.

148. Ibid., 127–30.

149. Anderson, *Quest for Jesus*, 142–43. Lincoln observes that "in setting his

Matson observes that it would be erroneous to present a demarcation between the incident and its theological implications and rather it should be viewed "as a prophetic symbolic act pointing to God's eschatological intervention, which would involve the Temple in some way."[150] Given the magnitude of this symbolism as a warning and forerunner of God's promised "destruction of the Temple" and his emblematic "rebuilding" of it in the person of Jesus[151], it is appropriate that the human parameters of Jesus' behavior should have been pushed to such an extent. The wrath of Jesus is, of course, in the first instance a sign and demonstration that he was an actual man of flesh and blood.[152]

The impact of this implication confirms that the ultimate significance of the Temple Incident is therefore christological and not primarily ecclesiological.[153] Further, in his discussion of the Incident being placed by John at the beginning of his Gospel Morris concurs that this is due to the fact that he has a theological rather than a chronological approach.[154] The question is then raised as to what these christological and theological implications are in terms of Jesus himself, his character, purpose and actions; with the additional repercussion of what might be added to an understanding of God's nature.

Jesus' actions are described by Anderson as those of a "northern prophet" who, when confronted with the mercantile character of the sacrificial system, saw it as a sacrilege and sought to expunge its flaws. His didactic conclusion is that in all four Gospels this incident pits Jesus against

interpretation of the temple incident at the beginning of Jesus' public mission he wants his readers to understand from the outset the significance of what has happened in Jesus." Lincoln, *Saint John*, 143. Conversely, whilst acknowledging scholarly argument over chronology, Herzog argues that, "Consensus does seem to place the incident at the end of Jesus' ministry rather than at the beginning, thereby favoring the Synoptics over John . . ." He concedes that "beyond this point, agreement ends." Herzog, "Temple Cleansing," 820. Given his acceptance of the chronological argument, he might accede that the placing of this incident remains controversial with no definitive conclusion.

150. Matson, "Temple Incident," 147. On this historical incident's symbolic meaning this account is an example of history and theology intertwined from the start of the tradition until its canonical finalization. Anderson, *Quest for Jesus*, 143.

151. Matson notes that the Fourth Evangelist "understands the restoration of the Temple to be metaphorical in and through the body of Jesus, not a building in Jerusalem. By indicating that the "temple" is a metaphor for Jesus himself, FE (Fourth Evangelist) makes Jesus' resurrection the fulfillment of the Temple's restoration." Ibid., 148. Cf. Evans, "Jesus' Action in the Temple," 237–70, for a full discussion of the potential symbolic connotations of the Temple incident.

152. Stählin, "Wrath of Man," 427.

153. Beasley-Murray, *John*, 42.

154. Morris, *John*, 167.

the central cultic and national institution of Judaism leading directly to his opposition and demise at the hands of religious leaders, though carried out by the Romans.[155]

Likewise, Casey observes that in throwing people out of the Temple Jesus stopped those trading in it; he also prevented those carrying vessels through it.[156] He notes, therefore, that overturning the tables of the money changers was not a symbol of the Temple's destruction or of anything else but rather it was part of the practical action of stopping commercial activity in the house of God. For Casey, the reason that Jesus was not arrested immediately was because he had too much power, not too little and that he was crucified for exactly the same reason.[157]

Lincoln, however, questions the "cleansing of the temple" as a response to commercial abuse, arguing that this disruption of one of the most significant feasts of the year is understood and interpreted as a symbolic action that temporarily brings to a halt the sacrificial system understood to be ordained by God in the law.[158] Sanders contends that the turning over of even one table points towards destruction, questioning whether Jesus' choice to break something would have been a better symbol, before conceding that he will leave it to others whether the assessment of "overturning" is a self-evident symbol of destruction, before concluding that to him it appears to be quite an obvious one.[159] Not as obvious to those whose business was curtailed, however, who might understandably "interpret" Jesus' actions as a direct, personal and violent attack upon them and the precursor to his literally throwing them out of the Temple environs. A symbolic understanding of the Incident requires exploration, but not to the exclusion of the blatant and literal, historical action which Jesus enacted.

In order to retain focus on violence in the New Testament, discussions pertaining to the pericope's purpose and debates about motivation and *raison d'être* in Jesus' actions will not be undertaken.[160] The centrally portant

155. Anderson, *Quest for Jesus*, 143.

156. Casey, "Culture and Historicity," 319.

157. Ibid. Ellens describes the Temple incident as the event that ultimately killed Jesus, stating that "there is a straight-line cause-and-effect sequence of actions that led from the cleansing of the temple to his death on the cross." Ellens, "Violent Jesus," 17.

158. Lincoln, *Saint John*, 137.

159. Sanders, *Jesus and Judaism*, 70.

160. "Jesus' action was very vigorous, and it might be perceived as disrupting the arrangements for divine worship. Two points follow. Jesus must have had a reason for his action, and he would have had to explain what that reason was. He would also have had to have some means of doing something so authoritative." Casey, "Culture and Historicity," 311.

element of this event for Ellens and the one of which he contends that truth can be told is that it was a case of Jesus having "one of his fits of violence."[161] Our focus will remain upon what the Temple Incident demonstrates about God's character as manifest in the person and actions of Jesus in terms of wrath, judgment, and violent activity in achieving his purposes.

The issue under consideration is therefore Jesus' addressing, confronting and expelling people and animals from the temple area.[162] Commenting on verses 14–17 of John chapter 2, Beasley-Murray notes of this ejection of the traders from the Temple with their beasts and birds for sacrifice, in addition to the scattering of their money, that it equates to an act of wrath which the traders were powerless to resist—thus fitting the previous definition of violence, especially in regard to irresistibility.[163]

Controlling a large area such as the massive outer court or possibly the Royal Portico would, according to Borg,[164] have required a para-military or mob action involving scores of followers, possibly even a larger group, and with the utilization of force; he suggests that controlling the area without such force would have been virtually miraculous.[165]

Casey counters that,

> As for the Romans, they were confronted with a minor distur-
> bance at which a Jewish preacher persuaded most Jews to follow
> his view of what should and should not be done in the court
> of the Gentiles. This did not give them enough reason to risk
> life and limb or to cause carnage. They would surely need the
> chief priests and scribes to tell them whether or not Jesus' action
> should be regarded as seditious. When the Roman governor
> was told that it was, he had Jesus crucified. Borg's description of

161. Ellens, "Violent Jesus," 16. For Ellens, "These happened more frequently than Christian tradition is willing to acknowledge." Ibid., 16. He cites John 2: 3–4; Mark 8: 27–33; John 9: 1–34 and Mark 3:33 as other incidents in which Jesus demonstrated fits of inappropriate response to people.

162. For a detailed consideration of the *Sitz im Leben* of the Temple incident, see Casey, "Culture and Historicity," 306–32.

163. Beasley-Murray, *John*, 39. He notes, "Observe that the wrath was directed not against those engaged in or leading worship, but against those detracting from it." Ibid., 39.

164. Assessing Borg, Wright notes of his early work that he proposes the integration of political, social and theological themes in Jesus' work. Wright, *Victory of God*, 75. The Temple incident is a microcosm of these themes.

165. Borg, *Conflict, Holiness and Politics*, 182. He suggests that in this confrontational situation, "the non-intervention of the Roman troops and the temple police is incomprehensible." Ibid., 182.

these proceedings as non-intervention is inaccurate. His objections should not be accepted.[166]

Again, rather than appealing to miracle, others have explained the Incident in terms of Jesus' charisma and "holy gravitas." Morris, for instance, insists that it is clear that it was not so much Jesus' physical force as his moral power that was employed to empty the courts.[167] He nonetheless implicitly infers acknowledgement of "physical force," noting the prosaic nature of attempts to estimate the effectiveness of Jesus' "whip" as a weapon; it may have been considerable, but he contends that it was rather the blazing anger of the selfless Christ rather than the weapon he carried which cleared the Temple Courts of what he calls its noisy, motley throng.[168]

Casey, however, counters Borg's proposition of the need for para-military action to achieve a clearing of the temple, arguing that he underestimates the role of sacred texts and their interpreters in communities which adhere to them.[169] If this were the case and Jesus were able to evict all those present, going about their legally and religiously sanctioned business, by means of an appeal to scriptural precedent then it is difficult to understand why he found need both for a whip, of whatever kind, and for the over-throwing of the moneylender's tables.

If it is decided a priori that Jesus could not exhibit an act associated with violence, the task for the theologian becomes one of interpretation and re-interpretation. The threat of physical violence, implicit in the carrying of a weapon, is in some way nullified when the "weapon" is construed as a mere "stage prop" rather than a blatant implement of violence. For example, Morris presents it is a "weapon" which can only be called such in its most innocuous manifestation, so that the "whip" (or rather "as it were a whip") which Jesus brandishes is perceived as probably being "a lash of twisted rushes."[170] Likewise, for Turner, it is understood as a "scourge of small cords (a clutch of rope ends)."[171]

It is only in John's Gospel that the account of Jesus having "made a whip out of cords" with which he "drove them all out of the temple" (John

166. Casey, "Culture and Historicity," 321.

167. Morris, *John*, 171.

168. Ibid. Casey concludes that "inferring that Jesus' performance in the temple was a remarkable display of religious authority and power, as we must, we should not refuse to believe it." Casey, "Culture and Historicity," 320.

169. Ibid.

170. Morris, *John*, 171.

171. Turner, *Jesus*, 325.

2:15)[172] is mentioned. With such an implement he "drove them all out of the temple" (John 2:15), but who does this "all" refer to? Lincoln contends that the more likely construal is a reference to the sheep, cattle and humans too particularly in the light of the Synoptic tradition which, he asserts, clearly has the human sellers and buyers being driven out.[173] Commenting on the word "whip" in the account, Lincoln adds that some manuscripts interpret ὡς φραγέλλιον as being «like a whip» or «a sort of whip» and that despite the early date of two of the witnesses—p66 and p75—this appears to be a clear scribal attempt to soften the portrayal of Jesus' action.[174] Beasley-Murray supports this, noting that both these sources and some other MSS prefix ὡς φραγέλλιον to infer «a kind of whip," concluding that despite the age of these witnesses the addition nonetheless looks like an attempt to tone down the action of Jesus.[175] Michaels adds that Jesus was, "Quickly fashioning a whip out of cords . . ."[176], again inferring that Jesus' activity was rushed, spontaneous and unprepared; thereby lessening its potential power, threat, impact and violence.

In regard to this "down-grading" of the potentially violent nature of the passage, Croy notes,

> The editors of the modern critical text have deemed the absence of ὡς more likely original, but whether it was absent or present, it would mean that someone—either the evangelist or later scribes—felt the need to soften the image.[177]

Further, in comparing the "whip" used by Jesus with the more familiar *flaggelum* used by Roman soldiers, Croy also notes that it was an instrument fashioned (ποιήσας) on the spot from available materials; the latter did not

172. In the Johannine passage (John 2:15) ἐξέβαλεν is used, which is the second aorist verb of ἐκ-βάλλω meaning "to cast out of, from, forth." In fact, "In the NT ἐκβάλλειν has particularly the sense of 'to expel' or 'to repel,' especially in the case of demons, who have settled in men as in a house into which they have unlawfully penetrated." Hauck, "βάλλω," 527. It has the further sense of "drive out" and is used to convey the idea of "forcible throwing out, rejection and driving out of enemies, demons and similarly unwelcome beings from a house. Not until the 1st and 2nd cent. A.D. is it used in the favourable sense of sending out." Bietenhard, "ἐκ-βάλλω," 453. "The New Testament uses the word regularly and illustrates 'the whole gamut of its range of meanings,' including the notions of 'casting out,' 'excluding,' 'removal—implying the use of force' and the 'expulsion of demons.'" Ibid. The primary theme is the forcible and irresistible nature of the respective activities.

173. Lincoln, *Saint John*, 137.

174. Ibid., 136.

175. Beasley-Murray, *John*, 38.

176. Michaels, *Gospel of John*, 158–59.

177. Croy, "Messianic Whippersnapper," 557.

likely include, he argues, leather thongs, bone fragments, or bits of metal.[178] He concludes that such an implement would have been made from items such as rushes or reeds which, for him, are akin to rattan or wicker material which might have been available as the animals' bedding or perhaps were already fashioned into ropes or traces.[179] In other words, hardly a weapon to be used for violent purposes.

Such toned-down versions of events mean Jesus' actions become more passive, moral and righteous and merely the acting-out of a dramatic illustration; this presents a more palatable option excusing Jesus from charges of using excessive force, let alone violence.[180] The process of explicating Christ's actions in the Temple Incident has become an object lesson in mitigation as to why that which would normally be construed at face value as one thing, a confrontational and violent act, is actually something else, a piece of drama or a moment of charisma and strength of personality, when it is "perpetrated" by Jesus Christ.

Others, such as Stibbe, explicitly ignore this Incident[181] whilst Lincoln debates the *reasons* for Jesus' actions to the exclusion of the action itself.[182] Alternatively, Morris acknowledges the Incident, detailing how Jesus overturned the tables used by the money changers, pouring their coins upon the floor; he then makes no comment whatsoever on these actions, choosing to ignore the seemingly blatant connotations that such avert and antagonistic deeds would normally elicit.[183]

Whatever reason Jesus had for his actions in the Temple in which he patently provokes a confrontation with the religious authorities[184], the fact remains that the Incident, at the very least, raises the specter of the possibility of "divine violence" in the person of Jesus and at most that Jesus may have perpetrated a violent act, whether it is construed as parabolic or not.[185]

178. Ibid.

179. Ibid.

180. "Some have sought to escape this fact [of Jesus' use of violence in the Temple] by speaking, not very convincingly, of Jesus' moral authority." Borg, *Conflict, Holiness and Politics*, 182. He cites Rawlinson and Scott as two scholars who present what he perceives to be a less than convincing assessment of Jesus' activity. Rawlinson contends that "we must suppose [Jesus] to have dominated the crowd of traffickers by moral and not by physical means: they simply quailed before His holy indignation" (*St. Mark*, 156); whilst Scott contends that Jesus "gave his order and all who heard him were conscious at once that this was their Master" (*Life of Jesus*, 83).

181. Stibbe, *John's Gospel*.

182. Lincoln, *Saint John*, 141–44.

183. Morris, *John*, 171.

184. Lincoln, *Saint John*, 136.

185. "John's interpretation has most in common with the view that the historical

Whether Jesus' actions were symbolic, political, metaphorical or parabolic there is, however, very little suggestion that they did not happen at all.

Adding these various adjectives to Jesus' activities in the Temple is a means, consciously or not, of mitigating their obviously forceful and perhaps violent content. An example is seen in Yoder who, having briefly considered the Temple Incident, concludes that if one sought to reach behind the canonical Gospels to what he calls "the real historical Jesus," such an effort would increase rather than decrease the sociopolitical dimensions of our picture of his work.[186] He gives little evidence for this conjecture, although it should be noted that his own writing and work was produced in the context of his being a professor of theology at the University of Notre Dame where he was a fellow of the school's Joan B. Kroc Institute for International Peace Studies.

Whatever the sub-text for Jesus' disruption in the Temple area, he blatantly manifests actions that in any other context would be construed as confrontational, antagonistic, irresistible, adversarial and therefore violent.[187] The argument that the event was symbolic in some way does not lessen the incident's historicity, power, impact or potential to be interpreted as an incident of New Testament violence perpetrated by no less a person than the incarnate God in Christ. Herzog agrees. Having assessed the divergent claims for respective interpretations of Jesus' actions in the Temple Incident he concludes that it is more than a symbolic action and that it involved violence against the exploiters of the people.[188]

In the Temple Incident the theological conjunction of the two Testaments is demonstrated in terms of message and method. Jesus' audience was predominantly Jewish; representative of a Judaism directly linked, historically and theologically, with what Christians later came to call the

---

Jesus temporarily disrupted trade by a symbolic action that was an attack on the divinely ordained sacrificial system in anticipation of the coming new order." Ibid., 143. Gaston affirms this view, contending that, "Jesus' action can be best understood as an acted parable, a symbolic action which is important not in itself but in what it signifies and which collects an audience for the following interpretation." Gaston, *No Stone on Another*, 85–86.

186. Yoder, *Politics of Jesus*, 41.

187. Hays concedes that "certainly, there is a sense in which the actions described here are violent, particularly the overturning of the tables; Jesus does not politely ask the sellers and moneychangers to leave." Hays, *Moral Vision*, 334. Neufeld endorses a deconstructionist view of Jesus' use of a whip, claiming that it was probably made on the spot with straw that was "lying about" and yet nonetheless admits that, "At the same time, 'throwing out' cautions us not to downplay the forcefulness or the disruptiveness of Jesus' actions as depicted by the evangelists." Neufeld, *Subversion of Violence*, 61.

188. Herzog, "Temple Cleansing," 820.

Old Testament. Jesus was acting in a manner familiar to Jews in terms of his stark, antagonistic and violent engagement with that which stood in the way of his and God's soteriological purposes. Jesus was not trying to destroy and surpass Judaism, on the contrary, he wanted to bring it to its destined goal in the eschatological order of worship in the new creation; this event being initiated both through and in his own deed and presence, as the one who would be crucified and resurrected.[189] Jesus undertook this undeniably dramatic action in order to open up a way for true worship of God and this motif is central to the narrative and dialogue of the pericope.[190] It can be seen that when the intention of an action is soteriological God is willing, in either Testament, to exercise whatever means are necessary to accomplish his purposes—even if these means are occasionally confrontational and violent.

Concluding his thoughts on the Temple Incident Morris observes that one of John's great themes is that in Jesus God is working his purposes out; every critical moment, he argues, sees the fulfillment of Scripture in which those purposes are set forth.[191] Another interpretation of these events is possible—the purposes of God are manifest in Christ and the fulfillment of Scripture is demonstrated in God's violent activity, mediated through Jesus, in an act and moment of epoch-making soteriological significance.

Jesus was confronting Judaism and heralding both its fulfillment and its passing as the means of human engagement with deity—a paradigm shift of this magnitude required a dramatic, demonstrable, irresistible, emphatic and violent, action—just as the heralding of a "new covenant in his blood" heralds another Violent Incident at the crucifixion.[192] Divine violence, therefore, is constant throughout the New Testament, in its most explicit forms only manifest at moments of profound and essential soteriological significance; at the fulfillment and end of Judaism and its sacrificial system and then at the inauguration of the era of the cross and the subsequent genesis of Christianity.[193] The Temple Incident, therefore, provides an essential

189. Beasley-Murray, *John*, 42.

190. Ibid., 40.

191. Morris, *John*, 172.

192. "[Jesus'] coming has brought radical implications for the central symbols and institutions of Judaism, anticipating the end of the sacrificial system and, even further, the replacement of the temple itself through his indestructible crucified and risen body." Lincoln, *Saint John*, 143–44.

193. Matson notes that the Temple incident in John's Gospel "marks the beginning of Jesus' public messianic ministry, as well as the beginning of opposition by "the Jews," a fundamental Johannine theme." Further, the Temple incident "anticipates the Passion, thus providing an initial frame with which to interpret the entire gospel story." Matson, "Temple Incident," 145. Beasley-Murray concurs, stating that the Fourth Evangelist is

interpretative key to the New Testament as well as a lens through which to regard God's nature, purposes and, in this instance, his violence.

We conclude and assert that it is, therefore, impossible to imagine a historical scene in which moneylenders were plying their perfectly legal, state and religiously-sanctioned trade with a full entourage of staff, including a retinue of various animals, and in which an unknown and unauthorized interloper arrives, overturns their tables, spills their money and drives them and their animals out of their area of business and for it *not* to be considered an act of violence. To arrive at an alternative explanation requires not only a strong a priori agenda, disallowing and disavowing violence, but rather a denial that violence could ever, in any context, be associated with Jesus, with God and with his character, purposes, being or function.

Eschatological Violence

An important element of New Testament violence is found in the eschatological writings which Stott refers to as pertaining to the "last things," which include death, the Parousia, the resurrection, the last judgment and the final destinies of heaven or hell, and which together form the focus of eschatology; he asserts that these issues have always fascinated Christian minds.[194]

Certainly it is the case that much has been written on the interpretation of the Christian eschaton and thereby universal agreement on a definitive set of events is little short of impossible. Instead, as Stott has already noted, some concepts emerge on a regular, historical basis in order to provide at least a thematic framework if not a full-blown, definitive theological structure. Moltmann, for example, notes that in Catholic dogmatics up to about 1960 the treatise on eschatology treats first "the eschatology of the individual," with death, judgment, purgatory and hell, and then "the eschatology of the human race," with the Last Day, the resurrection of the dead, and final Judgment.[195]

Each of these themes, in their own way, is linked to and constitutive of an overall framework which would potentially not be alien to the notions of violence and, in particular, divine violence. Or rather, when considering,

---

not so much guilty of correcting the timing of the Temple incident by placing it at the beginning of his gospel, but rather that he did so to highlight its significance for understanding the course of Jesus' oncoming ministry, enabling readers to grasp the nature of Jesus' work, his words and actions, his death and resurrection, and the outcome of it all in a new worship of God, born out of a new relation to God in and through the crucified-risen Christ. Beasley-Murray, *John*, 38–39.

194. Edwards and Stott, *Liberal-Evangelical Dialogue*, 306.

195. Moltmann, *Coming of God*, 236.

for instance, death, judgment and hell it would be difficult to imagine them without at least the possibility of the shadow of violence falling across them.

To further explicate this "shadow," in the contention that in the Second Coming and Judgment Jesus confronts the world in the present, and will do so personally and visibly in the future, Wright reaffirms Jesus as the one to whom every knee shall bow (Phil 2:10–11) as well as being the one who took the form of a servant and was obedient to the death of the cross (Phil 2:6–8). Indeed, he concludes that, as Paul stresses, Jesus is the first *because* he did the second; God will therefore, Wright asserts, put the world and everyone in it "to rights" so that death and decay will be overcome, and God will be all in all.[196]

Wright does not dwell, however, upon exactly how God might both cause every knee, whether willingly or not, to bow to Jesus or, indeed, how a recalcitrant humanity might be put "to rights" without the exertion of a potentially irresistible force. Instead, whilst acknowledging traditional understanding of eschatology in terms of death, judgment, heaven and hell, Wright chooses to push divine violence entirely aside and focus rather on the over-arching and violence-free theme that history is going somewhere under the guidance of God.[197]

Revelation Chapter 14

In order to be more specific in our consideration of eschatological violence we will focus upon just the book of Revelation and, in particular, chapter 14. Kreitzer argues that Revelation contains perhaps the most detailed treatment of the judgment theme in the New Testament, interweaving complex images of judgment (past, present and future) within the apocalyptic vision related by the Seer. He concludes that the use of the Divine Warrior motif might be seen as an extension of this judgment theme which is so central to the book as a whole.[198] In terms of Jewish eschatological expectation Bauckham further notes that the theme of holy war plays a prominent role in which the future will bring the final victory of this Divine Warrior over

196. Wright, *Surprised by Hope*, 142–43.

197. Ibid., 122. Fiddes makes the summation that "the Christian understanding of the last things—the final advent of the Lord of the cosmos, the last judgment, heaven and hell—is located in a story, the death and resurrection of Jesus Christ, and is dependent on certain basic texts." Fiddes, *Promised End*, 6.

198. Kreitzer, "Parousia," 871.

his people's and his own enemies.[199] There could hardly be a more explicitly violent conceptual and linguistic framework for this apocalyptic vision.

In the overall eschatological themes presented in Revelation chapters 12–14 they provide, according to Beasley-Murray, the longest interruption in the judgment visions and are chapters which set the opposition between the emperor worship and the church in the context of the age-long conflict between the powers of darkness and the God of heaven.[200] Likewise, Bauckham posits a violent, cosmological macro-narrative in his observation that in these chapters the church's role is portrayed primarily by means of the image of warfare with the forces of evil; the church being the army of the Lamb, the messianic conqueror of evil (Rev 14:1–5).[201] For this to be the case, of course, there would need to be an acceptance of at least an extrinsically violent God who proposes to fight, when necessary, via human means utilizing the medium of his chosen vessel, the church.

The Grapes of Wrath

Throughout Revelation 14 there are explicit and detailed references to the nature of this expression of divine violence; in equal measure it is shown who is commanding the violence, by what means and against whom and for what reason. In Revelation 14:10b, for example, it states that the one who worships the beast and receives his mark will drink the wine of God's fury, "which has been poured full strength into the cup of his wrath." This metaphor of the "cup of wrath" is found with some frequency in the Old Testament, Aune cites numerous occasions,[202] concluding that their common element is that Yahweh is presented as one compelling his enemies to drink a cup resulting in their drunkenness, which is considered a judgment.[203] It should also be noted that the term ποτηριον, "cup," can be used as a metaphor for destiny[204] and, rather more stridently, for violent death[205], either the fact of violent death or violent death as the consequence of divine punishment.[206]

199. Bauckham, *Climax of Prophecy*, 210.

200. Beasley-Murray, "Revelation," 1031.

201. Bauckham, *Climax of Prophecy*, 285.

202. Pss 11:6; 75:9; Isa 51:17, 22; Jer 49:12; 51:7; Lam 4:21; Ezek 23:31–33; Hab 2:15–16; Obad 16; Zech 12:2.

203. Aune, *Revelation 6–16*, 833.

204. Isa 51:17, 22; Lam 4:21; Ps 75:8; John 18:11.

205. Isa 5:13.

206. Mark 10:38–39 = Matt 20:22–23; Mark 14:36 = Luke 22:42; John 18:11. Aune,

In terms of the "wrath" of Yahweh's "cup," in classical Greek θυμος is used of the inner emotion of passion and anger while οργη is used for its external expression, though these terms are used interchangeably in the LXX as they are in Revelation.[207] The emphasis on the wrath of God, provoked and deserved by the wicked behavior of humans, which results in the judgment of offenders, is a biblical motif found frequently in Revelation.[208] One would have to take an almost obtuse a priori non-violent hermeneutic in order to interpret these concepts as anything less than suggestive of very aggressive divine activity, let alone explicit divine violence.

In Revelation 14:19b it is further stated that the "grapes" will be cast, "into the great winepress of the wrath of God"—a clause which, according to Aude, is an allusion to Isaiah 63:1–6, which depicts the Lord as the divine warrior coming with garments stained with the blood of his enemies in comparison with the garments of one who treads grapes in the winepress.[209] This represents yet another explicit reference to divine violence and its being unleashed upon those who have incurred God's wrath.

In a reference to the cultural and biblical context of these fabled "Grapes of Wrath," Barker notes that when the prophet Joel foresaw the Great Judgment in the valley of Jehoshaphat he spoke of harvesting grain and of trampling grapes. The nations would assemble there on the Day of the LORD, the sun and moon would be darkened and the stars cease to shine, and then the LORD would give his command:

Put in the sickle, for the harvest is ripe.

Go in, tread, for the wine press is full.

The vats overflow, for their wickedness is great. (Joel 3:13).[210]

In his summation of Revelation chapter 14 Beale therefore asserts that the divine violence delineated there of God wreaking destruction upon the irreligious is as thoroughgoing as one mowing down the ripe harvest and crushing grapes in the winepress. He concludes that the building up of sin throughout history reaches its zenith in the final generation of history and has made the impious ripe for wrath.[211] Those destroyed thereby earned and

---

Revelation 6–16, 833.

207. Rev 14:10; 16:19; 19:15.

208. The term is used eighteen times in the New Testament, ten of which are in Revelation, with all of the latter uses, bar one, connoting divine wrath. Büchsel, "thymós," 339.

209. Aune, *Revelation 6–16*, 846–47.

210. Barker, *Revelation of Jesus Christ*, 256–57.

211. Beale, *Book of Revelation*, 776.

deserved their destruction and God was therefore justified in this expression of his nature in the furtherance of his overall purposes.

THE SHEDDING OF BLOOD

The stark language and metaphor of violence continues on into Rev 14:20b where it states that the "blood flowed from the winepress to the height of the bridles of horses for one thousand six hundred stadia." Bauckham argues that this is an instance of hyperbole which consists of an extraordinary amount of blood to indicate a slaughter of exceptional proportions and is, he argues, a *topos*, frequently found in ancient literature.[212] Whether a *topos* or not, the reference is, at the very least, one of excessive bloodshed and violence and refers, according to Aune, to God's climactic victory in the final eschatological battle.[213]

This being the case, then however these metaphors and descriptions might be translated and interpreted it is difficult to get away from both their original and overt militaristic and thereby violent connotations and of their association with God. This linkage to divine victory, of course, raises the violence above that of mere human militaristic endeavor and instead equates it to the accomplishment and fulfillment of God's purposes. It becomes, therefore, not merely violence, but rather *divine* violence manifest through human means. Beale observes that as in the Old Testament, so in Revelation 14 these two metaphors of harvest and vintage connote the thoroughgoing and definitive judgment of sinners by God. He concludes that blood rising up to "the bridles of horses" is figurative battle language and functions hyperbolically to emphasize the severe and unqualified nature of the judgment.[214] Figurative or not, the language chosen could hardly have been any more explicit in its manifestation of violent imagery.

TWO SIDES OF THE SAME COIN?

Within the same pericope, Rev 14:17–20, it is stated that the fire "spread out across the world" which Prigent interprets as the fire on which has been poured the incense of worship, that is, the prayers of the saints. Here, he contends, the angel of fire comes out from before the altar, showing once again that worship is not without relation to judgment; the wrath of God is

212. Bauckham, *Climax of Prophecy*, 40.

213. Aune, *Revelation 6–16*, 849.

214. Beale, *Book of Revelation*, 781.

therefore, for him, not the unleashing of a hateful vengeance but is rather the other side of the Gospel.[215]

In equating these two elements of wrath and love as being two sides of the same conceptual coin Prigent exhibits and expresses his fear of biblical ideology that might be construed as violent. Likewise, Collins, too, concedes that one criticism of the Apocalypse is its perceived focus on violent language. She asserts, however, that such language by no means advocates violence of humans against others and yet she cannot avoid the fact that violent imagery is prominent in the text, concluding that the attitude towards violence in the book of Revelation thus seems ambivalent.[216]

Having also seemingly accepted the notion of violence, both human and divine, and particularly of violent confrontation in Revelation, Bauckham, too, sets up an interpretative schema in which language that is otherwise apparently violent indeed only *seems* to be so. Rather, he argues that the lavish use of violent and militaristic *language* is invariably used in a non-militaristic *sense*; in the eschatological destruction of evil in Revelation, he concludes, there is no place for real armed violence—instead, he asserts, that there is ample space for the *imagery* of armed violence.[217]

Again, Collins's interpretation of the indisputable violence, both human and divine, in the book of Revelation is based on what she sees as the subjective benefit that it can facilitate for the individual engaging with it. She posits:

> Meditation on the violent images, symbols, and narratives in the Apocalypse can have a variety of effects. Instead of ignoring or rejecting these portions as distasteful, one can use them as an occasion to discover one's own hostile, aggressive feelings. Critical reflection is then needed to determine the most constructive way of dealing with these feelings. It may be that they should be released in the imagination in a way analogous to Revelation's resolution of tension.[218]

Attempts of this kind to downplay, reinterpret or ignore violence, and especially divine violence, can lead to a degree of confusion and contradiction in those advocating such an approach. Even after having previously down-played the use of violence and violent language, for example, Bauckham nonetheless concedes that in the book of Revelation the call to readers or hearers to "conquer" is fundamental to the structure and theme of the

215. Prigent, *Apocalypse of St. John*, 452.
216. Collins, *Crisis and Catharsis*, 156.
217. Bauckham, *Climax of Prophecy*, 233.
218. Collins, *Crisis and Catharsis*, 173.

book. In fact, he argues that such a call demands the readers' active partici-pation in the divine war against evil.[219]

Quite how one would "fight" such a "divine war" without the use of divine violence is an issue that Bauckham leaves unanswered.

The Satan & The Demonic Realm

We have established that God, at least extrinsically, accommodates violence and now it is time to consider the identity, being and function of that or whom he had to overcome at the atonement, whether primarily or second-arily, metaphorically or in actuality—the Satan, the Devil, the Evil One.[220] Or one, who Perry concedes, when presented as an explanatory hypothesis, is now mythological and pre-scientific.[221]

Whilst acknowledging what he perceives as the imprudence and na-ivety of seeing demonic forces along the lines of "them" and "us," however, Wright is willing to grant that there is, nonetheless, an enemy at work, but one who is subtle and cunning and much too clever to allow itself to be identified simply with one person, group or nation. He concludes that the line between good and evil is clear at the level of God, on the one hand, and the Satan, on the other and yet asserts that it is much less clear as it passes through human beings, individually and collectively.[222]

Conversely, according to Macquarrie, what was previously attributable to "demons" is now explicable through reason, leading to the province of the demons being shrunk away; Occam's razor, he concludes, demands the exci-sion of the concept of the demonic from the categories of modern thought.[223]

219. Bauckham, *Book of Revelation*, 88.

220. "Σατάν and Σατανᾶς are transliterations of the Heb *śāṭān* . . . or the Aram *sāṭānāʾ* and mean 'adversary.' In such instances 8HevXIIgr and the LXX translate the Hebrew expression with *Diabolos* . . . meaning 'the Slanderer'; *Ho Satanās* (rarely used without article) thus designates the opponent of God. In the NT *Satanās* and *Diabolos* can refer to the same supernatural being (cf. Rev 20:2) and can thus be interchanged (cf. Mark 1:13 and Luke 4:2). This highest evil being can also be referred to as *ho ponēros* ('the evil one,' cf. Matt 13:19) and *ho peirazōn* ('the tempter'—cf. Matt 4:3; I Thess 3:5)." Breytenbach, "Satan," 726–27. In the interest of consistency, *Satan* and *Devil* will be capitalized in light of their being referred to at least as alleged "persons," and due to their unique status, both will be preceded by the definite article.

221. Perry, "Taking Satan Seriously," 109.

222. Wright, *Simply Jesus*, 120.

223. Macquarrie, "Classic Idea of the Atonement," 3. Elsewhere Macquarrie ob-serves that "among all ancient peoples, and also among the more backward peoples of our own time, [circa 1956] we find a firmly established belief in demons, invisible and quasi-personal forces of evil which threaten the well-being of men." Ibid., 3.

This is an issue which polarizes religious opinion, producing a tendentious area of theological penumbra, engendering controversy and debate, but little congruence.[224]

> That the "devil," shorthand for evil at its most potent, truly exists is unquestionable. "He" was present throughout the witch-craze but in the hearts not of its victims but its inquisitors. He was present at Auschwitz. His face appears only too often in the daily papers. The danger in demonology is not that it has over-emphasized the need to struggle with the "powers of darkness" but that, too often, it has misplaced and perhaps even belittled the extent of their true identity.[225]

Hastings's quote is a microcosm of current theological debate and understanding of the Devil adding to the overriding malaise around his/its identity. He starts with a depersonalized view giving way to dropping the inverted commas with the later acknowledgement that *his* "face" appears only too often in the media. He is conflicted about evil and the Devil, the linking of the two and the personhood of the latter; he is not alone.

Biblical Background

A robust theological foundation for understanding the Devil must, of course, be built upon testamental evidence and it is therefore important to initially note that every writer of the New Testament makes mention of either the devil, the Satan, the evil one or the deceiver of this world.[226] Macquarrie acknowledges that belief in demonic powers does appear in the pages of the New Testament but argues that "it could hardly be said to be prominent."[227] Certainly the relative prominence or priority of the Satan and demonic powers is open to interpretation and debate. Perry again challenges the notion that Paul is more concerned with sin than the Satan in his theology and asserts that, in fact, Paul not only has a great deal to say about the Satan but further, this element of his theology could only be removed from his

---

224. For a modern overview of the debate see, Johnson, "Powers and Principalities," 14–17. Having assessed the modern theological milieu on the perception and identity of the Satan and having failed to reach a definitive position, Johnson nonetheless concludes of the study of principalities and powers saying that "it is serious and necessary work, for whatever else he may be, the Devil is no joke." Ibid., 17.

225. Hastings, "Devil," 166.

226. Perry, "Taking Satan Seriously," 106.

227. Macquarrie, "Classic Idea of the Atonement," 3.

presentation of the Gospel with serious loss.[228] Conversely, in comparing the Gospels and St. Paul, Macquarrie asserts that whilst removing demons from the former can be done without much difficulty, it would prove rather less easy to eliminate them from Paul because they enter into the very texture of his theology.[229]

Likewise, in terms of the Gospel as Jesus himself preached and understood it, Hastings acknowledges that the Satan and the demonic was central for Jesus; he adds the caveat, however, that it is less clear that this is true of Jesus' own thought and that perhaps it owes rather more to his interpreters.[230] Perry counters such assertions with his view on Jesus' self-understanding of the Satan and the demonic realm and whether he represents a reliable theological source. He contests,

> What we cannot do is to say that Jesus really knew there was no such entity as a personal devil but that he spoke and acted as though there were, in order to accommodate his teachings to what would be credible and accessible to the people in whose culture he had become incarnate. That is to reduce the incarnation to play-acting, and cannot be seriously entertained.[231]

Any attempt to look at the historical and cultural context of Jesus' life, teaching, death and self-understanding must facilitate a broader theological vista that, whilst incorporating God's overall soteriological purposes, does not stop short of putting them into their ultimate, framing context of the eternal and everlasting purposes of a Sovereign God. Noble, for example, warns against what Hanson called a "washing line theology"[232] in which an attempt is made to delineate each and every topic with its own theology—such as a "theology of gender" or a "theology of science"—rather than acknowledging Christian theology as an organic whole, incorporating each of these separate and yet related theological elements into one overarching, inclusive and inter-dependent model. Noble argues that such an outlook is dangerous in its perception of a "theology of the spirit world" which might be presented as separate to an overall and otherwise consistent all-in-one, holistic Christian theology.[233]

Further, it is also essential to be aware of First Century cultural context which necessarily affects perceived meaning, understanding and

---

228. Perry, "Taking Satan Seriously," 106.

229. Macquarrie, "Classic Idea of the Atonement," 3.

230. Hastings, "Devil," 166.

231. Perry, "Taking Satan Seriously," 108.

232. Hanson, *Attractiveness of God*, 47.

233. Noble, "Spirit World," 187.

interpretation.[234] Indeed, acknowledgement must be made of the spiritual and over-arching biblical milieu in which these teachings and theology find their original and thereby potentially ultimate soteriological purpose, meaning and resonance; failing to do so will mean producing a theology which will necessarily fall short of recounting a truly authentic theological picture, for those either in the First or the Twenty First Century. It is therefore not without irony, given his perspective on demythology, that Bultmann nonetheless contests that to understand the theology of parables it is first essential to recapture the culture that informs the text; in the context of the synoptic parables, that of first-century Palestine.[235]

This testamental background is, however, not limited to the New Testament. Rather, in the Old Testament the Satan was originally presented as being one of the angels whose role was to tempt people and to test their faith; he challenged the LORD to let him test the faith of Job (Job 1:1–12) and tempted David to take a census of Israel (1 Chr 21:1). He even stood before the LORD in the holy of holies to challenge Joshua's right to be the high priest (Zech. 3:1). In his origin, however, the Satan, according to Barker, appears to have been an aspect of the LORD himself, insofar as later texts attribute to him what had formerly been described as actions of the LORD.[236]

Barker's assertion raises a problem in diabolic provenance, especially in regard to the issues of the Devil's origin and character, his fall and his future. On these matters Hastings argues that there is remarkably little in Scripture outside the book of Revelation resulting in what he calls a "scriptural paucity" leading to the church being extremely parsimonious in dogmatizing in these areas.[237]

Notwithstanding this dogmatic caveat, there is still a great deal that the Scriptures either explicitly state or at least allude to in regard to the Satan and his activity. In his commentary on the three angels that fly in mid-heaven in Revelation 14:6–11, for example, Bauckham observes that this means that they fly between heaven, which since the Devil's fall is now the uncontested sphere of God's kingdom, and the earth and the sea, where the devil and the beasts rule.[238]

---

234. In his study of the apostle Luke's parables, Bailey notes that they "confront the exegete with what can be called the cultural problem." He notes that whilst Paul expressed his theology in conceptual language the parables were expressed "in stories about particular people who lived in a given cultural setting at a specific time in history." Bailey, *Poet & Peasant*, 27.

235. Bultmann, *Synoptic Tradition*, 166.

236. Barker, *Revelation of Jesus Christ*, 215.

237. Hastings, "Devil," 165.

238. Bauckham, *Climax of Prophecy*, 286.

A cosmological duality of this kind is therefore not alien to the biblical text and has in fact been evident from the very first occurrences of scriptural Satanic references. There are multifarious scriptural occurrences which include a large number of names for the principalities and particularly for the Satan; showing, according to Schlier, how much early Christians were preoccupied with these phenomena. He observes that their names are derived only in a few cases from the Old Testament, which describes the Satan as accuser and tempter,[239] but mentions him only three times.[240]

In an Old Testament incident in Genesis 6:1–4, however, the spirits of the deceased offspring of the sexual liaison between the angels and human women continue to roam the earth as evil spirits and, because of their corrupt nature, continually seek to destroy humanity. Wright posits that their former physical nature is most likely responsible for the implied desire to reoccupy a human body as identified in the Gospels.[241] In the DSS (Dead Sea Scrolls), he claims, the evil spirits develop as a group that operate under the leadership of a chief spirit who is known by the names of Belial, Beliar, and Mastema, and who is probably, he concludes, the "Satan" figure in later Christianity.[242]

Certainly, the term maśṭēmâ originates from the Hebrew root שׂטם (śāṭam) which is a derivative of שׂטן (śāṭān). The origins of this personification are found in the Hebrew Bible whilst the LXX uses the term διαβολος to translate the Hebrew השׂטן thirteen times as a proper name (in Job, Zechariah and 1 Chronicles). In these instances, Wright argues, it could be implied that השׂטן is a member of the bĕnê ĕlōhîm; however, it could be understood that he has been singled out, thus leaving room to recognize him as some other type of being.[243] Maśṭēmâ also appears in Hosea 9:7–8 as a noun that is translated "hostility" and has likely evolved from the concept of hostility or adversarial conduct to the personification of this concept in

---

239. "In fact the different Greek roots for the Devil in the Septuagint—*diabolos/apollyon*—are of very little importance, for what emerges is the concept of the Devil as the supreme Evil One, the Dark Power. He is not only the tempter and accused: he is 'god' and 'prince.'" Walker, *Enemy Territory*, 29.

240. Schlier, *Principalities and Powers*, 12. Wink confirms that, "Satan is mentioned only three times in the Hebrew Scriptures, all of them quite late, and demons go virtually unnoticed." Wink, *Unmasking the Powers*, 174. Dunn reiterates this position, acknowledging the three Old Testament instances (Job 1–2; Zech 3:1–2; 1 Chr 21:1) and noting that in mention of the Satan, "the definite article probably reflects the continuing influence of the original concept, that of a force hostile to God but permitted so to act by God to serve his will." Dunn, *Theology of Paul*, 38.

241. See Mark 5:12.

242. Wright, *Origin of Evil Spirits*, 222.

243. Ibid., 157–58.

postbiblical Judaism in the figure of Satan, *Mastema* (Jubilees), *Belial* (DSS), and other designations in the New Testament.[244]

So, whilst there are many references to a Satan figure in the Old Testament there nonetheless remains a lack of specific and detailed description and ascription of the Satan's characteristics. Hastings, in fact, states that the devil has rather a complicated history before acknowledging that the Old Testament has remarkably little to say on the subject concluding that only in the later books are there hints about him and his function.[245] In response, Langton nevertheless posits the first small beginnings of a stream of Hebrew thought concerning a supernatural enemy of God and humanity; detailing one which/whom was later destined to exercise a predominating influence upon the whole body of Jewish and Christian teaching concerning God and humanity in all succeeding centuries.[246]

By the first century, however, the Satan had developed, Barker asserts, into the antitype of Melchizedek and according to the Qumran fragments 4Q280 and 4Q544 the Satan had three names: the first is Melchiresa, meaning "My king is evil," whereas Melchizedek means "My king is justice"; the second can also be read Satan, meaning "the tempter, the accuser," the antitype of the Paraclete, meaning "the advocate, the intercessor." The third name in the fragment has not survived but Barker conjectures whether it was perhaps the Prince of Darkness, as his followers are called the "Sons of Darkness" and the followers of Melchizedek are called the "Sons of Light."[247] Again, the Satan is seen as the "anti-divine" and an apophatic theological realisation as God's nemesis, adversary and enemy.

The initial association of the devil with the introduction of evil into the world is made, according to Murdoch, in Wisdom 2:24 and the link between devil, Satan and serpent is in Revelation 20:2. That the devil fell from Heaven, so was presumably originally an angel, he notes, is supported by Luke 10:18, and a plurality of angels-become-devils is implied in Matthew 25:41, II Peter 2:4 and Jude verse 6, just as the Heavenly hosts are attested in Genesis 32: 2 and Daniel 7:10. That a third of the stars of Heaven fall in Revelation 12:4–9, and the reference to the war with Michael, provide additional circumstantial details, he states, as does the most significant addition

244. Ibid., 158–59.

245. Hastings, "Devil," 164.

246. Langton, *Essentials of Demonology*, 53. Conversely, Breytenbach argues that the Hebrew Bible's mentions of a celestial śāṭān are probably dateable to the sixth century BC or later and that none of the texts indisputably use śāṭān as a proper name; concluding that, "given these data, it is difficult to maintain, as many scholars have, that we can see in the Hebrew Bible a developing notion of Satan." Breytenbach, "Satan," 730.

247. Barker, *Revelation of Jesus Christ*, 213.

to this complex, Isaiah 14:12–14, the death-song to the arrogant King of Babylon, referred to as Lucifer, the day-star, who wanted to set up his throne above that of God.[248]

Later scholars built upon this diabolic foundation and some, according to Murdoch, went further in their ascriptions and descriptions than the Scriptures themselves. He notes,

> In medieval thought we encounter what might be termed a process of logical extrapolation of the Bible, which is then presented as if it were actually biblical itself. Thus although the devil does not appear in Genesis, assuming his presence means that he has to originate somewhere, and indeed to have a motivation. Medieval treatments of Genesis almost invariably begin with the fall of an angel, usually (but not always) named Lucifer, and of other angels, driven out by Michael. Lucifer is transformed into the head of a council of devils, and various explanations are given for the integration with the serpent for the purpose of causing the downfall of man.[249]

Overall however there is, according to Girard, a biblical and theological centrality of the Devil in the Scriptures which he notes that, especially in spite of his considerable role in the Gospels,[250] modern Christian theology nonetheless scarcely takes into account. If these references to the Satan are examined, he claims, they do not deserve the oblivion into which they have fallen.[251]

Diabolic Definition

Considerable influence has been exerted by Wink and his understanding of the Satan and the demonic realm in the Twentieth Century and on into the Twenty First.[252] He asserts that nothing commends the Satan to the modern mind, acknowledging the difficulty of perceiving and representing him as a spirit, when the modern worldview has banned spirit from discourse and

248. Murdoch, *Medieval Popular Bible*, 21.

249. Ibid., 20–21.

250. Likewise, Hastings agrees that the main argument for Christian belief in the Satan remains undoubtedly the large place he occupies in the New Testament. Hastings, "Devil," 166.

251. Girard, *Satan Fall*, 32.

252. "The quick, sharp glance is just about all theologians of the second half of the twentieth century have allotted to the spirit world; with one exception . . ." Wink is presented as that exception. Noll, "Thinking About Angels," 23.

belief. The Devil is evil in a culture which resolutely refuses to believe in the real existence of evil, preferring to regard it as a kind of systems breakdown, fixable with enough tinkering. Worst of all, he claims, the Satan is simply not a very good intellectual idea, arguing that once theology lost its character as reflection on the experience of *knowing* God and became a second-level exercise in *knowing about*, its experiential ground began to erode and with it a clear dialogue and understanding of the Satan, his being and function.[253]

Throughout history the concept of the Devil has moved with the times. Perceived as a great Christian myth in an age when Western people could not chose their religion, when heretics were persecuted and witches burned, the notion of the Satan infiltrated the romantic symbolisms of an age of revolt and rebellion. More recently, the notion of the Devil has metamorphosed endlessly in societies increasingly drawn to individualism.[254] In terms of perceiving Satanic personhood and to paraphrase the biblical ascription to Paul: the Devil has become all things to all people in order to confuse, confound and delude many.

Against this backdrop a unanimous theological understanding and definition of the Devil is both illusive and elusive; a fitting context and an appropriate metaphor for a "being" who has, throughout the history of theology, been a continual cause of contention, denial and controversy.

Diabolic Theology

From the earliest days of Christianity attempts have been made to dogmatize diabolic theology, with each era seemingly apt to disregard the findings of former times. In terms of addressing and potentially rejecting out of hand Patristic teaching on the Devil and Christ, however, Aulén notes,

> It should be evident that the historical study of dogma is wasting its time in pure superficiality if it does not endeavour to penetrate to that which lies below the outward dress, and look for the religious values which lie concealed underneath.[255]

253. Wink, *Unmasking the Powers*, 9. Kelsey agrees, stating that, "With only sense experience and reason to go on, and with no rational place for an evil first cause, enlightened people simply dropped the devil from consideration. With direct psychic experience no longer admissible as evidence of his reality, the devil was as good as dead." Kelsey, "Mythology of Evil," 16.

254. Which Muchembled presents as a powerful rising tide forcing into retreat all systems of thought which might otherwise aim to impose their blanket certainties. Muchembled, *History of the Devil*, 227.

255. Aulén, *Christus Victor*, 47.

So, whilst Macquarrie argues that the concept of the demonic is, at best, not what he calls "of first-class importance" he yet acknowledges that this is not the case with the Fathers. The reason for this, he postulates, is that in the Fathers the idea of the demonic has become closely connected with the central Christian doctrine of the Atonement. With variations of emphasis, he notes, the teaching of the Fathers is that the meaning of the death of Christ for faith lies in the victory which he won at the Cross over the powers of darkness. Macquarrie concludes that, for the Fathers, Jesus put to flight the demons, destroyed their dominion over man, and so rescued man from sin and death.[256]

These biblical ideas and ontogeny germinated and eventually found expression in the theology of Calvin who describes the Satan as one who opposes the truth of God with falsehoods, who obscures light with darkness, who entangles men's minds in errors, stirs up hatred and kindles contentions and combats; all to the end of eventually overturning God's Kingdom and plunging humans, with himself, into eternal death. Calvin concludes that the Devil is in nature a depraved, evil, and malicious being.[257] Such dogmatic certainty and detailed personification has had a bearing on certain elements of theological and ecclesiastical history ever since.[258]

Conversely, in speaking of the expectation of an imminent arrival of God's Kingdom on earth, Bultmann concludes that the hope of Jesus and the early Christian community was not fulfilled, demonstrated by the fact that the same world still exists and history continues. The reason for this, Bultmann argues, is that the conception "Kingdom of God" is mythological, as is the conception of the eschatological drama and the presuppositions of the expectation of the Kingdom of God, namely, the theory that the world, although created by God, is ruled by the devil, the Satan, and that his army, the demons, is the cause of all evil, sin and disease. The corollary of his position is that the idea of the intervention of supernatural powers in the inner life of the soul, the conception that men can be tempted and corrupted by the devil and possessed by evil spirits, is likewise mythological.[259]

Certainly, overly literalistic images of a personified and ontologically evil being have long provided a "wicker man" for liberals to rail against and

256. Macquarrie, "Classic Idea of the Atonement," 3.

257. Calvin, *Institutes*, 174.

258. Calvin makes his dogmatic assertions whilst noting that "some persons grumble that Scripture does not in numerous passages set forth systematically and clearly that fall of the devils, its cause, manner, time, and character. But because this has nothing to do with us, it was better not to say anything, or at least touch upon it lightly." Ibid., 175.

259. Bultmann, *Christ and Mythology*, 14,15.

fundamentalists to use the acceptance of as a mark of theological ortho-doxy.[260] Such polarities do little to further understanding of such an elu-sive and controversial figure who, in whatever manifestation is presented and accepted, nonetheless occupies, as demonstrated, a place of central importance in both theology and the biblical narrative whether literally or metaphorically.

Acknowledging this figure in an overarching assessment of the vari-ous enemies ranged against God and Israel throughout history, Wright con-cludes that the pagan hordes surrounding Israel were not the actual foe of Yahweh's people. Instead, standing behind the problem of Israel's exile was the dark power known in some Old Testament traditions as the Satan, or the accuser.[261] Even with acknowledgement of this accuser, conclusive adjudica-tion of identity and function has been difficult to ascertain. The parameters of theological speculation on the Devil are wide and few conclusions are deemed universally heterodox, stimulating a wide spectrum of conjecture within diabolical theology.

Assessing the role of the Satan in the book of Job, for example, Wink concludes that whilst God alone is supreme; the Satan is thoroughly inte-grated into the Godhead in a wholly non-dualistic fashion. The Satan is not evil, or demonic, or even fallen, let alone God's enemy; this adversary is merely a faithful, if somewhat overzealous, servant of God, entrusted with quality control and testing.[262] It is, after all, the Satan who prompts God and humanity, in the person of Job, to explore the problem of evil and righteous-ness at a depth never before plumbed—and seldom since.[263] Whilst this is a somewhat unorthodox representation of the Satan, it is nonetheless one in which he is personified and given identity. Wright notes the difficulty such a view raises for Satanic ontology and God-talk, arguing that a position

260. Acknowledging the ontological nature of the Satan Wright concurrently seeks a redefinition; stating that the Devil has no true ontology and yet he does "have an *ontological ground* or a point at which he might emerge in the existence of humankind. He is the construct—albeit a real one—of fallen society. Without a created ontology he is none the less real, but in the same way that a vacuum or a black hole or death itself are real." Wright, *Theology of the Dark Side*, 70.

261. Wright, *Victory of God*, 451. Further, he observes that "stories of the kingdom of YHWH were thus essentially stories of conflict, and that conflict thus came to play a symbolic role within the worldview as a whole. The true god was not at the moment ruling the world in the way that he intended to do. Evil powers had usurped his author-ity, and they would have to be defeated if he was to regain his rightful throne." Ibid., 448–49.

262. "Demons in mythological vision are divine-anti-divine beings. They are not simply negations of the divine but participate in a distorted way in the power and the holiness of the divine." Tillich, *Systematic Theology*, 3, 105.

263. Wink, *Unmasking the Powers*, 14.

such as Wink's confers legitimacy upon the devil if he is thought to have an existence *of the same order* as that of God.[264] He asserts:

> God is the Living God who possesses fullness of being and is Being Itself. God and the devil stand in mutual contradiction. To make God's existence even notionally dependent on or akin to that of the devil is close to blasphemy.[265]

Further, Moser notes that for God to be considered divine he needs to go beyond mere kindness or even mercy to seek what is morally best, not just for God's allies but for all concerned—without which such a goal would be a divine purpose in which one would not be divine; God, Moser concludes, is not to be confused with the kind of evil being called "Satan."[266]

In the post-exilic, inter-testamental period the Satan, his person, identity and function, entered Jewish religious consciousness and the traditional idea of an evil spirit, warring against God, mysterious in origin and fearful in power, takes shape.[267] Acknowledging the evolution of understanding and representation between the Hebrew "Satan" of the Jewish Bible and the New Testament "Devil" Walker accedes that there is considerable evidence that the view of the New Testament Evil One is influenced by apocryphal literature, which in turn was influenced by Persian Zoroastrianism.[268] There have always been outside cultural influences on theology but in this instance there is a thread running through the entire biblical narrative affirming the existence and purposes of this evil being.

This thread ineluctably culminates in the clash of evil with God incarnate, Jesus Christ, at the crucial crucifixion.[269] For Green, any model of the atonement with a "solid claim" to being biblical cannot represent the death of Jesus in terms that do not integrate seriously the reality of his crucifixion as the consequence of a life in the service of God's purpose and in opposition

---

264. Wright, *Theology of the Dark Side*, 30.

265. Ibid., 31.

266. Moser, *Severity of God*, 13.

267. Hastings, "Devil," 164.

268. Walker, *Enemy Territory*, 29. He argues that such acknowledgement does not necessitate undercutting the reality of this Evil One, stating, "To provide an aetiology is not to pronounce on matters of authenticity." Ibid.

269. In his assessment of the centrality of the cross in Christian theology Moltmann reflects upon Luther's *Theologia crucis*, asserting that "the theology of the cross is a practical doctrine for battle, and can therefore become neither a theory of Christianity as it is now, nor the Christian theory of world history." Moltmann, *Crucified God*, 72. It is this notion of *battle* that commends it to our study, both for God in his battle against evil and the Satan, and then for humanity in its battle against sin, self, and the Satan.

to all manner of competing social, political, and religious agenda.[270] In addition to these earthly opponents are the cosmological and spiritual elements of the Satan and his demonic hordes; in making a link across the testaments with his previous comments on conflict for the people of Yahweh against such "evil hordes," Wright concludes this later meant for Jesus Christ that the struggle coming to a head was cosmic and not merely martial in nature.[271]

Modern Understanding: Satanic Personhood

At the end of the Twentieth Century Wink addressed the concept and possible identity of the Satan and the demonic realm and, whilst thoroughgoing in his comments on demons and principalities, he demurred at explicitly addressing the Satan's personhood;[272] referring to "Satan" (speech marks his) as the "world-encompassing spirit of the Domination System."[273] Wink's problem is the impasse reached if personal identity or being is given to what he views as an impersonal spiritual reality at the center of institutional life.

Wink's main objection to personification is that demons would be regarded as having a body or form separate from the physical and historical institutions of which he believes them to be the interiority.[274] Wink has no hesitation in speaking of Satan, demons, powers or angels;[275] neither does he baulk at acknowledging their reality. In fact, after criticizing those possessing a simplistic "Pentecostal political naïveté" in regard to their ascriptions of a too-active demonic realm he counters that it is equally naïve to blindly refuse to recognize the reality of the demonic in this most demonic of centuries.[276] Where he demurs is in describing adequately what "the Satan" is and whether it/he has an ontological being apart from his/its manifestation in the systems and structures in which its/his activity is made known.

---

270. Green, "Kaleidoscopic Response," 165.

271. Wright, *Victory of God*, 451.

272. Russell notes that although Wink describes the radical evil embodied in the Satan as a "brute and terrifying fact," he is nonetheless unwilling to locate evil in a personal will or being; see Russell, *Prince of Darkness*, 276.

273. Wink, *Engaging the Powers*, 9.

274. Ibid., 9. Ricoeur shares Wink's perspective, stating that, "I do not know what Satan is, who Satan is, or even whether he is Someone. For if he were someone, it would be necessary to intercede for him." Ricoeur, *Symbolism of Evil*, 260.

275. Noll acknowledges that "the great contribution of Walter Wink to angelology is his identification of real intermediary realities in the fallen world order." Noll, "Thinking about Angels," 25.

276. Wink, *Engaging the Powers*, 9–10.

Such a perspective calls to mind Harnack's quip in regard to Marcion's deference to Paul—that only one Christian in the second century—Marcion—took the trouble to understand Paul, but he had actually misunderstood him.[277] It might likewise be said of Wink that he was one Christian in the twentieth century who took the trouble to understand the Satan and the powers and yet he misunderstood them! At the very least he failed to explicate their identities, even though they formed the foundation of his whole thesis.[278]

Wink's position seemingly answers both those accepting the Satan's importance and those balking at ascribing the Satan being; on the contrary, Wink's position furthers the need to continue searching for the Satan's personhood within the ontological context which he has ignored. Girard likewise observes that the Devil's "quintessential being," the source from which he draws his lies, is the violent contagion that has no substance to it; concluding that the Devil does not have a stable foundation, having no *being* at all.[279] To himself in the mere semblance of being, he must act as a parasite on God's creatures. He is, for Girard, totally mimetic, which amounts to saying *non-existent as an individual self* and therefore not to be regarded as an ontological reality.[280]

Girard and Wink express reticence at conferring personality, identity and ontology upon the Satan but fall short of denouncing attributes and prescriptions entirely. Wink notes that he reluctantly refers to the Satan as "he," after trying "it" without satisfaction. I have done so, he concedes, because every archetype must find some image by which to present itself to consciousness and the satanic seems above all to be personal in its assaults on us; and because the form of action we call satanic is most often "agentic," a type of behavior culturally associated with crass masculinity unleavened by any feminine qualities.[281] He presents an amorphous outline of Satanic personhood whilst simultaneously ascribing a negative descriptor of masculinity, thereby necessarily conferring a degree of personal identity.

277. Harnack, "Marcion," 534.

278. Noll notes that in failing to distinguish the holy angels from the powers, Wink turns the Satan into God's negative parent in which he becomes the "negative possibility that resides in God and he/it is incarnated by us when we sin." Noll, "Thinking about Angels," 25.

279. Barth agrees: "Evil as such does not and cannot receive any individuality or autonomy from God. From all eternity this gift is denied to evil." Barth, *CD* 2/2:178.

280. Girard, *I See Satan Fall*, 42. The accusation can be made, however, that since humans are, according to him, also "totally mimetic," they are, therefore, also to be perceived as *non-existent as an individual self*.

281. Wink, *Unmasking the Powers*, 174–75.

In this regard and whilst admitting that because of "silly and unhelp-ful caricatures of evil" he cannot blame non-Christians for dismissing the possibility of a personification of evil, Walker states why he nonetheless still accepts this position. Contrary to Wink he adds the caveat that the Devil is an "it" rather than a "him" because of the connotation of attributes normally associated with personhood that the Satan lost when he rebelled against God.[282] God, according to Walker, is therefore only truly personal and hu-mans only persons in so far as they bear God's image.[283] Küng, too, in regard to the use of the term "person" when attributed to God, observes that

> God is not a person as man is a person. The all-embracing and all-penetrating is never an object that man can view from a dis-tance in order to make statements about it. The primal ground, primal support and primal goal of all reality, which determines every individual existence, is not an individual person among other persons, is not a superman or superego. The term "person" also is merely a cipher for God. God is not the supreme person among other persons. God transcends also the concept of per-son. God is more than person.[284]

On the other hand, the Devil, according to Walker, is instead all that God is not and is, therefore, not a person and subsequently remains an "it." He has no objection in personifying evil per se but is loath to over-personal-ize by awarding the Satan predicates that "he" has lost, or never had.[285]

Further, Barth describes the Satan as

> the rebel angel who is the very sum and substance of the pos-sibility which is not chosen by God (and which exists only in virtue of this negation); the very essence of the creature in its misunderstanding and misuse of its creation and destiny and in its desire to be as God, to be itself a god.[286] Satan (and the whole kingdom of evil, i.e., the demonic, which has its basis in him) is the shadow which accompanies the light of the election of Jesus

282. Calvin concurs: "Yet, since the devil was created by God, let us remember that this malice, which we attribute to his nature, came not from his creation but from his perversion. For, whatever he has that is to be condemned he has derived from his revolt and fall." Calvin, *Institutes*, 175.

283. Walker, *Enemy Territory*, 10.

284. Küng, *Does God Exist?*, 632–33.

285. Walker, *Enemy Territory*, 10.

286. "The demonic is not [therefore] conceived as the divine in some way imma-nent in the world, but something that happens to the world to throw it out of kilter." Further, Gunton states, "The demonic is what happens when what is in itself good is corrupted into its opposite." Gunton, *Actuality of Atonement*, 71.

Christ (and in Him the good creation in which man is in the divine image).[287]

The ways of expressing the concept of the Satan may differ, but the belief in a personalized Prince of Evil, Perry notes, is common both to the Synoptists and to John.[288] He further notes that even if Epistle and Gospel are not by the same hand, they come from the same community, thereby showing that it could not have been a community which ignored the existence of the Satan.[289]

As has been demonstrated, there of course exists a broad spectrum of perspectives on the Satan—from impersonal force and metaphor for evil, to ontological being as source and personification of evil; two extremes which could hardly be further removed from one another. If atonement is, to whatever degree, a means of overcoming the Satan (or impersonal "satanic evil"), it is imperative to establish what or whom has been overcome, by what means and whether violence was utilized by God.

According to Hastings, regardless of the position held,

> Whether or not the devil is a "personal" reality or a symbol appropriate within a society which believed in the existence of a multitude of invasive invisible beings, the power of evil is unchanged together with the Christian duty to resist it.[290]

Seeking the Via Media

In Christian theology, Macquarrie contends that demonic powers have always been considered to be creatures, even if creatures of superior force and cunning; simultaneously affirming that they were never considered to constitute an independent reality equiprimordial with God.[291] Conversely,

287. Barth, *CD* 2/2:122. Further, Barth notes that, "Sin, death and the devil do exist within the sphere of the divine creation, of *res creatae*, as principles of disobedience, evil and rebellion. But they do not belong to these *res*. They are not themselves created by God. Their being is simply the non-being which disturbs and denies God's creation." Ibid. 2/1:560.

288. Perry, "Taking Satan Seriously," 106. "Finally, for all that the fourth evangelist seldom mentions Satan, the author of the First Epistle of John mentions him, verse for verse, about ten times as often." Ibid.

289. Ibid.

290. Hastings, "Devil," 166.

291. As was the case, he argues, in some eastern dualistic religions. Macquarrie, *Principles of Christian Theology*, 237. Further, "While the concept may have been borrowed from neighbouring, more dualistic religious systems, Babylonian or Persian,

attempts to demythologise the Bible come with a resultant effect on understanding demonology and the Satan; his part played as the lord of this world limited in a peculiar way, or else, if this is to be said, then "this world" standing in peculiar dialectical relation to the world as the creation of God.[292] There is little room for maneuver between these recalcitrant positions and even less attempt to find a *via media* between what otherwise remain diametric, contradictory and potentially mutually exclusive theological positions.

Commenting on this dilemma, Walker concludes that if scholars are "modernist" they reject the Devil and the fallen angels; not because of a lack of evidence or authentic bases for their existence in the New Testament canon, but rather because they do not believe in him. As heirs of the philosophical Enlightenment and the modern scientific world-view, he claims, they simply cannot grasp the possibility that Evil could be personified or exist as a spirit opposed to God and his creation.[293] This means that there exists, in an a priori manner for modern theology and for the Church, the danger of rejecting the Satan as ontological reality.

A modernist exemplifying this reluctance to personify the Satan whilst concurrently prioritizing "him" is Girard who, as noted by McDonald, identifies the foundational principle of culture as "Satan," arguing that it mirrors perfectly Christ's description of "the Prince of this world," moved by envy and "a liar and a murderer from the first." Girard, he observes, contends that by laying down his life to expose and overthrow this kingdom built on violence and untruth, Christ introduced the world to another kingdom, one "not of this world," whose fundamental principles are repentance for sins instead of the catharsis of scapegoating and love of God and neighbor rather than the warfare of mimetic desire.[294]

Girard explains his understanding of this "satan" in terms requiring acknowledgement of the Satan's importance but without conferring personhood. He claims that the interpretation that assimilates the Satan to rivalistic contagion and its consequences will for the first time enable acknowledgement of the importance of the prince of this world without also having to endow him with personal *being*.[295] At best Girard appears

---

it did not undermine the fundamental monism of Hebraic ontology: Satan is not an alternative principle but a 'fallen' creation of Yahweh." Hastings, "Devil," 164.

292. Bultmann, "New Testament and Mythology," 17.

293. Walker, *Enemy Territory*, 31.

294. McDonald, "Violence and the Lamb Slain," 41.

295. Girard, *I See Satan Fall*, 45. It is apposite to note the previously quoted idea that Girard does not place any importance on answering the question whether he sees the Satan as a "being" or a "structure." When asked, he responds, "Well, I don't know. Does

confused about the Satan's identity and at worst he simply does not care about it as a theological issue.

Conversely, Bell has suggested that "person" could be a tensive term in that the Satan is a person because the biblical witness suggests it[296] and yet is still *not* a person, in the commonly perceived sense, because he remains incapable of being redeemed.[297] It is this redeemability, the ability to respond to love that, for Bell, is the essence of personhood and since this is lacking in the Satan, the claim for person-status is ultimately undermined.

In terms of Girard's views, however, whilst he remains ambiguous on Satanic identity he has nonetheless been persuasive, his influence perceived, for example, in Beck who contends that the construct of a strong "Satan figure" exists as an attributional locus, fulfilling a psycho-theological role in the lives of some Christian believers enabling them to explain misfortune and pain while simultaneously protecting their God-experience from negative affect.[298] What he does not address, like Girard before him, is whether there is any ontological status for this "Satan figure." He is right to acknowledge the beneficial praxeological corollary of belief in such a "being"; he falls short in not exploring whether such a being might, in fact, *actually exist*.

A Cosmic Power-Encounter: The Great Battle

It has been established that violence is certainly accommodated by God and sometimes actively endorsed and utilized by him, primarily as an extrinsic, functional divine attribute; it has also been concurrently shown that a God devoid of violence is alien to the biblical evidence. Grimsrud argues, however, that this is only the case because understanding of God has been influenced by the idea that he is constrained in terms of providing salvation pending the offering of an appropriate sacrifice. The basis of this constraint, he argues, is in regard to a particular notion of God's justice, holiness or

it really matter? Whether Satan is a personal being or not, he is still the 'prince of this world.'" McDonald, "Interview with Rene Girard," 43.

296. In his response to Wink's denial of this perspective (Wink, *Engaging the Powers*, 8–9) Bell concludes that "one problem of this approach is that it so plainly contradicts the New Testament where demons (and angels) clearly have 'personality.'" Bell, *Deliver Us from Evil*, 350.

297. "Even though the devil has deceived himself, he is in no sense a victim and is culpable for his actions because he technically could still admit goodness . . . I would argue that the soul of Satan is in a similar state to that of Christ: it retains its power to choose (αὐτεξούσιον), but because Satan has consistently chosen evil, and turned his whole mind towards this end, the moral choice (ἐφ ἡμῖν) of good is impossible because his mind is consumed with evil." Holliday, "Will Satan Be Saved?," 21–22.

298. Beck and Taylor, "Emotional Burden," 151.

honor carrying tremendous weight in his ability to relate to human beings.[299] Further, we have demonstrated that the most biblically and theologically consistent representation of the Satan, both pragmatically and ideologically, is one in which he is personified as an ontological being; opposed to God and his creation and the general of malevolent spiritual forces perennially at war with God and all he loves, most notably, Jesus Christ and human beings.[300]

In terms of looking back to the theology of a bygone era in order to gain insight on this cosmic battle, or indeed to reject these earlier understandings, Macquarrie notes what he sees as the danger of jettisoning the teaching of the Fathers on demonology. This is because, for him, to throw out the demonic myths would necessitate, as we have already noted, the concurrent scrapping of the atonement which the Fathers closely conjoined with their demonology. Instead, Macquarrie proposes a reinterpretation of the Fathers' theology in order to preserve the essential meaning of the death of Christ from their perspective. In order to do so, however, he adds the caveat that in this reinterpretation, "We reject the demonic mythology, assuredly."[301]

His justification for this rejection is that the critics who have taken these mythical statements as facts have, in his words, not surprisingly found them to be childish and even repellent.[302] Such an outlook pre-supposes that a modern hermeneutic is de facto more accurate and insightful, for no other reason than that it *is* more modern. It is, however, not a compelling argument to suggest that any biblical narrative or event that the interpreter might find "childish" or "repellent" can a priori be disregarded. Indeed, Macquarrie sets up a theological impasse in his assertion that Aulén fails in the explication of his thesis because he represents his argument for the Christus Victor model in what Macquarrie contends are mythical terms. Or put another way, Aulén is caught in a theological vicious circle of presenting a spiritually-focused doctrine in spiritual terms; which is, for Macquarrie, an endeavor doomed before it begins as Aulén will have to first remove all mythical references because only by so doing can he make it intelligible and

---

299. Grimsrud, *Instead of Atonement*, 4.

300. Dunn says, in the context of ascertaining a hierarchy of spiritual beings, "the hostile angels and demons, whose leader is . . . named as Satan . . ." Dunn, *Christology in the Making*, 151. Likewise, Aulén speaks about Paul's view of the order of the powers of evil such as demons, principalities and powers which rule in this world because God has permitted them for a time to have dominion, concluding that "Satan stands at the head of the demonic powers." Aulén, *Christus Victor*, 65.

301. Macquarrie, "Classic Idea of the Atonement," 4.

302. Ibid.

convincing to people who no longer think, according to Macquarrie, along such mythical lines.[303]

Following this theme, Walker contends that instead the New Testament should be understood not as a resource for abstract theological thinking, but rather as a divine drama: the story of the Great Battle.[304] He asserts that the early church, in particular during the great Patristic era of the first five centuries AD, despite many internal disagreements on matters of doctrine, saw redemption in thoroughly expansive and dramatic terms. He concludes that if—for whatever reason—the Devil is taken out of the redemption story, this divine drama is lost.[305]

Certainly, the role of the Satan in the book of Revelation, according to Collins, is determined by what she calls the "combat myth." In chapter 12, she argues, the Satan's role as *katēgōr* in the heavenly court is subordinated to his role as warrior and his activity on earth after having been cast down is characterized as waging war on those who observe the commands of God and hold the witness of Jesus (12:17). Finally, she concludes, all of the subsequent activities of the Satan are dominated by battle language.[306]

In the context of the overall prevalence of terminology describing the demonic world in the New Testament Wink concedes that the use of "demons" and "evil spirits" there is too extensive to review. He notes that *daimonion* is used 63 times in the New Testament; in the Gospels it refers to possession, in Acts, Paul, and Revelation it refers to demons worshipped as gods, whilst *daimōn* is used but once, exactly like *daimonion*.[307] He further states that it must suffice to note that Jesus regarded his healings and exorcisms as an assault on the kingdom of Satan and an indication that the kingdom of God was breaking in; concluding that the gospel is very much a cosmic battle in which Jesus rescues humanity from the dominion of evil powers.[308] In terms of this New Testament battle language Twelftree argues that in what he calls "our sophisticated society" and with theologies to some

---

303. Ibid.

304. The view which Aulén brought to attention again in his seminal Aulén, *Christus Victor*; there, he renames the "Classic" view of the atonement the "Dramatic." Ibid., 4.

305. Walker, *Enemy Territory*, 24.

306. Collins, *Combat Myth*, 161. Further, Collins posits that the traditional motif of Satan in Revelation posits him as the deceiver and is interpreted in military terms and that deceiving the nations is equated with gathering them for battle (Rev 20:8). Ibid., 161.

307. Wink, *Naming the Powers*, 26.

308. Ibid.

extent still dependent on nineteenth-century liberalism, it is often forgotten how important exorcism is in the Synoptic Gospels.[309]

Perry goes further; asserting that at the center of the New Testament is the conviction that, in Jesus, the kingdom of God is coming. Signs of its coming, he notes, are manifold, but they all boil down to the assertion that humans are in the last days, and that the Satan is meeting his match. His conclusion is that Jesus is in the front line of this battle, provoking a head-on clash with the Satan.[310]

Wright identifies evidence of Jesus' interaction with the Satan early in his ministry as the point at which Jesus gained a demonstrable, but not final or definitive, victory. So, whilst this "victory" enabled Jesus to announce that God's Kingdom was beginning to happen and thereby make inroads into the Satan's realm, this same Kingdom, according to Wright, would only be firmly established through the Final Battle. At this time enemy troops will mass again and do their worst to repair the earlier damage, but it would be a war that should not be represented militaristically in terms of a battle, either against Rome or Herod. Instead, Wright contests, Jesus saw this Final Battle in terms of something much deeper, in fact, as the manifestation of a battle against the Satan himself who, whilst he no doubt uses Rome, Herod and Chief Priests, Jesus keeps his eye rather on the fact that the Satan is not identified with any of these entities per se and that actually to make such an identification would equate to already giving up, thereby losing the real battle.[311]

According to Wright, Jesus believed that the only way to defeat this great anti-creation, this Satan, would in fact be for him, "anointed with God's spirit to fight the real battle against the real enemy, to take the full power of evil and accusation upon himself, to let it do its worst to him, so that it would thereby be exhausted, its main force spent."[312]

Twelftree conjectures that there was a two-stage unfolding of Christ's plan to ultimately and definitively destroy the Satan. From what we see reflected in the authentic Jesus tradition, he claims, this is how Jesus understood the destruction of the Satan: his exorcisms were the first stage of binding him but the final defeat would take place in the final judgment.[313]

---

309. Twelftree, *Christ Triumphant*, 55.

310. Perry, "Demonic and Exorcism," 139.

311. Wright, *Simply Jesus*, 123–24.

312. Ibid., 184.

313. Twelftree, *Christ Triumphant*, 82.

This parallels the idea that violence itself was "mortally wounded" at the cross of Christ and would be finally and irrevocably defeated at the Parousia.[314]

In his conclusion to Jesus' perception of his own mission and purpose Wright concludes that the battle Jesus was fighting was against the Satan and whatever we think of this theme he asserts that it was clearly centrally important for all the gospel writers, thus giving reason to suppose it was central for Jesus as well.[315]

In the end however, Perry concludes, there is no *proof* that the evil in the world is to be explained by the activity of a supernatural creature who has rebelled against his Creator; additionally, there is no *proof*, in the sense of a logically irrefragable conclusion from neutral premises, that the good in the world comes from a personal God.[316] Perry instead suggests a pragmatic approach in which believers in God should, whether they actually believe in Satan's actual existence or not, *act* as if the Devil is real in order to better serve God and to live a more effectual Christian life. Such a life and choice, he argues, enables a hypothesis which facilitates the facts falling more smoothly into place and which are also consonant with the revelation offered in the Holy Scripture.

Divine Violence against the Satan

The position of this thesis is that academic and chronological humility is once again required to facilitate a dynamic tension between ancient and modern perspectives. This acknowledges that original, historical doctrines might be capable of understanding and presenting a worldview that does not, de facto, have to be redundant to post-modern sensibilities and theology. To remove, or demythologize central biblical and theological themes could irreparably damage both ancient and modern understanding and engagement with the canonical Scriptures.[317] Further, it is theologically pompous, short-sighted and academically disingenuous to reject a perspective on the grounds that it is outdated and erroneous solely because it is not of this time. Wink, for example, argues that it is as impossible for most people to

314. Kreitzer concedes that the parousia is a multi-faceted concept whilst noting that it "has been understood as an act of vindication, a time of visitation, a decisive moment of judgment, a time of deliverance and the climactic event of consummation." Kreitzer, "Parousia," 858.

315. Wright, *Simply Jesus*, 118. Wright goes on to delineate numerous NT biblical instances to highlight his contention. See ibid., 118–19.

316. Perry, "Taking Satan Seriously," 111.

317. Boyd argues that the spiritual warfare motif is extant across the biblical testaments. Boyd, *God at War*, 63–72.

believe in the real existence of demonic or angelic powers as it is for them to believe in dragons, or elves, or a flat world.[318]

Conversely, Boyd argues that this represents a discredited and redundant Western rationalistic perspective which, when pushed to the point of the total relativism of Christian truth claims through their deconstruction, presents a perspective not merely philosophically problematic for Christianity but rather disastrous since Christianity, he concludes, is inextricably rooted in a number of objective historical and metaphysical truth claims.[319] Indeed, this practice of assuming a "primitive human past" to be contrasted with a more "advanced" ethical modern consciousness embodies, according to Blumenthal, the historical fallacy of the wholly unwarranted assumption of human moral progress.[320]

Consequently, our conclusion is that it is necessary to present an inclusive, macro-vision of God and theological understanding of him and his character. Also, we contend that his soteriological purposes are not seeking to accentuate divine violence at the expense or diminution of divine love but rather they are an attempt to demonstrate how the conjoining and coexistence of the two in the divine economy might be understood.[321] Divine violence, coupled with the necessity of overcoming the Satan, the tyrant, is central to both the biblical message and the overall perception of God's character and his soteriological intent.

In fact, the denial of divine violence and its consequences and biblical centrality can lead to the desire of presenting God in entirely non-violent terms. This desire, as noted, leads to the inadvertent construction of a divine passivity which might itself become or be perceived as neglectful, or even "abusive." God would then stand accused not just of the violence he has advocated, accommodated or sanctioned—he would also face the charge of choosing passivity in the face of human violence and chaos. On this point Volf concedes that his thesis on the practice of nonviolence, which requires

---

318. Wink, *Naming the Powers*, 4.

319. Boyd, *God at War*, 62.

320. Blumenthal, *Facing the Abusing God*, 243.

321. This conjoining is notoriously controversial and difficult to substantiate. Ray alludes to a potential linkage before baulking and setting a clear and incontrovertible demarcation between the two, concluding that in the context of the cross of Christ it is apparent that, "Fighting violence with violence may result in momentary victory, but it will never bring true peace and justice. To be liberated from evil in a world that remains so clearly in its grasp means refusing to let evil define our options and existence." Ray, *Deceiving the Devil*, 144.

a belief in divine vengeance, is one that will be unpopular amongst Christians, especially with "theologians in the West."[322]

Volf issues a pragmatic challenge to those apt to dismiss his contentions that they should imagine themselves delivering a lecture in a warzone on the topic of "A Christian attitude toward violence," with the thesis that people should not retaliate since God is perfect non-coercive love. He posits that the one doing so would soon discover that it takes the quiet of a suburban home for the birth of the thesis that human nonviolence corresponds to God's refusal to judge. Instead he concludes that in a scorched land soaked in the blood of the innocent, such a thesis invariably dies; and that as its demise is watched, one would do well to reflect about many other pleasant captivities of the liberal mind.[323]

Conversely, the centrality of a violently overcome tyrant and the attendant forceful institution of God's Kingdom, in dramatic rather than metaphorical or religious terms, is presented by Wright in his conclusion that Jesus' death, as seen by Jesus himself, and manifest via the crucifixion,

> was the ultimate Exodus event through which the tyrant was defeated, God's people were set free and given their fresh vocation, and God's presence was established in their midst in a completely new way for which the Temple itself was just an advance pointer.[324]

Not a salvation won then by the actions of a non-coercive God, but rather a stark, violent, full-frontal attack on a deadly nemesis, heralding the release of previously subjugated captives.

Decisions on the Devil

Before considering soteriological purpose and accomplishment and acknowledging the post-modern uncertainties of Girard and those he influences about the Satan's identity, ontology and purpose; it is essential to conclude about what or whom is overcome in the atonement.

It has been argued that right understanding of God's freedom of will makes dualistic thought impossible; Barth notes:

> We deceive ourselves if we think that we should take sin, death, and the devil seriously in the sense of ascribing to them a divine or semi-divine potentiality or the rôle of a real antagonist to the

322. Volf, *Exclusion and Embrace*, 304.

323. Ibid.

324. Wright, *Simply Jesus*, 181–82.

living God.[325] It is when we see them as powers which are in their own peculiar way subordinate and subject to the will of God that we really take them seriously as powers of temptation, evil and eternal destruction. It is only then that we know conclusively that we ourselves do not have the power to combat and conquer them. We cannot do this because it is not our business. They are powers combated and conquered by God, and our business is to acknowledge and accept the decision about them made by God's will and to deal with them accordingly.[326]

A theological *via media* between Barth and Walker is articulated by Gunton who argues that the language of possession by demonic forces expresses the helplessness of human agents in the face of psychological, social and cosmic forces in various combinations; theologically, he contends, it is important to see the origins of bondage in the idolatrous worship of that which is not God. When any part of the created world is given the value of God, humanity comes into the power of a reality which, because it is not divine, operates demonically.[327]

Acceptance of a guarded personification of the Satan and powers and principalities is also forwarded by Schlier who argues that the manifold principalities which unfold the one satanic power are encountered as a kind of personal and powerful being. He simultaneously accepts that these principalities exercise their being by taking possession of the world as a whole, and of individual men, the elements, political and social institutions, historical conditions and circumstances, spiritual and religious trends.[328]

---

325. An example of theological "sectarianism" and "dualism" in research about the Satan is posited by Walker who, after describing God's on-going war with the Devil, describes it, as we have seen, as "the Great Battle," conceding that "this may seem a very primitive way of talking, but this book is primarily a work of propaganda for a primitive gospel. Such a gospel insists on a proper Christian dualism that understands Christ and his church to be confronted by a real and terrifying enemy. The early church fathers called him the Evil One." Walker, *Enemy Territory*, 9–10.

326. Barth, *CD* 2/1:563.

327. Gunton, *Actuality of Atonement*, 70. Tillich observes, "for the demonic is the elevation of something conditional to unconditional significance." Tillich, *Systematic Theology*, 1:155.

328. Yoder comments on each group or leader trying to ascertain the power-source of their enemy—whether correctly or not; this is why, he argues, rambunctious students occupied the office of the dean and why Che Guevara, after coming to the belief that peasants would prove to be the backbone of the coming Latin American revolution, went to live with them in the hills of Bolivia. Neufeld, *Subversion of Violence*, 229. Similarly, Schlier "covers his bases," arguing that the Satan is both a personal being and yet one able to manifest "himself" through impersonal institutions.

Above all, Shlier concludes, their possession is exercised mainly through the "atmosphere," which is the immediate site of their power.[329]

It is apparent that whilst the personification of evil manifest in the Satan is currently out of theological and cultural favor it is likewise true that the concept of the Satan is not yet entirely redundant. The perception of the Satan as ruler over the world expresses the insight that evil is not only found here and there in the world, but that all particular evils make up one single power which in the last analysis grows from the very actions of men and which form, Schlier argues, an atmosphere and a spiritual tradition, which overwhelms every human.

This outlook represents the imperative that whilst the Satan might not be perceived how he has been traditionally and historically, demons nonetheless express, in at the very least a mythological way, truths about evil which will be lost if too superficial a view of the subject is taken. Amongst these truths, according to Macquarrie, are: the depth and mystery of evil; the superhuman dimensions of evil; its sometimes apparently systematic character; and the fact that a spiritual nature is no safeguard against evil and may indeed issue in the worst forms of evil.[330]

The task of steering a *via media* between the opposite ends of theological perspectives on the Satan is highlighted, as we have seen, by Walker who warns that if the Devil has no reality or active role in the divine drama of salvation then the vision of the Great Battle is lost.[331] Likewise, even though Gunton cautions of the dangers of taking talk of "the powers" and the devil too literally, leading to misunderstanding of the use of metaphor and myth,[332] he is nonetheless cautious not to discount that the forces are in some sense "cosmic," whilst simultaneously bearing an earthly manifestation through political, social, economic and religious structures of power.[333]

329. Schlier, *Principalities and Powers*, 67.

330. Macquarrie, *Principles of Christian Theology*, 238. Gunton argues that "the contribution made by a theology of the demonic, and the consequent taking seriously of the place of Satan in the New Testament, is that it presents a picture of evil as an appalling and irrational corruption of the good creation, something that cannot be explained away because it is a denial of the purposes of God." Gunton, *Actuality of Atonement*, 84.

331. Walker, *Enemy Territory*, 23.

332. He balks at too-literal an understanding of the devil and the failure to appreciate metaphorical language, arguing that in passages like Mark 10:45, where it reports that Jesus came to give his life as a ransom, that one would be left "to speculate about how much money was to be handed over and to whom." Gunton, *Actuality of Atonement*, 64.

333. Gunton is influenced by Caird who argues that Paul uses "mythical language of great antiquity and continuing vitality to interpret the historic event of the cross." Caird,

Like Gunton we are keen to steer a middle course between a naively supernaturalist view of the demonic and a reductionist one, which is construed as a way of speaking of merely finite or psychological influences. Gunton endorses indirect description as the best means of expressing this cosmic realm; concluding that "an indirect description is still a description of what is really there."[334] We concur, therefore, with Barratt that this equates to there being a Devil who is defeated, but is not yet entirely destroyed.[335]

Further, Newbigin argues that in the past 150 years scholarly readers of the New Testament have chosen, for all practical purposes, to ignore what was said about hostile spiritual powers and the Satan. This outlook, he contends, feeds into the dominant reductionist materialism of the day, preventing the discernment of realities that Paul and other New Testament writers talk about, and which, according to Newbigin, *are* realities.[336]

Those who have demurred at ascribing the Satan personhood, such as Wink and Girard, have nonetheless, at least grammatically, conferred being on the Devil by the addition of masculine pronouns as descriptors. So, this "force" of evil, even if not a person per se should still be perceived as one, as this is the only route that "makes sense." Whilst there will always be contention about the precise, ontological reality and personhood of the Satan we are in accord with the Fathers and Walker that belief in him as a being remains a central element of atonement doctrine and therefore of soteriology and it therefore remains incumbent upon modern believers to uphold the dogma that, "To be a Christian is to be at war with the Devil."[337]

In terms of "being a Christian" and of a person thereby having secured salvation Harrison notes that human nature is, in fact, the foundation of what people are and what everyone shares, making them alike; he observes:

> Being according to the divine image is intrinsic to our nature. It gives us the capacity to become like God or not, to choose between good and evil, to live a life of virtue, to love God and neighbours, to be rewarded by God in the age to come or not, and to enjoy communion with God in heaven. Their nature thus makes people capable of likeness to God, communion with him, and eternal life in the age to come—that is, salvation.[338]

Language and Imagery, 242.

334. Gunton, *Actuality of Atonement*, 65.

335. He concludes that "the Church was historically too well acquainted with his devices to suppose that Satan had died." Barrett, *Holy Spirit*, 52.

336. Newbigin, *Pluralist Society*, 200.

337. Walker, *Enemy Territory*, 13.

338. Harrison, "Human Person," 80.

In regard to the one who is the enemy of this salvation, the Devil, we conclude that "it" is a being, but not a person (in as far as a "person" is determined as one with the potential to love, is redeemable and on whom personhood has been conferred by a loving God)[339], the personification of evil, its source and loci and the one who through Christ's death and resurrection would be mortally wounded to herald God's eschaton and the ultimate salvation of humanity otherwise under his influence and sway.

339. "Fundamental to any Christian view of the person is love. Persons gain their dignity and value from their capacity to give and receive love." Further, Pyper states that the value of the human person is grounded in "the self-disclosure of a God constituted by love, who accords the dignity of personhood to each human individual . . ." Pyper, "Person," 533.

3

Metaphor & Models

Penal Substitution—Judicial Violence

AMONGST MANY CONSERVATIVE PROTESTANT and, in particular, evangelical scholars, preachers and apologists in the twenty-first century the Penal Substitutionary view of the atonement (PSA) holds predominant sway in much the same way that the Ransom Christus Victor model (RCVM) and then the later Christus Victor model (CVM) did amongst Greek theologians during the patristic era. One emblematic demonstration of this is the 20th anniversary edition of Stott's, *The Cross of Christ*,[1] where he presents his adherence to the PSA view of atonement. Stott's book has gone through nearly twenty reprints since it was first published in 1986 and prominent Protestant, evangelical scholars such as D.A. Carson, G. Goldsworthy, W. Grudem, J. I. Packer and D. F. Wells, amongst others, have written their endorsements for its contents and message. Another representative title which defends and presents the PSA model is the collection of articles written by key Reformed and evangelical scholars, *The Glory of the Atonement*.[2] The Protestant evangelicals who contributed to this book include B. K. Waltke, H. Blocher, C. E. Hill, S. P. Rosenberg, B. L. McCormack and S. B. Ferguson. Other recent titles defending or promoting PSA include, *The Wondrous Cross: Atonement and Penal Substitution in the Bible and History*,[3] *Pierced for our Transgressions: Rediscovering the Glory of Penal Substitution*[4] and

---

1. Stott, *Cross of Christ*.
2. *Glory of the Atonement*.
3. Holmes, *Wondrous Cross*.
4. Jeffery et al., *Pierced for Our Transgressions*.

Aspects of the Atonement: Cross and Resurrection in the Reconciling of God and Humanity.[5]

Among the available interpretative models of the atonement, not only is PSA the "controlling" one but is, in fact, the *sine qua non* of evangelical soteriology.[6] Hilborn charts a historical timeline of theologians who have held or been sympathetic to PSA, in much the same way that Aulén does in regard to the CVM in *Christus Victor*. He argues that this historical pedigree has laid the foundation for the Protestant position of deeming PSA as the primary means of interpreting the soteriological role of the cross.[7] Weaver observes that, on the other hand, Catholicism has not accorded the status of dogma to a specific theory of atonement, whilst acceding with Hilborn that nineteenth- and early twentieth-century conservative Protestants gave almost creedal status to satisfaction atonement.[8] This assertion of Weaver reiterates that whilst PSA is not exclusively associated with conservative Protestants it is primarily so and, as we have seen, by evangelicals in particular.

Anselm, of course, reflected on the significance and purpose of Jesus' death in *Cur Deus Homo*[9] and whilst the PSA theory which evolved out of his ideas is a thoroughly different means of understanding the atonement, it is nonetheless a hybrid of his position with many adherents. Weaver, in fact, notes that since Anselm some version of satisfaction atonement has been the majority view for both Catholics and the communions of Protestant Orthodoxy.[10] Further, Rieger argues that Anselm wanted to prove the necessity of the atonement through reason alone, without relying on Scripture; in doing so, Rieger observes, he set a pattern that influenced thought about the atonement for the next millennium.[11] The great influence of Anselm is such that whilst the majority of Protestants might not have read his text, its explanation retold countless times in hymnody and evangelistic illustrations, remains in their blood.[12] Anselm's ideas are, therefore, not explicitly extant within modern PSA and yet their teaching of a wronged and dishonored God seeking appeasement by a sacrificial offering in a judicial context

5. Marshall, *Aspects of the Atonement*.

6. Hilborn, "Atonement," 15–33.

7. Ibid., 19.

8. Weaver, *Nonviolent Atonement*, 19.

9. Anselm, *Cur Deus Homo*. What Bartlett calls a "landmark work" and, for him, "unquestionably the major single document in Western atonement doctrine." Bartlett, *Cross Purposes*, 76.

10. Weaver, *Nonviolent Atonement*, 19.

11. Rieger, "Good News," 381.

12. Rauser, *Faith Lacking Understanding*, 96.

has remained constant. In regard to each of these key assertions Anselm entitled chapters to address their concerns in his seminal tome. In terms of a wronged God, book 1, chapter XV is "Whether God would suffer his honor to be profaned even in the very least; for appeasement by a sacrificial offering." Book 2, chapter VI is "That the satisfaction whereby man can be saved can be effected only by one who is God and Man; for judicial fairness." Whilst book 1, chapter XX states, "That the satisfaction should be proportionate to the transgression, nor can man make it for himself."[13]

Modern proponents of PSA have objected to what they see as the oversimplification and concomitant vilification of this doctrine.[14] Whilst restating support for PSA Tidball counterattacks those questioning it; concerned that critics are not attacking the model but rather a distorted caricature of it.[15] Tidball does not distance himself from PSA, but a "crass version" which highlights only its negative elements; advocates of PSA likewise seek to represent it in a positive manner. Rather than Jesus' death being construed as the appeasement of a Father unable or unwilling to forgive, these apologists offer a constructive model in which those facing the judgment of a wrathful God can approach him, claiming mercy with Jesus having borne their judgment in his death.[16]

The irreducible claim of PSA is that Jesus Christ in his death offered himself on behalf of mankind and in its place. A wrathful God acts as Judge to fulfill his desire for justice and judgment and provides his Son as a payment otherwise required from a sinful, guilty humanity. Marshall considers key words related to God's response to humans in terms of their sin and need of salvation; primary are judgment, wrath and vengeance. He admits, in regard to what he considers the most contentious issue of all, that

> there have been numerous attempts to argue that this wrath is not the divine equivalent of what, in human terms, would be a feeling or emotion, still less an arbitrary outburst of rage. Some would understand it simply in terms of the inevitable self-inflicted wounds of sin that God allows to happen. However, I can see no legitimate way of avoiding the fact that these terms refer to the attitude of God himself that results in actions being taken against sinners.[17]

13. Anselm, *Cur Deus Homo*.
14. Tidball, "Penal Substitution," 345–60.
15. Ibid.
16. Marshall, *Aspects of the Atonement*, 59–60.
17. Ibid., 19.

This kind of judicial metaphor represents, for Marshall, ultimate sacrifice by God for God, fulfilling the divine requirement for payment.

PSA has been caricatured as a law-based "pay-off" and although advocates claim that God cannot be persuaded through sacrificial offerings this is implied in doctrines of intercessory atonement; even defenders of PSA fail to recognize their inherent violence.[18] Additionally there is a trinitarian problem within certain atonement models in which it is said that the Father punishes, the Son expiates, the Spirit forgives and the Father demands satisfaction, whilst the Son pays it, and the Spirit interposes between.[19]

This presents problems for perichoresis in the Trinity so that instead of eternal, divine unity there is internal conflict both ontologically and functionally. Augustine derives problems from terminology associated with PSA in which the Son "appeases" the Father. He denies that God the Father can be "placated" by the Son's death. If this were so there would be inherent difference, even conflict, between Father and Son which, for Augustine, is unthinkable, because the Father and the Son eternally enjoy perichoretic union and harmony.[20] So, whilst it is difficult to conceive of conflict in the soteriological plans of God, it is impossible to accept in terms of the ontological Godhead since the triune perichoretic unity of person and purpose precludes any possibility of division or conflict.

Gunton considers such Trinitarian ramifications of the atonement in regard to the three main interpretative models noting that the metaphors enable the expression of something of the work of the triune God through, in and with his creation.[21] Gunton highlights the unity in the trinity regarding God's response to the world and the atonement in particular, further commenting that the purpose of the Father achieved by the incarnation, cross and resurrection of the incarnate Son has its basis in the creation by which the world took shape, and which will find its completion in the work of the Spirit who brings the Son's work to perfection.[22] If any doubt remains about the strength of Gunton's claims of perichoresis in the triune Godhead he asserts that the human career of Jesus is also the decisive action of God in and towards his world and is, therefore, both the center point of, and clue to, the way in which God is related to the world from beginning to end.[23]

18. Finlan, *Problems with Atonement*, 9.

19. Richard of St. Victor, *De Verbo Incarnato* 11 (PL 196:1005), quoted in Gorringe, *God's Just Vengeance*, 116.

20. Aulén, *Christus Victor*, 58.

21. Gunton, *Actuality of Atonement*, 154.

22. Ibid.

23. Ibid., 155.

For Gunton, there is no room for conflict in this ontological, perichoretic schema.

Away from these issues, those supporting PSA argue for a re-alignment of thought that presents the cross as not merely divine response to sin but as "condign penalty" for those rejecting God and his will and purpose for creation as expressed in commandments of divine love. The disobedience of humanity thus causes a fatal break in personal relationship with God making it wholly appropriate for him to respond by excluding them from his kingdom. Marshall states that final judgment is therefore the execution of a condign penalty after God, in his mercy, has provided a way of salvation that has been persistently refused and rejected.[24]

"Condign" may be apposite in terms of God's penalty, but regarding "severity," not being "well-deserved"; PSA thus seeks to defend God against charges of violence in the atonement. Following this feudal schema of a wronged God, rebellion and concomitant punishment it is reasonable to postulate whether any human law, judge or court would consider God's *eternal* punishment a proportionate response to those who "persistently refused and rejected" God's salvation during *finite time*.[25] PSA makes an assumption about justice and retribution, closely linking the finite and the infinite, the human and the divine. It draws favorable comparisons between that "above" and that "below," conferring continuity, union and parity between these realms.

The charge of projecting anthropomorphic, human sensibilities onto divine purposes can be made against theologians and doctrines of every era and yet PSA may be particularly guilty of placing primary emphasis on the human realm before it has properly addressed and understood the divine realm.

Moral Influence—Denied Violence

PSA has been presented as the predominant means of interpreting the atonement for Catholics and many Protestants denominations; equally it can be claimed that liberal Protestantism has broadly embraced MIT. So,

---

24. Marshall, *Aspects of Atonement*, 33.

25. Edwards, in his dialogue with Stott, comments on the prospect of "eternal separation" from God, which is restricted by the Lausanne Covenant to those who condemn themselves because they "reject Christ." It is a concept, he argues, "that avoids the teaching that one 'mortal' sin earns the same punishment as a lifetime of total wickedness. By this teaching God was alleged to condemn the guilty to hell without adhering to the elementary principle of justice that the gravity of the punishment must fit the gravity of the crime." Edwards and Stott, *Essentials*, 292.

while the MIT can be broadly characterized as being aligned with liberal Protestantism, it is not confined to this group; many modern Anabaptists, pacifists and Mennonite groups also hold this doctrine.[26] To explain, ignore or deny the charge of divine violence liberals have long turned to this doctrine to uphold the view of a non-violent God who would otherwise be associated with violence.[27]

Abelard (1079–1142) is usually portrayed as the originator of MIT and is certainly its most influential purveyor; MIT's ideals had, however, been extant before his version with the early Fathers highlighting issues that would later come to be associated with the model.[28] As with other theories, key theologians and movements are associated, but each experiences a genesis, growth, evolution and adaptation to reach its modern manifestation.

Given Abelard's influence on MIT it is important to consider ideas that framed his thinking. He had thought it "cruel and wicked," for instance, that the blood of an innocent person should be demanded as the price for anything. He also considered it abhorrent that an innocent man should be slain at all; much less that God would demand this to reconcile the world to himself.[29] These sentiments are foundational to Abelard's view of God's character and the means of accomplishing the divine will.

Abelard concluded:

> Our redemption through the suffering of Christ is that deeper love within us which not only frees us from slavery to sin, but also secures for us the true liberty of the children of God, in order that we might do all things out of love rather than out of fear—love for him who has shown us such grace that no greater can be found.[30]

The means by which he interpreted and understood the centrality of God's love served as a locus to which all other propositions were subsidiary.[31]

---

26. Historically, key adherents who have held variations on the theme of Moral Influence have included Schleiermacher, *Christian Faith*; Bushnell, *Vicarious Sacrifice*; Ritschl, *Christian Doctrine*; and Rashdall, *Idea of the Atonement*.

27. "Beginning with Schleiermacher . . . there was a renewed interest in an Abelardian-type approach that continued throughout the nineteenth and twentieth centuries among many." Green and Baker, *Recovering the Scandal*, 142.

28. Boersma, *Violence, Hospitality and the Cross*, 116.

29. Ray, *Deceiving the Devil*, 13.

30. Abelard, "Love of Christ," 184.

31. Ray sums up Abelard's position, noting that for him, "the event of atonement, then, is an event of creative love: God created the universe out of love; God becomes incarnate in Jesus out of love; and in and through the incarnation, God elicits from human beings a responsive love." Ray, *Deceiving the Devil*, 14.

This pervasive echo of love resonates throughout his doctrinal reflections and for Abelard the central atonement issue was not how to change an offended God's mind toward the sinner, but how sinful humankind could be brought to see that the God they perceived as harsh and judgmental, was in fact loving.[32]

One of the central themes of MIT is the atonement as living metaphor, demonstrating God's intent and actions as an aspirational model for humans; there are, of course, multifarious biblical instances to support this. For instance, God exhorts Israel, the Church or individual believers to either imitate the divine or Jesus Christ. To illustrate this claim, in the Old Testament the people of Israel are addressed corporately on God's instruction through Moses and encouraged to emulate God and his functions. Moses is told, "Speak to the entire assembly of Israel and say to them: 'Be holy because I, the LORD your God, am holy'" (Lev 19:2).

In the New Testament Paul speculates on the role of the Church in God's purposes and sees it as not merely an instrument of God, but an extension of God's reality, not only to those on earth, but cosmologically. Paul also eulogizes that, "his intent was that now, through the church, the manifold wisdom of God should be made known to the rulers and authorities in the heavenly realms" (Eph 3:10). Finally, Jesus exhorts individual believers to have the highest aspirations in terms of outlook, behavior and purposes; he encourages individuals to, "Be perfect, therefore, as your heavenly Father is perfect" (Matt 5:48). In all cases, corporate and individual, emulation and expression of God, his character and purposes is paramount.

God thereby serves as "exemplar" for imitation, to be copied and aspired to in terms of thoughts, outlook and behavior. From an exemplarist perspective, whatever else the story of Jesus expresses it represents a supreme pattern to follow (Heb 12:2) and the one example of a genuine human life in the midst of a fallen world.[33]

MIT places a new soteriological emphasis of responsibility with humans, making it possible to conclude that,

> for Abelard, Jesus died as the demonstration of God's love. And the change that results from that loving death is not in God but in the subjective consciousness of the sinners, who repent and cease their rebellion against God and turn towards God. It is this psychological or subjective influence worked on the mind

32. Weaver, *Nonviolent Atonement*, 18.

33. Gunton, *Actuality of Atonement*, 157.

of the sinner by the death of Christ that gives this view its name of moral influence theory.[34]

A theological paradigm shift in emphasis of this kind will, of course, elicit those who welcome it and those who oppose it. Some question the emphasis accorded to humans and consider its subjective and anthropocentric pole to be a weakness.[35] Others, like Boersma, believe it represents God taking human response seriously, not coercing believers, but using genuine persuasion to draw them to himself.[36] Certainly MIT presents newfound soteriological responsibility for humans in that whilst the divine expression of love is utterly God-initiated, nonetheless huge onus is put upon humans who will be held accountable for whether they rightly respond to Christ-as-exemplar.

Rather than worshipping a distant, judgmental, and potentially violent God humans find themselves, according to MIT, at the heart of divine soteriological purposes, deciding whether to emulate God or not. They either bear the consequences or reap the rewards of their actions and choices rather than remaining dependent upon a potentially wrathful and unpredictable God. This soteriology has been seen as both admirably simple and ethically appealing, replacing the disconcerting notion of divine violence evident in other theories with a God ready and willing to receive those who choose to approach him.[37]

Conversely, it is argued that MIT fails to take full measure of the power and influence of evil and sin. Sin should be understood as a slavery which cannot be overcome by mere appeals to follow a good example. Instead, the requirement is for a tangible act of setting free, of re-creation, indeed, of a redemption which fully respects the humanity of its object.[38] An appeal to follow an example, however seminal and inspirational, is unable to change the ontological status of individuals ensnared by the Satan, the demonic realm and sin.[39] Whilst it is biblical to set God and others as exemplars, a successful imitation can only occur *after* atonement has been made, the

34. Weaver, *Nonviolent Atonement*, 18.

35. Schmiechen, however, notes that the love of God as demonstrated in the death and resurrection of Jesus and as understood and presented by Abelard is an objective event, concluding that "the theory is not completely reduced to the subjective response of humanity." Schmiechen, *Saving Power*, 294.

36. Boersma, *Violence, Hospitality and the Cross*, 132.

37. Rauser, *Faith Lacking Understanding*, 105.

38. Gunton, *Actuality of Atonement*, 160.

39. "One of the objections to 'moral imitation' as a basis for atonement is that it offers no necessary purchase on the world; it refers to no ontological change brought by Christ that achieves its goal regardless of human response." Bartlett, *Cross Purposes*, 15.

Satan defeated and with the nullifying of Satanic power and the attendant overcoming of sin.

Abelard disliked the emphasis on God's judgment required in the satisfaction theory; he also objected that God's attitude is understood to change in regard to the person who accepted Jesus' death on their behalf. Such teaching was impossible for him because the perfect God is entirely impassible.[40] The responsibility for change within MIT therefore shifted from God, whether impassible or not, to human beings who have high degrees of passibility and either a desire or a need for change.

Abelard's atonement theory is primarily epistemological, presenting humans with a message of God's love and the weight of their sin; it is also volitional, offering motivation for humans to make a positive response.[41] MIT is therefore principally concerned with human function rather than divine or cosmological ontology. The human seeking salvation through Jesus Christ is encouraged to see the cross as a supreme visual aid and stimulus for moral and praxeological change. This moves the emphasis away from the Satan, sin and any encounters that might occur between God and malevolent forces, thereby removing any accompanying need for divine violence. What is required is that a lesson be learnt and an example applied to the individual in a subjective manner such that their response lifts them out of sin and into right relationship with God through their choice and endeavor.[42] Scant regard is given to the Satan or evil forces actually existing, other than in a metaphorical or symbolic manner.

MIT presents a way by which God can be absolved from the charge of violence, ontologically and functionally. Boersma notes, however, that, "A moral theory of the atonement only truly avoids the problem of divine violence if it focuses entirely on the life of Christ, so that there is no way in which God uses the death of Christ as a redemptive event."[43] This particularity and focus on one soteriological element at the expense of others to explain or deny the charge of divine violence belies an inherent weakness of MIT.

---

40. Weaver, *Nonviolent Atonement*, 18.

41. Rauser, *Faith Lacking Understanding*, 105.

42. This issue is further highlighted by Rauser when he compares the MIT to the CVM and PSA theories. He notes that, "While these other theories are objective (that is, they see the primary force of the atonement in the objective work achieved by God in Christ), the example/influence theory is subjective insofar as it sees the primary work of the atonement in the effect it has upon individuals (revealing the love of God to us) and the response it invokes in them (motivating us to be like Christ)." Rauser, *Faith Lacking Understanding*, 104.

43. Boersma, *Violence, Hospitality and the Cross*, 117.

Another problem emerges in the stark disparity between Jesus as exemplar and humans as imitators in that Jesus is an example because he alone is the incarnate Son who by the enabling of the Holy Spirit remained unfallen whereas humans universally fall.[44] By analogy, this is like a great athlete being an example to a small, physically-challenged child. The athlete could inspire the child to achieve its best in response to her example and exhortations and yet, by definition, because of his inherent limitations, the child would ultimately be unable to attain all that the role-model requires. This scenario provides the definition of an exercise in futility and frustration—both for model and imitator.

Christus Victor—Cosmological Violence

The CVM will be considered in more depth later; for now it suffices to introduce only its central features. Aulén veers away from using "model" to describe Christus Victor, instead speaking of it as a "drama," a "classic" view, or an "idea,"[45] noting,

> Finally, I would call attention to the terminology which I have employed. I have tried to be consistent in speaking of the classic *idea* of the Atonement, never of the, or a, classic *theory*; I have reserved the word *theory*, and usually the word *doctrine*, for the Latin and the "subjective" types. For the classic idea of the Atonement has never been put forward, like the other two, as a rounded and finished theological *doctrine*; it has always been an idea, a *motif*, a theme, expressed in many different variations. It is not, indeed, that it has lacked clearness of outline; on the contrary, it has been fully definite and unambiguous. But it has never been shaped into a rational theory.[46]

Likewise, Gunton is cautious in ascribing a description, noting that against Aulén it must be emphasized that a basis for a theory of the atonement is not found, particularly if such a theory is opposed to other supposed options; instead, for Gunton, the CV "model" is merely a group of metaphors.[47] Whilst acknowledging these caveats, the term "model" will, however, continue to be used for ease of reference, primarily because it is

---

44. Gunton, *Actuality of Atonement*, 158.

45. See Aulén, *Christus Victor*, 4–7, where each of these terms is used and explained.

46. Ibid., 157.

47. Gunton, *Actuality of Atonement*, 61.

how it is understood and referred to by the majority of theologians in atonement studies.

Once again, what PSA is to mainstream Protestantism and MIT is to Protestant liberals, so CVM was to the early Church in its inception and in the first centuries of theology. The RCVM will be considered shortly, but suffice it to say that it provided the foundation and basis for the CVM to take shape. There was some level of overlap between the models, both of which see God and the Satan in direct opposition and through their respective interpretations, God overcomes or deceives the Devil thus securing humanity's salvation. In case the temptation to read anachronistically into the Patristic era overtakes today's theologian, however, Kelly advises that

> the student who seeks to understand the soteriology of the fourth and early fifth centuries will be sharply disappointed if he expects to find anything corresponding to the elaborately worked out syntheses which the contemporary theology of the Trinity and the Incarnation presents. In both these latter departments controversy forced fairly exact definition on the Church, whereas the redemption did not become a battle-ground for rival schools until the twelfth century, when Anselm's *Cur Deus Homo* (c.1097) focused attention on it. Instead he must be prepared to pick his way through a variety of theories, to all appearance unrelated and even mutually incompatible, existing side by side and sometimes sponsored by the same theologian.[48]

In regards to these early centuries, therefore, Aulén argues that the CVM held complete, almost unchallenged, sway as an interpretative model for nearly one millennium; he contends, in fact, that if it is asked how widely spread was the classic idea in the early church, it may be said that it dominates the whole of Greek patristic theology from Irenaeus to John of Damascus who, Aulén argues, is commonly regarded as marking the close of the patristic period.[49] Over time it evolved and changed until it eventually came to be surpassed in the Western Church by PSA theories. A number of reasons have been posited for this transition, Boersma contending that primarily the influence of Enlightenment thought on the Western Church and what he calls its "myopic naturalism" made it difficult to accept supernatural influence in the realm of history.[50] Aulén also unpacks numer-

48. Kelly, *Early Christian Doctrines*, 375. He chooses not to differentiate between the CVM and the RCVM, deciding to characterize Patristic soteriology in terms of the latter (see ibid., 163–83).

49. Aulén, *Christus Victor*, 37.

50. Boersma, *Violence, Hospitality and the Cross*, 194.

ous reasons for the neglect of the CVM and its replacement by PSA (and other models) noting that an implied demand of the Christian faith is that it must be clearly expressed in the form of a rational doctrine.[51] Aulén also acknowledges that the CVM is not primarily a doctrine of this kind, but rather a dramatic *idea*.[52]

In the first half of the Twentieth Century Aulén's *Christus Victor*[53] proved a seminal book, heralding a re-consideration of this ancient doctrine. His ideas have been influential in leading many to revisit CVM as a means of interpreting and understanding the atonement; Aulén synthesized the doctrine:

> The central idea of Christus Victor is the view of God and the Kingdom of God as fighting against evil powers ravaging in mankind. In this drama Christ has the key rôle, and the title *Christus Victor* says the decisive word about his rôle.[54]

Summarizing his perspective, Boyd concludes that Jesus came to end the cosmic war that had been raging from time immemorial and to set the Satan's captives free.[55] CVM has therefore been called the dramatic view[56] as it presents an understanding of the atonement that is broad in its schemata and vivid and poetic in its representation of the eternal, cosmic battle between God and the Satan and his malevolent spiritual forces that stand counter to divine purposes for humanity. It also speaks to God's ultimate victory over these forces via the birth, life, death and resurrection of Jesus Christ, not merely because of his passion through the cross.

This "whole life soteriology" is the first of two key differences between CVM and other views of the atonement. It is seen as a doctrine concerned with all that Jesus experienced and accomplished, including his incarnation and not only with his death and resurrection.[57] The second is that it is cosmological, taking into account the full sweep of salvation history whilst

51. Aulén, *Christus Victor*, 9.

52. See Aulén, *Christus Victor*, 7–15 for a full description of Aulén's causes for the neglect of the CVM. Further, Boyd considers the postmodern context of the rejection of the CVM in Boyd, *God at War*, 61–72.

53. Aulén, *Christus Victor*, 1931.

54. Ibid., ix.

55. Boyd, "Christus Victor," 23–49.

56. Aulén compares the CVM with other models highlighting its nature as dramatic, noting that within it "Atonement is not regarded as affecting men primarily as individuals, but is set forth as a drama of a world's salvation." Aulén, *Christus Victor*, 6.

57. Aulén notes that Gregory of Nazianzus sums up the purpose of the incarnation thus: "that God by overcoming the tyrant, might set us free and reconcile us with Himself through His son." Ibid., 42.

embracing a thorough-going theology of the Satan and the demonic realm, not as metaphors or symbols, but as ontological beings; it has been some time since even the Church has embraced this kind of "biblical dualism."[58]

The Enlightenment's promotion of naturalism has made it difficult for many, including Christians, to accept supernatural influence in the historical realm. The idea of a cosmic battle between God and the powers of evil has been hard to sustain in an environment where science and technology hold pre-eminent sway.[59] Previously in church history and theology, a majority had been comfortable in speaking literally of this eternal battle; Athanasius, for example, observed:

> The air is the sphere of the devil, the enemy of our race who, having fallen from heaven, endeavours with the other evil spirits who shared in his disobedience both to keep souls from the truth and to hinder the progress of those who are trying to follow it.[60]

Articulating the issues that CVM addresses he added that the Lord came to overthrow the devil and to purify the air in order to make "a way" for humans up to heaven.[61]

For advocates of CVM it follows as a (super)natural corollary of their support that holding this doctrine necessarily leads to a belief in a spiritual dimension and acceptance of a dualistic understanding of the cosmos. Boersma, whilst not an advocate of the CVM nonetheless concedes, for instance, that the Christus Victor theme cannot function without at least some degree of metaphysical or cosmic dualism; observing that Boyd and others are right in reclaiming this dualism as part of the Christian heritage.[62] Such theologians, therefore, express their understanding through the lens of a first-century worldview, or at least an outlook sympathetic to this perspective.[63]

---

58. Ray argues that the problematic element of Patristic dualism is that its "clear-cut" distinction leads to moral absolutism with the concomitant bypassing of "the complexity and subtlety of evil as we know it, feeding illusions of purity and innocence, on the one hand, and permitting the demonization of those people and groups viewed as unclean or damaged, on the other." Ray, *Deceiving the Devil*, 126.

59. Boersma, *Violence, Hospitality and the Cross*, 193.

60. Athanasius, *On the Incarnation*, 55.

61. Ibid.

62. Boersma, *Violence, Hospitality and the Cross*, 199.

63. Rieger asserts that "a New Testament metaphor-complex for the atonement, so-called *Christus-Victor*, was adopted and ardently articulated by the church fathers . . ." and, after its rejection by scholastics of the high medieval period, this motif "should be repopularized in the church's evangelism of the postmodern world." Rieger, "Good

A position acknowledging continuity between ancient Judaism, early Christianity and then Judeo-Christianity is thereby endorsed; it is also accepted that early Christians inherited this dual focus of Judaism and Christianity. This provides a basic framework within which Christian thinkers have understood atonement through the ages. Within these two separate and yet not disparate religions, atonement involves establishing right relationship between God and world *through* the confrontation of evil.[64] Not primarily through the defeating or forgiveness of sin and *then* the corollary of evil being dealt with. Rather, as seen in CVM there is a direct, violent, pro-active and primary confrontation with evil; all other issues are secondary and subsidiary.[65]

CVM does not, therefore, perceive atonement as a visual or moral stimulus or the placating of a wrathful God; nor is it a response to one carefully chosen element in the life, ministry and death of Jesus Christ. In the fullest sense it is not even a metaphor, rather, for its advocates, it is a doctrine about the very character of God and about everything that stands against divine purposes. It is the attempt to paint with broad and dramatic brush-strokes an all-encompassing overview of the eternal unfolding of salvation history. It is, therefore, a doctrine concerned more with ontology than function and one providing not only an aid to understanding but a full-blown insight into what *actually happened* and *is* happening in terms of God, salvation, the cosmos and the spiritual realm, both divine and evil. Gunton notes that

> the problem that the atonement engages with is primarily *theological*. It does not consist primarily in morally wrong acts whose effect is on human life alone and which therefore can be rectified by merely human remedial action, but in a disrupted relationship with the creator. As a result of the disruption there is an *objective* bondage, pollution and disorder in personal and social life, encompassing all dimensions of human existence and its context. By virtue of both truths, that the problem is one we cannot solve and that our being clean and free and upright is the gift of the creator, there needs to be a recreative, redemptive

News," 379.

64. Ray, *Deceiving the Devil*, 1.

65. "Its central theme is the idea of the Atonement as a Divine conflict and victory; Christ—Christus Victor—fights against and triumphs over the evil powers of the world, the 'tyrants' under which mankind is in bondage and suffering, and in Him God reconciles the world to Himself." Aulén, *Christus Victor*, 4.

divine initiative in which the root of the problem, the disrupted personal relationship, is set to rights.[66]

In CVM atonement is portrayed as a salvation battled for, a powerful, real adversary overcome and a *war* actually won by the Victor God.

A criticism of CVM, however, is its perceived lack of compelling and explicit biblical evidence. Critiquing Weaver's *Narrative Christus Victor*,[67] Finlan notes this paucity, adding that the idea of a battle between cosmic forces of good and evil seems characteristic of the worldview of the first and second centuries and is thereby de facto inadequate to answer humanity's philosophic needs today.[68] This said, Finlan could be guilty of what Lewis called "chronological snobbery";[69] it is "present-centric" to disregard an opinion because of its perceived anachronism. Instead reconsideration of the original application of CVM is required, only after which should a decision be made as to whether its theological themes might require revisiting. This is especially the case in regard to its engagement and understanding of divine violence and of the way in which it addresses, perceives and responds to an actual adversary of God personifying evil in the ontological being of the Satan.

Few support such a position today.[70] Even those, like Girard, who seemingly endorse a personified malevolent being, on closer reflection are less than fulsome in their support. So, whilst Girard's understanding of the functioning of the cross is of revelation and imitation, seen in terms redolent of MIT, the revelatory power of the cross serves, and turns out to

---

66. Gunton, *Actuality of Atonement*, 160.

67. See, Weaver, *Nonviolent Atonement*.

68. Finlan, *Problems with Atonement*, 99.

69. A friend of Lewis, Owen Barfield, had been seeking to convert Lewis to the perspective of Anthroposophism. Lewis withstood his attempts but admitted, "his counterattacks destroyed forever two elements in my own thought. In the first place he made short work of what I have called my "chronological snobbery," the uncritical acceptance of the intellectual climate common to our own age and the assumption that whatever has gone out of date is on that account discredited. You must find why it went out of date. Was it ever refuted (and if so by whom, where, and how conclusively) or did it merely die away as fashions do? If the latter, this tells us nothing about its truth or falsehood. From seeing this, one passes to the realization that our own age is also "a period," and certainly has, like all periods, its own characteristic illusions. They are likeliest to lurk in those widespread assumptions which are so ingrained in the age that no one dares to attack or feels it necessary to defend them." Lewis, *Surprised by Joy*, 207–8.

70. Bell, however, argues that "today we can speak of the 'existence' of the devil and demons." The devil, he contends, "has an ontological status which one can compare to Adam . . ." Bell, *Deliver Us from Evil*, 344.

METAPHOR & MODELS   133

be for him Christ's victory over Satan.[71] This appears to be incontrovertible advocacy for CVM and belief in an actual being called the Satan who stands against God's purposes. The position crumbles, however, when it is understood, as we have seen, that for "Satan" in Girard's thought, as with Finlan, one needs to read—the very process of "violent contagion" and not someone who really exists.[72]

Girard apparently gives tacit endorsement of CVM, even its ransom element, although for him their themes are dramatically demythologized. This is part of a broader process, coupled with the de-prioritizing of an awareness of the Satan per se, that originally led to the ransom motif being left in antiquity. It was relegated to being at best irrelevant, a theological "museum piece" and at worst a grotesque abrogation of the Gospel and in particular of God's character and soteriological plans.[73] It will be argued, however, that a demythologized CVM is no Christus Victor model at all.[74]

Ransom Christus Victor—Deceitful Violence

The final metaphor is one out of which CVM evolved, its narrative again depicting the atonement in terms of conflict and victory; it is a view that was especially popular between the second and sixth centuries.[75] RCVM is the first to be widely held by Christians as a means of understanding God's achievements through the birth, life, ministry, death and resurrection of Jesus Christ of Nazareth; in particular highlighting the soteriological significance of the Satan's overthrow and defeat. Stott crystallizes this central role of the Satan in early understanding of the salvation drama by noting

---

71. Boersma, *Violence, Hospitality and the Cross*, 147.

72. Girard, *Satan Fall*, 35.

73. Boersma concedes of the Ransom theory that "the notion is fascinating, but I remain unconvinced of the deception theme of the fishing analogy." Boersma, *Violence, Hospitality and the Cross*, 191.

74. Milbank claims that the gospel account is immune to an idealist reading and inherent within it is an absolutely exceptional phenomenon leading to a unique understanding of the gospel in terms of the fact that "its meaning *is* that meaning has sloughed off its fallen impotence and is now fully actual and effective. If Christ be not raised, then our faith is in vain, because the new meanings offered in Christ only have significance (unlike all other meanings) if they are entirely effective. They must have arisen originally as events, indeed as hyper-events that more truly occurred than any other occurrences, else they would have no power now to be effective and to generate the event of reconciliation." Milbank, *Being Reconciled*, 95.

75. Ray, *Deceiving the Devil*, 119.

that in the early church it was perceived to be the devil who made the cross necessary.[76]

Although RCVM was almost universally popular during the first centuries of the Eastern Church, it is now perceived as either a theological anomaly or an historical aberration. Heim, for example, characterizes a recurrent response to the RCVM in noting that early Christian writers are famous for their fondness for two images which he argues have perplexed and often embarrassed later theologians; the two images he highlights are Jesus' death as a ransom and as a trick or "deceit" of Satan. He concludes that in discussions of atonement these views, whilst prominent in the early centuries, are now usually passed over lightly.[77] Certainly, no major part of the worldwide Christian Communion currently retains these two perspectives and, as will be demonstrated, many theologians not only deny the doctrine but distance themselves from it and its ramifications in regard to the character and purposes of God.[78]

So, whilst considering atonement models, Schreiner concludes that PSA provokes the most negative response[79] and certainly it has come in for its share of scholarly criticism of late and yet it nonetheless remains premature to affirm it as the least popular model. Historically, that accolade still goes to RCVM, a doctrine not merely discounted by the majority of scholars post-Anselm but, as noted, usually discounted *and* abused in the process, scholars and theologians outdoing each other in their quest to add the most discourteous adjectives to it.[80]

Regardless of its unpopularity, RCVM must be assessed in order to ascertain whether it retains theological relevance and might yet be a pertinent means of understanding soteriology, the atonement, God, the Satan and divine violence in a modern context. It is easy to heap approbation on RCVM model but this falls short of the standards of objective theological enquiry and, as noted when considering CVM, likewise invokes Lewis's

---

76. Stott, *Cross of Christ*, 133.

77. Heim, *Saved from Sacrifice*, 161.

78. The Orthodox Church ascribes to the CVM and, in regard to Western theology, "renounces not only their distortions but their foundational principle that the sacrifice of the Son is in any way demanded by the Father." Bouteneff, "Christ and Salvation," 98.

79. Schreiner, "Penal Substitution," 72.

80. Examining St. Basil's atonement terminology, Kelly noted that "Gregory's grotesque imagery of the bait and hook, we observe, is absent here . . ." Kelly, *Early Christian Doctrines*, 383. Dale goes further, describing such imagery as "intolerable, monstrous, and profane." Dale, *Atonement*, 277. Whilst assessing Gregory of Nyssa's vivid descriptions, Stott concludes on theology's behalf that "to us the analogy of the fish-hook is grotesque . . ." Stott, *Cross of Christ*, 134.

charge of chronological snobbery.[81] Aulén notes that it should be evident that the historical study of dogma is wasting its time in pure superficiality if it does not endeavor to penetrate to what may lay below the outward dress; it is incumbent upon the theologian, therefore, to look for the religious values which might otherwise lay concealed.[82]

Further, an additional method is needed. Finlan, for example, responding to Brown and Parker's critique of atonement theology, notes:

> [But] they do not fill this out with any biblical scholarship, any background in cultic theology or the metaphorical appropriation of cultic images, or any history of the phases of doctrinal development. Humanistic appeals are not enough to provide the ground for a new theology. It is necessary to give a sustained account of how and why these doctrines emerged. Strong biblical scholarship is needed; the case against traditional atonement cannot be argued with one's ethical instincts alone. Otherwise there is little mooring or depth to one's attempted new theologizing.[83]

Putting personal causes, concerns and agendas aside, each doctrine must be approached on its own merits, free from ideological constraints of denomination or heritage. Atonement doctrine has long existed as a vehicle for conveying information, primarily about salvation and, on occasion, the Incarnation. There are always many interpretative vehicles available, and there is no reason, as Finlan suggests, why the best one might not be a very old one.[84]

The oldest of all is RCVM and according to its early advocates the Fall had placed human beings in the power of the Satan and redemption was envisaged as humanity's emancipation from this actual, personal being of evil.[85] One of the chief theological concerns of the time was for God's justice; hence the emphasis that it was through free choice that humans had fallen into the Devil's clutches. This human decision gave the Devil the right to adequate compensation if he was to surrender humans that "belonged" to

81. Ray notes that "the patristic view of atonement is often rejected as anachronistic, bizarre, grotesque, and theologically incorrect; and no doubt a case can be made that it is each of these." Ray, *Deceiving the Devil*, 121.

82. Aulén, *Christus Victor*, 47.

83. Finlan, *Problems with Atonement*, 104.

84. Ibid., 120.

85. Stott asserts that the early church Fathers "all recognized that since the Fall, and on account of it, mankind has been in captivity not only to sin and guilt but to the devil. They thought of him as the lord of sin and death, and as the major tyrant from whom Jesus came to liberate us." Stott, *Cross of Christ*, 133.

him; for God to have exercised *force majeure* at this point would have been construed as unfair and tyrannical.[86]

Instead God offered Jesus as a ransom to the Devil who when he saw him, born of a virgin and a renowned miracle worker, decided the exchange was to his advantage. What he failed to realize was that the outward covering of human flesh concealed the immortal Godhead. Hence, when he accepted Jesus in exchange for mankind, he could not hold him; he was deceived, outwitted and caught, as a fish is by the bait which conceals the hook.[87]

In addition to the previously noted objections to this view of atonement it has been argued that "deceit" is beyond the Christian God's capability. This subjective interpretative caveat aside and taken at face value it seems, however, that there is still much to commend this outlook; Boersma, whilst ultimately unconvinced of the "deception theme," nonetheless admits that the notion of it is fascinating.[88]

Synthesizing central elements of this ancient doctrine, Aulén concludes that the most common view is that a postlapsarian Devil possesses an incontestable right over fallen man and therefore a regular and orderly settlement is necessary.[89] This idea of the Devil having "rights" over humans has caused much discomfort and consternation; there has been more recently, however, a willingness amongst some theologians to revisit and reconsider RCVM to re-appraise its claims.[90]

Sometimes, in fact, support has come from unexpected quarters, such as when Girard states that Western theology, in rejecting the idea of the Satan tricked by the Cross, has lost a pearl of great price in the sphere of anthropology.[91] Even given Girard's reinterpretation and demythologizing of "Satan" this statement retains force and it is not only anthropology that has lost out—theology has too. At the very least it has forgotten its historical forbears and thereby its foundations and mission and at worst is missing the possibility of a modern re-appropriation of a potentially key doctrinal understanding of the Christian God, divine violence and the means by which salvation has been won.

86. Gregory of Nyssa, "Great Catechism," 492.

87. Kelly, *Early Christian Doctrines*, 382.

88. Boersma, *Violence, Hospitality and the Cross*, 191.

89. Aulén, *Christus Victor*, 48.

90. At the forefront of this movement in the Twentieth Century was G. Aulén with *Christus Victor*. More recently various scholars have presented perspectives ranging from sympathetic appraisals to full treatises on the RCVM. These include Ray, *Deceiving the Devil*; Weaver, *Nonviolent Atonement*; Boyd, "Christus Victor," 23–49.

91. Girard, *I See Satan Fall*, 150.

In the context of ascertaining "what is," Anderson tells the joke of three umpires having a beer after a baseball game and reflecting on what it is "all about." One contends that there are balls and strikes and that he calls them the way they are; another responds that there are balls and strikes and he calls them the way he sees them. The third says that there are balls and strikes and they are *nothing* until he calls them.[92] This assessment of baseball metaphorically conjoined with theology needs to allow a fourth position—that there are balls and strikes and whether or not they are seen or called they are nonetheless real. The issue is about putting aside personal perspectives, the influence of others and the need to be "right" or palatable; what matters is being true to the call, whatever the call is and however unpopular it might be. It just is what it is.

It is of course understandable that some baulk at the notion that God practices deceit in order to overcome the Satan and of thereby potentially utilizing violence to finalize such a deception. There is also the issue, as noted, which particularly challenges modern sensibilities: the acceptance of an actual adversary for God—a personified evil being who ontologically exists. We will revisit RCVM later and so for the time being its potential and ongoing validity as a means of interpreting the atonement and the overall life, mission and accomplishments of Jesus Christ will be acceded. Having reflected on Reformation theories of the atonement, in particular the absolute depravity of humans, of universal guilt and the subsequent transfer of divine wrath to the undeserving Son, Finlan concludes their cumulative worth as "monstrous teachings."[93] He then asserts that the only atonement explanation that is consistent with the goodness of God is the old rescue theory, where God tricks the devil.[94]

RCVM is a contentious doctrine that has stirred controversy since its inception in the Patristic Era. This does not have to disqualify it, however, from further consideration, reappraisal and re-application to hearers in a postmodern context. Regardless of its challenging ramifications to the Christian God and divine purposes, it might yet remain a way by which God and his soteriological plans can be understood. In particular, RCVM could still provide a means by which divine violence can be explicated to incorporate God's endorsement and utilization of violence.[95]

92. Anderson, *Reality Isn't*, 75.

93. Finlan, *Problems with Atonement*, 78.

94. Ibid.

95. Conversely, Weaver argues in his five reasons for the demise of this atonement doctrine that one of them is "discomfort with the motif's military and battle imagery." Weaver, *Nonviolent Atonement*, 15.

The Use of Metaphor

Further to our assessment of some of the main atonement models and to aid understanding of whether divine violence might be intrinsic or extrinsic, a function or an ontological trait of God, it is important to reflect upon the nature and use of metaphor. This linguistic and conceptual device is used repeatedly in theology and the Bible to express otherwise inexplicable elements of divine existence, being, nature, praxis and purpose—particularly in regard to soteriology. It is in regard to life's great "unknowns" which, according to McFague, include mortality, love, fear, joy and hope, that the poets use metaphors as an epistemic bridge. Religious language, she argues, is deeply metaphorical for the same reason and it is therefore not a surprise, she concludes, that Jesus' most characteristic form of teaching, the parables, should be extended metaphors.[96]

Aware of this theological and linguistic conundrum, Weil suggests, in regard to the existence of God, that it is

> a case of contradictories, both of them true. There is a God. There is no God. Where is the problem? I am quite sure that there is a God in the sense that I am sure my love is no illusion. I am quite sure there is no God, in the sense that I am sure there is nothing which resembles what I can conceive when I say that word . . .[97]

To counter this seeming impasse metaphors become essential in the endeavor to speak of God; indeed, it is impossible to express ideas about God, his action and being, independently of the biblical metaphors in which they were first given.[98] Further, the study of metaphors may yet also provide important clues towards understanding the nature of religion itself.[99]

As already considered, there are various ways to interpret and understand the salvific significance of Jesus Christ dying on a cross.[100] The apostle Paul was particularly exercised in this area and yet for him the quest for a particular atonement metaphor was not of primary concern. In fact, the desire to promote one means of understanding at the expense of another

---

96. McFague, *Metaphorical Theology*, 15.

97. Weil, *Waiting for God*, 32.

98. Gunton, *Actuality of Atonement*, 47.

99. Tracy, "Metaphor," 104.

100. The theological use of the word "cross" inherently contains metaphor and interpretation; for Macquarrie, "the word 'cross' does not simply denote a particular kind of instrument of execution, but rather connotes all that Christ's death has come to mean in the Christian experience of salvation . . ." Macquarrie, *God-Talk*, 98.

was not an issue; instead he even used one metaphor to interpret another.[101] The issue nonetheless remains that throughout the whole endeavor he relied heavily, if not exclusively, on metaphors as a means of engaging with and explaining both Jesus Christ's death and all that this death accomplished. Perhaps this dependence was linked to Paul's realization early on that there is in fact, no explicit and distinct New Testament "doctrine" of atonement but rather, as den Heyer argues, only a "multiplicity of images" that "influence one another . . . but also contradict one another." [102]

Each image or metaphor could therefore be used, Heyer asserts, to illustrate or illuminate a particular element of understanding, but no one image should be allowed to take precedence in any ultimate sense. He concludes that there are no dogmas formulated in the New Testament but that there is instead a rather surprising and confusing variety.[103] The absence of explicit dogma or doctrine further highlights the use and value of the constituent metaphors that provide each element of insight. The prolific use of metaphors by such a seminal biblical figure as St. Paul is however, at the very least, indicative of their theological importance, again especially in regard to soteriology.

For example, Finlan notes that the various soteriological metaphors used in Romans 8 are judicial, commercial, and ritual images for the efficacy of the death of Christ, picturing that death as bringing about acquittal, constituting a payment, or functioning as a cultic event.[104] In this manner Paul is forwarding metaphorical ideas as an essential means of understanding and expressing atonement.

Further, Richardson notes that Paul and other New Testament writers do not offer theories but rather vivid metaphors, which can, if the recipient allows them, operate in the human imagination, making real the saving truth of redemption by Christ's self-offering on the behalf of humans.[105] He concludes, in fact, that it is a rather unfortunate kind of sophistication which believes that the only thing to do with metaphors is to turn them into theories.[106] The central importance of metaphorical language and imagery

---

101. Finlan, *Problems with Atonement*, 55. In considering Romans 8:3, for example, Finlan notes that "three principal metaphors are blended here: the judicial notion of condemnation (*katakrinō*), the technical term for the purification sacrifice (*peri hamartias*), and an implied scapegoat image (projecting all sin onto one body)." Ibid., 49.

102. Heyer, *Doctrine of the Atonement*, 130.

103. Ibid., 133.

104. Finlan, *Options on Atonement*, 19.

105. Richardson, *Theology of the New Testament*, 222.

106. Ibid., 223.

for Paul and other New Testament writers is therefore patent, both for theological understanding and for discourse on salvation and atonement.

This is not to say that the use of metaphors is without potential pitfalls. In fact, due to their central theological significance and powerful emotional resonance to the believer and their beliefs, metaphors are open to abuse and misuse.[107] They are, however, indispensable to the language of religion and their facilitation as a primary vehicle by which the otherwise inexpressible or incomprehensible or, in the case of divine violence, the unpalatable, can be made tangible; they nonetheless remain potentially dangerous.[108] The main concern for Combes in this regard is that over time metaphors might in some cases lose their obvious identity as metaphors, and instead become confused with literal truths.[109] The critical level of importance for metaphors, coupled with this scope for confusion and error, mean that it is essential to reflect on exactly what metaphors are and how they are used.

The Primacy of Metaphor

Given this level and means of engagement it is apparent why metaphors are invaluable to those seeking to delineate, understand and express theological truths, perhaps in particular theological expressions which, like divine violence, might otherwise remain inaccessible. Theology is concerned with those parts of existence and reality that fall outside the normal sphere of human understanding and therefore require a "bridge" to facilitate engagement and cognition.[110] The lens of metaphor is both informative and cognitive, giving access to fact which would otherwise be unobserved or to truth which would otherwise remain hidden.[111] It is this "bridge" or "lens" (both metaphors of course . . .) of metaphor that provide its efficacy as, an albeit shocking, way of facilitating understanding. Metaphorical talk effects a familiarity or "intimacy" between speakers and between them and their

---

107. See, Gunton, "Christ the Sacrifice," in *Actuality of Atonement*, 115–41, for a discussion of this problem.

108. Combes, *Metaphor of Slavery*, 11.

109. Ibid.

110. "In the concept of theology the truth of theological discourse as discourse about God that God himself has authorised is always presupposed. Talk about God that is grounded in humanity, in human needs and interests, or as an expression of human ideas about divine reality, would not be theology. It would simply be a product of human imagination." Pannenberg, *Systematic Theology*, 1:7.

111. Caird, *Language and Imagery*, 153.

world enabling people to feel "at home" and it is this quality that explains why metaphorical discourse is so pervasively engaged in.[112]

To understand God, his nature and purposes it is patent that without some degree of ideological and conceptual resonance all propositions would remain abstract and ungrounded.[113] To fill this conceptual chasm a system has been sought; a linguistic and perceptual method by which humans can span the otherwise insuperable gap between them and deity. Kittay argues,

> Some order, at least one intelligible to ourselves and to those with whom we share our space and our words, none the less remains crucial. And a systematic tolerance of a "disorder" that can be shown to be purposeful and intelligible is equally essential, if we are to remain in touch with the well-springs of our creativity and to keep our surroundings and our minds adaptable to the changing circumstances of our lives and our world. Understanding the workings and the meaning of this latter "disorder" is as much a part of understanding meaning and language as is understanding the "proper order." It is within a carefully conceived "chaos" that metaphors attain an irreducible cognitive content and their special meaning.[114]

In a rudimentary sense religious metaphor is the human attempt to draw upon that which they are most familiar with in order to explicate that which they are least familiar with. Thus, the everyday world of human activities and relationships is mined to create pictures of that which is unknown and thereby otherwise unintelligible. By these means humans can, to some degree, engage with, understand and express those areas of belief and existence that would otherwise remain outside the sphere of their lives.[115] Succinctly put, religious metaphors are the transcendent expressed through the mundane. Conversely for Bultmann, such a definition, rather than explicating "metaphor" rather describes "myth" which, for him, objectifies the transcendent into the immanent, and thus also into the disposable, as

112. Cooper, *Metaphor*,140.

113. Saint Paul is a prolific user of metaphors whose effective use is coupled with their obvious cultural resonance; Dunn observes that "Paul draws on metaphors from the customs of his time." Dunn, *Theology of Paul*, 328. If Paul had not thus utilized metaphors their communicatory efficacy would have been lessened.

114. Kittay, *Metaphor*, 327.

115. "The structures drawn, to a greater or lesser extent, from human relationships make it possible to define the terms under which the physical and spiritual worlds interrelate and provide assurance to the believer of his or her place in the order of things, specifying to a degree the behaviour expected from the believer and giving that individual the means to placate and influence the supernatural world." Combes, *Metaphor of Slavery*, 18–19.

becomes evident when cult more and more becomes action calculated to in-fluence the attitude of the deity by averting its wrath and winning its favor.[116]

Explicating Reality

It is important to note that metaphor is not a linguistic tool peculiar to Christian faith, rather all major world religions share a vision, or perhaps a re-description, of reality that is informed by a specific cluster of metaphors.[117] At the heart of Christian faith and therefore at the center of theology is the quest to engage with, understand and then communicate a perception of reality as ontological fact. Further and in particular regard to the concerns of this thesis, comes the quest to understand and delineate God's nature, particularly as it pertains to violence.

Metaphors, both new and historic, can have the power to define these realities in a manner that is unavailable to any other medium.[118] They do this through a coherent network of entailments that highlight particular fea-tures of reality whilst hiding others. The acceptance of a specific metaphor forces those accepting it to focus *only* on those aspects of experience that it highlights, thus leading to the view that the entailments of the metaphor are themselves *true*.[119] Throughout the Pauline letters, as we have seen, a rich and varied range of metaphors are utilized in order to express the sig-nificance of Christ's death.[120] These metaphors of the cross and atonement express and define their own version not merely of the reality of Christ's crucifixion, but of the concomitant aspects of response, action and lifestyle that ought to follow as a result of an acceptance of the central metaphor cho-sen. Dunn highlights the importance of recognizing the character of each of these options as a metaphorical assertion, warning against the danger of promoting any one metaphor at the expense of another; the metaphor, after all, is not the thing itself but a means of expressing the thing's meaning.

---

116. Bultmann, "Problem of Demythologizing," 99.

117. Tracy, "Metaphor," 93.

118. "Metaphor is a supreme instance of the harmony that can be attained between language and the world. Therefore: the world is the kind of thing that can be interpreted in language. It is, or has—metaphorically!—a kind of language." Gunton, *Actuality of Atonement*, 37.

119. Lakoff and Johnson, *Metaphors We Live By*, 157.

120. Dunn highlights what he considers to be the most important ones: "repre-sentation, sacrifice, curse, redemption, reconciliation, conquest of the powers." Dunn, *Theology of Paul*, 231.

Dunn concludes that pushing metaphors too far leads to the unwise practice of translating them into literal facts.[121]

A problem with conventional religious metaphors is that in the time between their creation and their current use they lose not only their relevance but also their original meaning and the fact that they are actually metaphors. Commenting upon the problem of religious language being rich in models, Soskice notes that theology is not alone in this regard; observing that science has failed to acknowledge its use and dependence upon models and metaphors to understand and explain its findings. She concludes that science too considers one entity in terms of another and speaks, for example, of the hypothetical light "wave" or magnetic "field" which lies beyond experience.[122]

The continued advocacy of metaphorical language in other fields demonstrates that theology and religion are not alone in facing the danger of metaphors no longer being acknowledged as such through protracted usage. Gunton, for example, notes that the word *muscle*, when first used, drew upon some of the associations of the Latin *musculus*, "little mouse." It was originally presented as a helpful metaphor precisely because, in its indirect way, it enabled physiologists to name and understand a part of human anatomy. Gunton observes that no-one thinks of those associations any longer, but that is because they have been so successful.[123]

This highlights the problem that metaphors can be perceived as "dead" metaphors, confused with literal truth so that the perceptual basis of those interpreting them is warped and conclusions drawn which were never intended.[124] In the dynamic of interpreting and understanding a metaphor there is a primary imperative to ascertain the literal meaning referenced in the metaphor as well as an acknowledgement of the vehicle's contrastive and affinitive relations which are transferred to a new domain.[125] It is also important to be aware both of the parameters of expectation in regard to the use of language, both literal and metaphorical, as well as similarly having an acceptance of particular limitations in modes of language, literal and metaphorical, which lead to the more modest demand and expectation of there only ever being the potential of achieving a partial or provisional success within the human desire to name and describe.[126]

121. Ibid., 231.

122. Soskice, *Metaphor and Religious Language*, 103.

123. Gunton, *Actuality of Atonement*, 34.

124. Combes, *Metaphor of Slavery*, 11.

125. Kittany, *Metaphor*, 301.

126. In defense of metaphor Gunton notes that its strength in explication is

Additionally, there is the issue of temporal constraint and to what extent metaphors are determined by their original context which, of course, is particularly relevant in regard to divine violence. Aware of these constraints McFague asserts that any attempt to speak about God is done by beings who are by definition social, cultural and historical and whose perspectives, therefore, are necessarily influenced by a wide range of factors.[127] Conversely, metaphors may be able to transcend such limitations and stand for all time as expressions of deeper realities and truths about religious belief. Certainly if the use of metaphors is dictated by the social environment and the era of the user some change or loss of the language correlating to these changes would be expected.[128]

If, indeed, historical context and original user are linked then perhaps metaphors de facto have built-in obsolescence; whereas if they are transcendent of such contextual limitations they retain meaning and value theologically and throughout subsequent history indefinitely. This commends their use in terms of an ability to capture a potentially problematic theme, such as divine violence, thereby encapsulating it to be safely unpacked from its cultural dressing in each subsequent era—whether or not the theme itself remains unpalatable or troubling.

The search for meaning free from historicity is notoriously difficult and it has been argued that no words are "literal" and therefore unchangeable in all times, places and contexts.[129] On the other hand, even if a metaphor is inextricably tied to its original cultural context, this need not mean that its eventual cultural irrelevance must equate to the loss of the understanding or truth for which it was initially formulated.[130] Each metaphor deserves to be considered individually, including its cultural context and original, accepted meaning to ascertain whether this meaning remains cogent even if the metaphor itself has long since lost its original potency and cultural relevance.[131] Further, this provides a basis to potentially link originally violent

---

enhanced by the fact that it "claims only an indirect purchase on reality, bringing to expression some but not all aspects and relationships of the segment of the world to which it is directed." Gunton, *Actuality of Atonement*, 34.

127. McFague, *Metaphorical Theology*, 3.

128. Combes, *Metaphor of Slavery*, 14.

129. Gunton, *Actuality of Atonement*, 34.

130. "Because the metaphor pivots therefore not on the nature of secular authority but on the nature of the Christian kerygma, it is the changes in the latter more than changes in the former that dictate the lifespan and nature of the metaphor." Combes, *Metaphor of Slavery*, 15.

131. "No metaphor is completely reducible to a literal equivalent without consequent loss of content, not even those metaphors for which one can specify an ostensive referent." Soskice, *Metaphor and Religious Language*, 94–95. If, however the attempt is

metaphors with a violent interpretation in a modern context; or at least not to decry such a link in an a priori manner.

Consequently, whilst issues of truth do inevitably arise for new metaphors, another question facing religious believers is what appropriate belief and action particular metaphors might elicit. Gunton goes further than stating the manner in which a believer might respond to biblical metaphors; rather than considering only praxeology and function he sets an ontological agenda for theological and biblical metaphor. Christian proclamation post-Easter for Gunton is not merely a message to be believed but a change in the *status* of believers and, indeed, the whole world and, "The metaphors of atonement are ways of expressing the significance of what had happened and was happening."[132]

What is at issue, therefore, is the dual concern for the truth or falsity of a metaphor integrally linked to the perceptions and inferences that follow from it as well as the actions sanctioned by it. There is, therefore, an essential link between ontology and function—between the reality and what response that reality requires. In all aspects of life, not just politics or love, reality is defined and expressed in terms of metaphors with the integral and essential concomitant process of ascertaining how to act on the basis of metaphors. Inferences are drawn, goals are set, commitments made and plans executed, all on the basis of how in part experience is structured, consciously and unconsciously, by means of particular metaphors.[133]

Soteriological Metaphors

In his attempt to explain salvation Finlan reverts to metaphors, observing that despite the theological influence of atonement-thinking no mention of a sacrificial death can be found. He notes that Jesus does not say that faith saves people contingent upon their acceptance of a soon-to-come interpretation of his death as a cosmic cleansing, a penal substitution, or a massive ransom payment. Rather, faith allows people to be saved because it allows God to reach into their lives and heal them; it is God, he concludes, who is doing this saving.[134] In his desire to circumnavigate metaphors, however,

---

made to attend exclusively to a metaphor's reference point its power is thereby misrepresented, "it is intended to refer to something other than the referent to which conventional usage has assigned it . . ." Macquarrie, *God-Talk*, 97–98.

132. Gunton, *Actuality of Atonement*, 46.

133. Lakoff and Johnson, *Metaphors We Live By*, 158.

134. Finlan, *Problems with Atonement*, 111.

he ironically remains heavily dependent upon them with references to God "reaching," "saving" and "healing."

Finlan does, however, highlight the soteriological primacy of God. The theo-centric nature of Finlan's position and his assertion that divine action is central to the gospel as a means of interpretation and understanding lends itself to the view that the whole arena of salvation is better viewed as an epic, spiritual conflict and drama rather than merely a delineation of definition and formula. Riddell agrees, admitting that many contemporary notions of Christian evangelism betray their modernist and rationalist origins with their "highly manipulative" agendas which are designed to get prospective customers to "sign up" to a particular understanding of doctrine and propositional beliefs.[135]

Likewise, Macquarrie notes that within theology there is instead a demand to find a truth that is not an abstraction, attained by mere intellectual effort, but rather for one requiring that those seeking it are true to each other and live in the sometimes hard and occasionally painful discipline of the spirit.[136] Again, Riddell observes that in Jesus' own attempts to "convert" people he did not ask them for a statement of belief or a commitment to a programme of action; instead, his invitation is one in which he simply asks them to accompany him as he moves on.[137] It is the response to this metaphorical invitation of "travel" and "journey" rather than the propositional nature of the message that causes Walker to assert,

> Christianity is in effect a rescue mission for humankind, for through the telling of the story, people find themselves enabled to indwell it, make the story their own, and discover in it ultimate concern—their true end.[138]

Such an outlook presupposes that humankind requires rescuing from something, or someone, whilst also taking the theologian and thereby theology into the realm of worship in addition to, or perhaps even instead of, mere academic theology. Indeed, McFague acknowledges what she calls the "great tradition" of deeply religious people, especially the mystics of all religious traditions, for whom the conviction of their belief in God is found at the level of experience—in worship, but who nonetheless maintain great uncertainty in regard to their words, which they know are inadequate

---

135. Riddell, *Threshold of the Future*, 145. Further, he argues that such methods are "about as far away from the story of Jesus of Nazareth as it is possible to get." Ibid., 145.

136. Macquarrie, *Paths in Spirituality*, 69–70.

137. Riddell, *Threshold of the Future*, 146.

138. Walker, *Telling the Story*, 8.

to express God's reality.[139] There is a further suggestion that the dramatic action of Christian worship might in fact serve as an indispensable metaphoric commentary upon all that the Church believes about God's action for humans in Christ.[140]

Such a movement equates to a shift in soteriology from the exclusive realm of words, propositions and theories; not supplanting them with metaphors and symbols, but adding these to an overall understanding of the living, indwelt and ongoing *Heilsgeschichte*. It is in the salvation story and its intertwined metaphorical accoutrements and means of engagement that the believer finds and lives faith; for example, the cross of Jesus itself, according to Middleton, whilst the center of the biblical salvation metanarrative, is not merely symbolic but rather a living element of the story.[141]

This is the story, Middleton claims, of the Creator's unsurpassing love for a world gone astray and a love that ultimately leads him to the cross, to enter into human pain, bearing human suffering and sin and then to hand it back to humanity as redemption. He concludes:

> This is the story of the unswerving narrative intent of the Author of creation to liberate his creatures from their bondage, untangling the dead-end plots of their stories by incorporating them into his grand design, through what Jesus has done.[142]

This dynamic perception of bondage, liberation, salvation, story and metaphor prompts Niditch to suggest that, if properly read, myths and metaphors may, in fact, be the truest indicators of essential human perceptions of existence itself.[143] Or rather, in terms of soteriology and metaphor, there can never be a case of having one without the other. Instead, an organic tension and link exists between the two such that a soteriology without metaphor would be impossible for humans to access and receive whilst metaphor without soteriology would lack substance and be incapable of saving.

Or as Newbigin puts it, the Christian story provides a set of lenses that provide the believer not with something to look *at*, but rather for them to look *through*. He concludes that the Christian community is one which is invited to *indwell* the story, *tacitly* aware of it as shaping their understanding but *focally* attending to the world they live in so that they are able to confidently, but not infallibly, increase their understanding of it and their

139. McFague, *Metaphorical Theology*, 1.

140. Paul, *Atonement and the Sacraments*, 308–9.

141. Middleton and Walsh, *Truth Is Stranger*, 105.

142. Ibid., 107.

143. Niditch, *War in the Hebrew Bible*, 37.

ability to cope with it.[144] Christian soteriology, therefore, is ultimately not a stagnant and static story to be read and assented to, rather it is a violent battle delineated and a narrative to be believed, indwelt and lived.

Further than the Christian gospel therefore being a set of propositions, further still in fact than it being a story to be indwelt it is, in its deepest and most profound sense, the offer of a relationship with God, on God's terms, his purposes being linked to humanity's purposes and his enemies becoming humanity's enemies. Or, as Walker puts it,

> [The gospel story] is not a set of propositional truths, or a manual
> of systematic theology. It is the story of Christ, that, once written
> on our hearts, shows us how we should treat each other, how to
> live together, how to become persons. Ultimately, if we cannot
> demonstrate the proof of our story by living it, we will never
> convince people of its truth by talking about it. A story is telling,
> after all, only if it produces a striking effect on its listener.[145]

It is this element that McFague refers to as the new "root-metaphor" of Christianity, relating to the Kingdom of God, exemplified in Jesus' parables and presented in Jesus himself as parable of God; it describes a mode of being in the world as the free gift of God. Its distinctive note, she argues, is not merely a new view of God or a new image of human being with neither divine nor human nature at its center—rather, it is a new quality of *relationship*, a way of being in the world under the rule of God.[146]

In such a scenario, Jesus is not merely another leader with a set of creeds and doctrines to be affirmed and accepted. In fact, according to Wright,

> All suggestions that Jesus was simply a "great religious teacher"
> telling his contemporaries about a new pattern of spirituality
> or even a new scheme of salvation must be set aside (unless, of
> course, we are to rewrite the gospels wholesale, which is what
> many have done in their efforts to domesticate Jesus and his
> message).[147]

Instead, Wright argues that Jesus himself was conscious of the various human and societal powers which opposed him but, more importantly

144. Newbigin, *Pluralist Society*, 38.

145. Walker, *Telling the Story*, 201.

146. McFague, *Metaphorical Theology*, 109. This new way of being, she states, "is highly metaphorical—abjuring identification, possession, absolutism, stasis, conventionality, and spiritualism." Ibid., 109.

147. Wright, *Simply Jesus*, 96.

he was also aware that if God was going to become king it would be and could only ever be attained by some kind of violent confrontation with these forces or, more saliently, the forces that actually stood behind them.[148]

Closing the Epistemic Gap

This accommodation and incorporation of metaphor into soteriology can be taken further to argue that not only is metaphor merely a good and appropriate way to engage in God-talk, instead it is the very *best* way to speak of God and salvation and his means of accomplishing it. This is because of the epistemic gap between finite, flesh-bound humans and an infinite, spiritual God which cannot otherwise be *directly* crossed. Although this is what God did literally and historically in the incarnation when Christ transcended the sociological reality of the Church, so that

> even while He was within history in the days of His flesh, He belonged at the same time to the fullness of eternity because He is God, not only in His Godhead but because His humanity itself transforms life—finite, precarious, transitory as we know it—into life eternal, stable and victorious.[149]

Mediated language is therefore required and this is the semantic domain of the metaphorical; comparison, of course, being one of the most valuable sources of human knowledge and a primary means of connecting the known to the unknown.[150] Such mediated language comprises both a large part of daily speech and almost all the language of theology; God himself speaks to humans in similitudes, and man has no language but analogy for speaking about God, however inadequate it may be.[151]

Perhaps the *only* way that this gap can be crossed is therefore via metaphorical language that facilitates associations enabling a sense of meaning where "literal" language is limiting, brittle and self-consciously finite. The very *indirectness* of metaphorical language gives it its inherent strength and

148. Ibid., 98.

149. Metropolitan Anthony of Sourozh, *God and Man*, 83.

150. Hart acknowledges Kant's influence on discernment of the difference between actuality and perception noting that, "The order and beauty which we perceive in the world are not the fruits of God's good creation; they are in fact the product of our own minds, which impose structure on the universe rather than discovering it there. What the mind knows, therefore, is not the world itself, but the product of a transaction between reality and the mind, a heavily processed version of the world out there, rather than the raw reality itself." Hart, *Faith Thinking*, 42.

151. Caird, *Language and Imagery*, 144.

value as the world can only be known indirectly and metaphor, being indirect is, according to Gunton, the most appropriate form that a duly humble and listening language should take.[152]

The ultimate function of theology, however, is not to explain the possibility of the person and work of Christ because in the presence of the unfathomable love of God all attempts toward a rational explanation remain useless.[153] Barth notes the "human impossibility" of the attempt to speak of God and yet does not advise against the endeavor of theology and the preached word to proclaim God's truth; instead he cautions those involved to operate with humility and care, conscious both that God does not belong to this world and that he also does not belong to the series of objects for which we have categories and words by means of which to draw the attention of others to them, thereby bringing people into relation with them.[154] Further, the word "God" itself can be seen as an embarrassment, even to theologians, in their attempts at Christian proclamation inasmuch as it prevents secular people from understanding the proclamation.[155] As such, the problems of attempting to understand and express ideas about God, his nature and his engagement with violence, whether metaphorical or not, are self-evident.

Thus it is appropriate to affirm that there is more to the truth than words can convey and yet since words remain the primary means of human communication, use them we must. In using them, however, we remain acutely conscious of their limitations so whilst not jettisoning their usefulness, the user must utilize them with the full incorporation of the mediums of analogy, myth, symbol and metaphor. In a postmodern context, there is undoubtedly a surfeit of words, information and modes of communication; metaphor and the imagery invoked could yet prove to be the most apposite means of engaging a populace jaded by this profusion.[156]

A startling modern representation of this postmodern principle is demonstrated by the character Beatrice, a donkey in a play about the

152. Gunton, *Actuality of Atonement*, 37.

153. Aulén, *Faith of the Christian Church*, 222.

154. Barth, *CD* 1/2:750.

155. Pannenberg, *Systematic Theology*, 1:64. He accedes that "the only problem is that without this word an appeal for faith in Jesus of Nazareth loses its foundation." Ibid., 64.

156. In a chapter entitled, "Boredom with Language," Ebeling notes, "Boredom with words seems to find a justification and compensation, obvious in human terms and yet Christian too, in the shift of emphasis away from words towards action." Ebeling, *Theological Theory*, 36. He is primarily referring to *praxeological* action yet it can be argued that metaphors themselves, when compared with prose, present themselves as an *active* form of communication and understanding.

holocaust within Martel's novel. She wryly observes that, "Words are cold, muddy toads trying to understand sprites dancing in a field—but they're all we have."[157] Whilst the observation is useful as a means of expressing the limitations of language, it is nonetheless poignantly inconclusive as evidence against the efficacy of words themselves, especially words that contain metaphors; "spoken" as they are in this instance by a donkey to a monkey in an allegorical novel about the holocaust set on the back of a striped shirt!

Just as in this case of arguments against the relevance and usefulness of words which are nonetheless made *using* words, likewise arguments against metaphor that depend heavily upon metaphor should be taken lightly. Two key areas of reflection for our thesis relate to how the significance of the work of Jesus Christ, that is the basis of salvation, is to be understood and how the presentation of the gospel is to be explained in contemporary society. These two closely related issues are the most important that can be put to biblical scholars and theologians by the church today.[158]

We have reached, however, along with Cooper, the "commonsense" conclusion that the presence of the metaphorical requires the presence of the literal.[159] This ineluctable union of ontological reality and that which reveals it is essential to our reflection upon both God and his engagement with and endorsement of violence.

God & Metaphor

Having considered the concept and use of metaphors the focus now is their application in understanding divine attributes and the relationship, if any, which violence has to God. There is a tendency to see metaphor as a poetic ornament illustrating an idea or adding rhetorical color to otherwise abstract or prosaic language. It can appear to have little to do with "ordinary language" except that such language is often composed of "dead metaphors," some blatant such as "the *arm* of the chair," others less obvious such as "tradition," meaning "to hand over or hand down."[160]

157. Martell, *Beatrice and Virgil*, 88.

158. Marshall, *Aspects of Atonement*, 1.

159. Cooper, *Metaphor*, 279.

160. See, "Tradition," *Concise Oxford Dictionary*, 1529. Macquarrie acknowledges the concept of "living" and "dead" metaphors (itself a metaphorical ascription!) noting that "some of the metaphors are living, as when we talk of the 'flesh,' in the Pauline sense. Many others are dead metaphors—words like 'spirit' and 'transcendence,' which we are no longer hearing as having anything to do with 'breath' or 'mounting up.'" Macquarrie, *God-Talk*, 98.

Metaphor is seeing one thing *as* something else, pretending "this" is "that" because there is no knowledge of how to think or talk about "this," so instead "that" is a way of saying something. Thinking metaphorically means spotting a thread of similarity between two otherwise dissimilar objects, events, or whatever, one of which is better known than the other, and using the better-known as a way of speaking about the lesser known.[161]

Given the aims, nature and content of theology metaphor is, as we have shown, an essential element—foundational and irreplaceable. The epistemic chasm between a transcendent, ethereal God and human beings can only be "bridged" (a metaphorical term) by means of metaphor since humans know little of "this" and so must lean heavily on "that." This does not mean that metaphorical language is conceptually or epistemologically secondary; rather, far from being an esoteric or ornamental rhetorical device super-imposed *on* ordinary language, metaphor *is* ordinary language; it is the *way* humans think.[162] Metaphorical language is, therefore, the means par excellence of exploring and explaining the attributes of God and his association and advocation of violence.[163]

Pushing Too Far . . .

There remains, however, the theological danger of pushing metaphors too far. For example, Scripture and tradition have often used juridical metaphors to describe the divine-human relationship; this does not mean that the metaphor can be pressed to the extent that it reduces human engagement with God to a merely legal transaction, rather than a true relationship.[164] Metaphors provide a means of pursuing, engaging with and understanding the attributes of God; they alone, like every other medium are, in and of themselves, incapable of providing definitive, ontological insights and answers. Instead they exist as signs along the traveler's journey towards realization and engagement rather than being literal definitions of what the journey and the destination are. Lakoff and Turner reiterate the pre-eminence and importance of this life-as-a-journey metaphor which, they

161. McFague, *Metaphorical Theology*, 15.

162. Ibid., 16.

163. "Philosophy's debt to metaphor is profound and immeasurable. Without metaphor, there would be no philosophy." Johnson, "Philosophy's Debt," 39. Philosophy's "debt," he notes, is no greater or less than any other significant field of human intellectual discipline because, "Philosophers must use the same conceptual resources possessed by any human being, and the potential for any philosophy to make sense of a person's life depends directly on the fact that all of us are metaphoric animals." Ibid., 39.

164. Sanders, *Atonement and Violence*, 107.

argue, is so taken for granted in the Judeo-Christian tradition that when it is used people instantly understand that God is a guide, that there are alternative paths of good and evil through life, and that death hangs over humanity throughout.[165]

Metaphors therefore serve the essential service of pointing the way towards God and offering *insight* into his ontology and (or) function; whilst never "just" metaphors, they nevertheless remain ontologically less than the reality they are expressing. Ricoeur acknowledges this in a chapter entitled "Ontological Clarification of the Postulate of Reference"; asserting that the relation of language to its counterpart, reality, concerns the conditions for reference in general, and thus for the meaning of language as a whole.[166] He postulates further on the limitations of language and yet accedes to the on-going centrality of the importance of language; arguing that in the relation of language to reality it is not possible to speak of such a relation because there is no standpoint, as we have shown, outside language and because it is and has always been *in* language that men claim to speak *about* language.[167] He therefore posits the adage that, "Something must be for something to be said," concluding that such a proposition makes reality the final category upon which the whole of language can be thought, although not known, as the being-said of reality.[168]

In the context of violence therefore, there might then be an extrinsic or intrinsic violent element of God's being, but this does not have to equate to him "being" violent per se but rather, for instance, that he *accommodates* violence when it is the only way to achieve his ends, particularly in a soteriological context.[169]

Cultic & Ritual Metaphors

If God does accommodate violence in an extrinsic manner it might be that he works via the ritual that metaphor is linked to; cultic metaphors, for instance, express God's choice to recognize the crucifixion as an effective ritual and respond to it. In this cultus Christ's death functions as the ritual act whilst the resurrection corresponds to God's positive response; reconciliation and justification therefore correspond to the transformed or cleansed status that ritual participants receive. This is the case whether in

165. Lakoff and Turner, *More than Cool Reason*, 10.
166. Ricoeur, *Rule of Metaphor*, 303.
167. Ibid., 304.
168. Ibid.
169. This idea will be pursued in greater depth when we consider Wolterstorff.

ritual or in ritual metaphors, the point being that what is *done* evokes and elicits a desired response from God.[170]

Consequently, God either uses and endorses or accommodates ritual and metaphor in his dealings with humans. The process whereby God utilises and humans understand atonement and its ritual uses a variety of metaphors, these together express the separated brought near, the distorted being untwisted and the broken mended and made whole. These metaphorical expressions present a further range of ideas including the battlefield, the courtroom and courtly love, whilst key concepts include those of justice, mercy, sin, love, obedience, compensation, substitution and representation.[171] A wide spectrum of metaphorical imagery is therefore employed to express a kaleidoscope of concomitant characteristics and attributes for the God behind them.[172]

The Poetry of Metaphor

Metaphors might be understood therefore as being to talk of God what songs and poetry are to the language of love. Zbikowski, for example, discusses the history and current understanding of how music has been understood both by those interested in semiotics and metaphor. He observes:

> The notion that music is language is the basis for some of the most prevalent metaphors used to describe music. But music is also *not* like language in at least one important respect: aside from a limited number of exceptional cases when music mimics natural sounds, music makes no reference to the outside world. Music *does* make reference to—or perhaps embody—the interior world of emotions or physiological states, but it is just this world that typically escapes the grasp of non-metaphorical language.[173]

170. Finlan, *Problems with Atonement*, 9. He also notes that "Paul did not initiate the sacrificial interpretation of the death of Christ, but he did formulate the version that has prevailed in Christian interpretation. In so doing, he took up and transmitted a primitive current in religious thinking, but spiritualized it with an emphasis on the heroic martyrdom of Jesus and the generosity of God. Paul emphasizes the outgoing love of God, but uses metaphors that imply that the death was a payment or offering to God." Ibid., 9.

171. Ray, *Deceiving the Devil*, 2.

172. "God is not just another superior with whom we must *deal*. Atonement doctrines turn God into a heavenly judge, an offended lord, or a temperamental spirit." Finlan, *Problems with Atonement*, 81.

173. Zbikowski, "Metaphor and Music," 503.

Schleiermacher too, in his consideration of the nature of religion, argues that if it is to be compared with anything it would be with music, which is closely connected with it. Music, he asserts, is one great whole, it is special and a self-contained revelation of the world.[174] Finally Žižek, reflecting on whether poetry might be redundant after Auschwitz, concludes that the opposite is true and that only poetic evocation is capable of succeeding where prose fails in expressing something of the unbearable atmosphere of a camp; he further suggests that no fear should be involved in taking a step further and referring to the old saying that music comes in when words fail.[175]

Power, insight and poetry are therefore presented as opposed to static, prosaic propositions that fall short of their aspirational aim.[176] The distinction between prose and poetry, or rhetoric and poetry, is usually accompanied by the assumption that the first is direct and the latter indirect. Ricoeur states that this, however, is a false dichotomy as the duality of rhetoric and poetics reflects a duality in the use of speech as well as in the situations of speaking.[177] He further observes the different purposes of these forms of speech; for example, for oration, persuasion and the purging of feelings concluding thereby that poetry and oratory mark out two distinct universes of discourse and that metaphor has a foot in each domain.[178] In fact, as we have seen, *both* prose and poetry are indirect for humans think by indirection; the difference is only that people have grown accustomed to the indirections of ordinary language which is then perceived as conventional.[179]

The Limitations of Language

A great deal of so-called mythical language is in fact analogical or symbolical language in which talk about the God laying beyond the grasp of literal expressions is undertaken with analogy to humans.[180] A case in point is the multiplicity of titular ascriptions for Christ in the New Testament; he is regarded as both Messiah and Last Adam and his death as both a sacrifice and

174. Schleiermacher, *On Religion*, 51.

175. Žižek, *Violence*, 4–5.

176. "In addition to elaborating conventional metaphor, poets go beyond the normal use of conventional metaphor to point out, and call into question, the boundaries of our everyday metaphorical understandings of important concepts. Indeed, the major poetic point being made can be the inadequacy of the conventional metaphor." Lakoff and Turner, *More than Cool Reason*, 68.

177. Ricoeur, *Rule of Metaphor*, 12.

178. Ibid.

179. Chalke and Mann, *Lost Message*, 16.

180. Marshall, "Myth," 451.

a cosmic event while God is portrayed simultaneously as Father and King. These seemingly diametrical statements are attempts to speak of transcendent realities which one human concept alone is unable to encapsulate; no contradiction is thereby incurred in using all of them at once.[181]

Accordingly, when the New Testament speaks of the life, and particularly the cross, of Jesus as a sacrifice, a victory and the justification of sinners, these are not "mere" metaphors but ways of incorporating new thinking into theological engagement with God. Here is *real* sacrifice, victory and justice, here too can be both divine love and divine violence so that what words were originally thought to mean is shown to be inadequate and in need of reshaping by that to which the language refers.[182] The use of language and metaphor may "restrain" those using it and yet these attempts remain a primary means by which expressions about God, his character and his purposes, including violence, are made. Metaphor and language must not be rejected, but their use must incorporate awareness of limitation in order to guard against the presumption that all that can be known and expressed about God could ever be encapsulated within *any* finite human medium.[183]

Anthropomorphism

Another shortcoming in the use of metaphors in theology, perhaps particularly in regard to God's use or endorsement of violence, is the anthropomorphism which can ensue. Ray observes:

> Metaphors intended to characterize God have a dual directedness. On the one hand, they point toward the absolutely indescribable—God, the infinite, ultimate reality, the ground of being. At the same time, they direct attention toward the finite, for it is only in and through the language and conceptualities of finite beings that any God-talk at all is possible. The problem with traditional notions of God, then, is not that they are metaphorical, since theological language is inevitably so. Rather, the problem is that they draw on and reflect only a small segment

181. Cairns, *Gospel Without Myth*, 93.

182. Gunton, *Actuality of Atonement*, 51–52.

183. Green and Baker explain God's "wrath" as being *just* metaphorical; see Green and Baker, *Recovering the Scandal*, 54. Conversely, Boersma opines that it is more accurate to say, "But isn't all language about God metaphorical?" Boersma, *Violence, Hospitality and the Cross*, 48. Whilst Macquarrie notes, "Whatever its limits, language is our most precise and reliable way of communicating. More than that, it is doubtful whether there could be any knowing or thinking worthy of the name that did not need to embody itself in language." Macquarrie, *Principles of Christian Theology*, 105.

of reality and experience, granting it unlimited, universal, and exclusive relevance and authority.[184]

Consequently, metaphors are essential in order to understand and express God's attributes, especially potentially difficult or unpalatable ones such as violence; Hanson observes of Gregory of Nyssa that he explains anthropomorphisms in the Bible as God accommodating himself to our understanding, rather like a mother talking baby-language to her children.[185] Likewise, Goldingay notes that this idea of God's accommodation is taken up by other Fathers such as Origen and Chrysostom, in part as an equivalent to the modern discussion in terms of analogical language. Origen, for example he argues, sees the anthropomorphisms of Scripture as instances of God's willingness to adapt language to hearers in this way.[186] Without such a concession, humans would be left gazing across an otherwise impassable epistemic chasm between their finite selves and an infinite God.[187]

Further, without divine violence, whether intrinsic or extrinsic, it is questionable whether God could both achieve a decisive victory against a violent enemy and whether violent humans would be able to engage with, understand and accept God's message of salvation, a salvation which could only be ultimately wrought by direct and violent means.

184. Ray, *Deceiving the Devil*, 37.

185. Hanson, *Christian Doctrine*, 722.

186. Goldingay, *Models for Scripture*, 342.

187. "If revelation has a cognitive element, as is commonly supposed, then there must be some possibility of verbally expressing what is revealed. The whole theological endeavor on which we have embarked is sustained by the recognition of the importance of trying to bring to verbal expression our most fundamental existential convictions." Macquarrie, *Principles of Christian Theology*, 105.

4

Scholars on Violence

Rudolf Otto

IT HAS BEEN DEMONSTRATED across both Testaments that God has been, at the very least, implicated in acts of violence and at most potentially has violence as an intrinsic or extrinsic element of his being. In fact, as Rollins notes, the supposed dividing line in the Bible between violence and nonviolence is not to be found, as commonly thought, between the Old and New Testaments. The fault line, he asserts, does not lie between two documents, but between two psychic attitudes that run longitudinally through both Testaments, and by inference through every stratum of the history of the human race.[1] These "two psychic attitudes" are the concurrent human desires for peace and the irresistible propensity for violence. This is a theologically controversial assertion and conscious of this, Otto's ideas are presented as a useful means of facilitating understanding of these violence-related claims.[2]

The problem that the proposition that God is implicated with violence raises is primarily connected to the nature of modern theology and the framing of dogma and doctrine itself; its practice, its modus operandi and its purpose and expression. These rather prickly issues exemplify a pursuit that has often found itself unable to do justice to the non-rational aspects of its subject; far from keeping these aspects alive in the heart of religious experience, orthodox Christianity has instead too regularly failed to recognize their value and by this failure has given to the idea of God a one-sidedly intellectualistic and rationalistic interpretation.[3]

1. Rollins, "Redemptive Violence," 175–76.
2. These ideas being originally expressed in Otto, *Idea of the Holy*.
3. Ibid., 3.

In Ware's reappraisal of Otto's position he argues that there are two main arguments to be considered. The first is the attack on Otto's epistemology in his attempt to account for the a priori necessity of the transition from numinous experience to "rational" religious faith. The second is Otto's relationship with mysticism, whereby he places the numinous, wholly other in contrast to the predominantly non-dual character of mystical experience.[4] It is this failure to acknowledge and explore supposedly non-rationalistic elements of divine attributes that has contributed to violence being rejected in an a priori manner because it is perceived as a non-rational concept which is inappropriate to align with a God perceived as being ontologically good.

Further, Raphael notes that Otto is "audacious" in requesting at the beginning of his thesis that those who have not actually experienced "a moment of deeply-felt religious experience" should "read no further."[5] She nonetheless concludes, however, that to reject Otto's claim that the numinous is *sui generis*, immediate experience, unconditioned by its context, does not mean that numinous experience is thereby vacated of meaning and function in theology.[6] Bultmann too acknowledges the need for the exegete to have a thoroughgoing understanding of the topic being studied in order for them to engage with and understand it correctly. In short, he argues that to have historical understanding presupposes an understanding of the subject matter of history itself and of the men and women who act in history; concluding that historical understanding always presupposes that the interpreter has a relation to the subject matter that is both directly and indirectly expressed in the text.[7]

Palatable Attributes

There is, however, no inherent, definitive reason why potential divine attributes have to be construed as either "acceptable" or "rational" in order to be considered theologically feasible.

The issue of God-talk and its concomitant problems, conceptually and theologically, are addressed by Hart, who notes:

> while in obedience we are called to speak of God in *this* language and not other language of our own choosing or devising,

4. Ware, "Otto's Idea of the Holy," 48.

5. Otto, *Idea of the Holy*, 8.

6. Raphael, *Rudolf Otto*, 149–50.

7. Bultmann, "Exegesis Without Presuppositions," 149. Bultmann speaks of the encounter that grows out of the individual's historicity as the "existential encounter." Ibid., 150.

the fact remains that of ourselves we do not know what we are saying when we say that God is love, so far as its reference to God himself is concerned. We do not, in other words, know the nature of the dissimilarity between what our human words signify in ordinary discourse, and what they signify in theological discourse. Precisely because, in revealing himself, God takes human form, all revelation is at the same moment a veiling.[8]

There is therefore no potential attribute which must be jettisoned a priori on the basis of it being comprehended, in some sense, as being either unpalatable or unacceptable. For this reason violence must not and cannot be disavowed in advance and certainly not before it has been acknowledged as a possible attribute or element within the Godhead and the functions and purposes thereof. Rather, it should be brought into theological reflection, regardless of any potentially negative praxeological consequences or perspectives and *then* be opened to consideration as to its viability and whether or not it might be allowed to stay.

The problem of Christians engaging with and responding to a theology of "God's violence" is difficult, in fact it has sometimes been linked with horrific acts perpetrated in God's name, based upon his supposed character and actions. A worst-case example is that of Michael Bray, a Lutheran Pastor and spokesperson for an extreme wing of the anti-abortion movement that justifies killing medical personnel involved in providing abortion services. Bray argues that Christians have long been willing to sacrifice their own lives and those of others in service of God's Kingdom, citing William Carey as an example.[9]

Bray further likens these sacrifices to those that might need to be made to protect unborn lives through the killing of "abortuary" workers; his justification based upon the understanding that God sanctions and supports violence in a "just cause" and his contention that, indeed, the Christian God, even the Lord Jesus Christ, is a forceful and some would say "violent" God.[10] Terrifying though such clumsy theological associations are, they should not a priori disavow theological exploration of God's possible advocacy of violence or whether violence can be an attribute of his being. This would be doing theology in reverse; a principle which will shortly be considered in more detail.

8. Hart, *Regarding Karl Barth*, 192.

9. Bray, "Time for Revolution," 56.

10. Ibid., 60.

The Numinous

In order to counter the "one-sidedness" of a de-spiritualized theology that is willing to sacrifice non-rational concepts so that a supposedly intellectually satisfying dogma can be presented, Otto coins the word "numinous"[11] from the Latin *numen* to suggest the theological concept of a spiritual element that cannot be taught or learnt but only perceived, considered, discussed and experienced through an individual having it stirred into their consciousness.[12] It is this elusive and yet, for Otto, tangible quality that commends it in the face of controversial and potentially divisive issues. The numinous provides an epistemic bridge linking the rational and the supposedly irrational, thereby providing the possibility of facilitating understanding of God's relationship to violence.[13]

Otto defines "*Mysterium Tremendum*" as part of his understanding of the numinous, noting that conceptually *mysterium* denotes that which is hidden and esoteric, beyond conception or understanding, extraordinary and unfamiliar.[14] If this is the case then a problem arises in Otto's argument as to whether this "wholly other" being can be perceived as truly numinous and if so, how can it truly be considered Divine; more specifically, how can it refer to the God referenced in the Judeo-Christian Scriptures. Poland notes how uncanny experiences can unsettle theistic descriptions of the transcendent; Otto's *mysterium tremendum*, she argues, seems both to entertain the possibility of a truly uncanny "wholly other" only to close it again, by finding that the uncanny is "completed" and "schematicized" by rational and moral ideas of the Western God.[15] Ware concedes that whilst Otto tries to close off and demarcate the theistic boundaries of the wholly other, the logic of his argument often caves in under its own pressure.[16] The way in which *mysterium tremendum* manifests itself for humans is to fill them with a "numinous dread" or *awe* of that beyond humanity or ordinary conception or

11. "The numinous presents itself as something 'wholly other' (*ganz andere*), something basically and totally different. It is like nothing human or cosmic; confronted with it, man senses his profound nothingness, feels that he is only a creature, or, in the words in which Abraham addressed the Lord, is 'but dust and ashes' (Genesis 18:27)." Eliade, *Sacred and the Profane*, 9–10.

12. Otto, *Idea of the Holy*, 6–7. Poland notes that "the numinous must be experienced to be understood, Otto insists; his task is not simply to analyze a religious phenomenon but to produce it in his readers." Poland, "Idea of the Holy," 175.

13. Otto affirms the ontological strength and substance of his theory by confirming that "the numinous is . . . felt as objective and outside the self." Otto, *Idea of the Holy*, 11.

14. Ibid., 13.

15. Poland, "Idea of the Holy," 187.

16. Ware, "Otto's Idea," 51.

experience; in other words, in the context of engagement with the divine, to "shudder" beyond horror and fear in the face of God and the spiritual realm.[17] Tillich echoes Otto, stating,

> In revelation and in the ecstatic experience in which it is received, the ontological shock is preserved and overcome at the same time. It is preserved in the annihilating power of the divine presence (*mysterium tremendum*) and is overcome in the elevating power of the divine presence (*mysterium fascinosum*). Ecstasy unites the experience of the abyss to which reason in all its functions is driven with the experience of the ground in which reason is grasped by the mystery of its own depth and of the depth of being generally.[18]

Otto admits that whilst this concept is deeply troubling and perplexing for modern people this was not the case for those extant at the manifestation of God's biblical wrath. Instead, for religious people of the Old Testament the wrath of God, so far from being a diminution of his Godhead, appears as a natural expression of it, an element of his "holiness" and a quite indispensable one.[19] Green and Baker challenge this, noting that "Old Testament scholars"[20] today are debating in what sense anger can be attributed to God "in any way other than metaphorical."[21] This is a one-sided way to consider the meaning of biblical teachings, utilizing a subjective and arbitrary decision to ascribe an unpalatable theological concept as metaphorical and therefore a diminution of "reality," whilst other, less controversial ones, are deemed literal and therefore a more accurate representation of reality. Green and Baker make no attempt to describe their methodology in choosing between the literal and their perception of the lesser concepts of the allegorical or metaphorical; instead leaving the charge unanswered that they make hermeneutical choices on personal a priori theological dispositions.

Numinous Wrath

The theological and biblical use of the word wrath, Otto argues, is not concerned with being perceived as a genuine intellectual "concept," but rather

---

17. Otto, *Idea of the Holy*, 14–15.

18. Tillich, *Systematic Theology*, 1:113.

19. Otto, *Idea of the Holy*, 18.

20. They cite three: Bergman and Johnson, "Πνάφ," and Herion, "Wrath of God."

21. Green and Baker, *Recovering the Scandal*, 53–54.

as an illustrative substitute for a concept.[22] Indeed, for Otto, "Wrath" is the "ideogram" of a unique emotional moment in religious experience, a moment whose singularly daunting and awe-inspiring character must be gravely disturbing to those persons who will recognize nothing in the divine nature but goodness, gentleness, love, and a sort of confidential intimacy, in other words, only those aspects of God which turn towards the world of men.[23] He concludes that ὀργή is quite wrongly spoken of as "natural" wrath; rather it is of an entirely non- or super-natural quality or, more pertinently, it is numinous.[24]

The Sublime

The concept of the sublime is used by Poland, linking it to the numinous, in order to present a similar argument to Otto's in regard to the responses it elicits from those experiencing it.[25] When it is encountered in the natural realm, perhaps in a scenario in which that experienced is beyond the usual human sensual limitations, then the sublime is that emotion that overwhelms the human receptor, evoking a sense of other so that in what is perceived to be a positive moment, dread gives way, not only to joy, but to an apprehension and engagement with transcendence; it therefore exists as a passage from external nature to internal force, from corporeal to spiritual.[26]

This is the same experience of being overwhelmed which is often recounted in the Bible as occurring when a human encounters God. Initially there is the moment of dread and fear in the face of a being of limitless, untamed potential; the exchange ultimately giving way to joy in the realization that this God, whilst capable of unimaginable and infinite power, is

22. "For Otto had read Luther and had understood what the 'living God' meant to a believer. It was not the God of the philosophers—of Erasmus, for example; it was not an idea, an abstract notion, a mere moral allegory. It was a terrible power, manifested in the divine wrath." Eliade, *Sacred and the Profane*, 8–9.

23. Otto, *Idea of the Holy*, 18–19.

24. Ibid., 19. Comparing numinous and mystical experiences Raphael observes that they "share a number of features such as an ineffability, a putative freedom from dogma, and a peculiarly heightened state of awareness." Raphael, *Rudolf Otto*, 156. This links the kind of features that might reasonably be expected when a human-being encounters God via an experience that includes, or alludes to, divine wrath or violence.

25. "Otto himself evokes the sublime as virtually identical in structure and content to the numinous . . ." Poland, "Idea of the Holy," 176. Otto notes, "A thing does not become sublime merely by being great. The concept itself remains unexplicated; it has in it something mysterious, and in this it is like that of the numinous." Otto, *Idea of the Holy*, 41.

26. Poland, "Idea of the Holy," 177.

nonetheless personal, knowable and ontologically good.[27] These predicates form the foundation of understanding this God and the context in which God then exerts, utilizes or endorses violence in the human realm.

René Girard

In terms of the level of influence exerted on the understanding of religion and violence across numerous and perhaps otherwise divergent academic disciplines, it is impossible to ignore René Girard. He is described by Mc-Donald as both one of the twentieth century's most prominent theorists of culture and a devout Roman Catholic.[28] Fleming, after describing Girard as one of the most original and influential cultural theorists on the contemporary scene goes on to enumerate Girard's considerable accomplishments, including honorary doctorates from half a dozen European universities, the awards of both the Prix de L'Académie Française and the French Academy's Grand Prix de Philosophie, the latter in recognition of his position as one of the outstanding philosophical anthropologists of his generation. Fleming also acknowledges the substantial and ever-growing body of secondary literature utilizing Girardian themes and hypotheses; his work, he concludes, has extended across a remarkably wide range of disciplines including psychology, systems theory, economics, political science, religious studies and even musicology.[29]

Finally, in his Foreword to Schwager's Girardian re-consideration of violence and redemption in the Bible, Daly proffers a wide-ranging overview of Western intellectual history, offering Machiavelli, Luther, Calvin, Hobbes and others such as Marx and Barth as influential cornerstones, concluding that whether or not posterity accords Girard a place in this august pantheon, the mere fact that he is thought of in such comparisons in attempting to assess the import of his work is some measure of its significance.[30] Girard comes to this issue of violence and to the Bible in particular, therefore, primarily as an anthropologist of religion rather than a theologian[31] and yet argues that the Bible, as a text available to anyone regardless of

---

27. "There is, in other words, something gratuitous about the scene of the sublime: a fantasy of injury, an imagined terror, so that the existence and nature of the transcendent order that one already knows can be affectively confirmed. It is as though the crisis has been staged so that Reason can arrive in aid; it provides Reason an occasion for its self-recognition." Ibid., 180.

28. McDonald, "Violence and the Lamb Slain," 40.

29. Fleming, *Violence and Mimesis*, 1–2.

30. Daly, "Foreword," in Schwager, *Scapegoats*, iv.

31. Ranieri, *Disturbing Revelation*, 187.

religious commitment, discloses a distinctive anthropological perspective, which because of its accessibility, brings to light essential insights into the workings of culture in a way in which other texts do not.[32]

Coupled with the primacy of biblical teachings, examples and stories, Girard has also been hugely influenced by key figures of world literature and draws upon the insights gained from selected works of Cervantes, Stendhal, Flaubert, Proust and Dostoevsky.[33] From the universe of novels imagined by these writers Girard has argued, or rather, as he puts it, has *allowed his subjects to contend*, that human desire is anchored neither in (desiring) subjects nor in (desired) objects, but in the imitation of the former from which the individual learns the value of the latter.[34]

Girard insists that these writers are a surer guide to human truth than present-day human and social sciences, a position which puts him in opposition to contemporary philosophical and aesthetic theory which postulates that literary texts can only ever relate to other fictional texts.[35] Kirwan, for example, asks whether literature has anything to do with the reality of human life, questioning whether anything can be learnt from writers like Dostoevsky, Proust and Shakespeare, about what human beings are like and how they should lead their lives. It should be noted, Kirwan contends, that Girard does not show much interest in literature as a whole, but only in a particular "canon" of texts—consisting, as it happens, of writers who are concerned with the same themes as he is![36]

At the very least Girard has prepared the way for further debate about the prevalence of deceit and violence in the Bible and at most he has presented a coherent, elegant and rational explanation to satisfy the needs of the exegete, the theologian and the Christian believer in regard to biblical and divine violence.[37] Daly reiterates that the Western Christian mind has

---

32. Ibid.

33. Fleming, *Violence and Mimesis*, 12.

34. Ibid., 5. "Girard's basic hypothesis concerning desire is most aptly schematized by the triangle; it is not, in other words, a theoretical schema which figures desire as a straight line of force which extends between (desiring) subject and (desired) object, but a complex of lines running from the subject to the mediator of desire and back again." Ibid., 11.

35. Fiddes challenges this, proposing that between creative literature and that of the doctrinal theologian there is "a relationship of mutual influence without confusion, where the images and narratives of literature can help the theologian to make doctrinal statements, while at the same time doctrinal thinking can provide a perspective for the critical reading of literary texts." Fiddes, *Promised End*, 7. Fiddes develops these ideas in his *Freedom and Limit*, 33–35.

36. Kirwan, *Discovering Girard*, 40.

37. Daly, "Foreword," in Schwager, *Scapegoats*, v.

been trained to skip over the massive presence of violence and deceit found throughout the Scriptures, usually in the form of self-deception.[38] Conversely, Williams notes of Girard's reading of the gospel narrative that it is certainly selective and even at times cavalier.[39]

Doubles Theory

His theory has been characterized by various versions of a story in which two children are playing in a room full of toys. At the moment in which one of them reaches for a particular toy, and not before, that one toy becomes the object of desire for the children, making them *doubles* in their focus; the first child becomes a model and the second child imitates the first. Or, in other words, both parties now desire to acquire the same item which thereby causes them to be in competition and to present themselves as a double of each other. As the children focus their attention on the toy, a rivalry ensues and the model issues a double-bind in her act of reaching. On the one hand, she makes the toy an object of desire by reaching out for it, occasioning mimesis, whilst on the other hand, as soon as she reaches for the toy an implied prohibition is expressed; the toy now "belongs" to her since she reached for it first. This rivalry, in one form or another, inevitably turns to violence which can only end with the expulsion or victimizing of one of the two rivals vying for the toy.[40]

Girard's radical theory of violence is controversial in both secular and religious communities, with both groups concurrently impressed and reviled by him; as McDonald illustrates,

> His cultural analysis has been praised by secular critics, even as his insistence that this very analysis should lead to Christian affirmation has shocked them. Christians are pleased that a giant of modernist and postmodernist thought is a solid Christian, but some are disturbed that he seems to "debunk" the propitiatory view of Christ's death on the Cross.[41]

38. Ibid., v–vi.

39. Williams, "Girard on Violence," 179.

40. Both Hardin, "Violence," 108, and McDonald, "Violence and the Lamb Slain," 40–43, use variations on this theme to explain Girard's theory. McDonald contends that "it would not be much of an exaggeration to say that Girard builds his whole theory of human nature and human culture through a close analysis of the dynamics operating in this story." Ibid., 40.

41. Ibid.

This position of being caught between two camps has not stymied his ability to produce influential work. His study and championing of contemporary fictional texts and mythology has, for example, led him to develop his theory of acquisitive mimesis and rivalry, from which all violence originates,[42] and the surrogate victim, from which originates ritual as the ameliorative factor for violence.[43] He believes these social mechanisms are hidden within the great novels, myths and historical texts and especially "texts of persecution," leading to their final revelation in the Christian Gospel.[44]

The beginnings of religion and culture are, for Girard, inextricably intertwined, and religion can properly be said to be at the origin of culture; indeed, archaic religion is the institution that recalls the founding violence in myth and ritual thereby legitimatizing a particular form of violence as the antidote to the ever-present danger of a relapse into a more primordial chaos.[45]

Mimesis

The most distinctive element of Girard's theorization of desire is that it is grounded in imitation, thus his invocation of the Greek term—"*mimesis*."[46] He points to the centrality of imitative behavior in human social and cognitive development and asserts that without the ability to copy the behavior and speech of others human capacity to inhabit a culture would be impossible.[47] Human *desire* is also constitutionally imitative and *mimesis* does not involve the simple representation of other forms of cultural memory—it rather incorporates acts of and intentions towards *acquisition*.[48] This second element is essential to his theory, as for Girard humans only learn what to desire from copying the desires of others.[49] Mimetic theory grapples with

42. Girard, *Deceit, Desire, and the Novel.*

43. Girard, *Violence and the Sacred*, 1977.

44. Girard, *Deceit, Desire, and the Novel*, and Girard, *Scapegoat.*

45. Ranieri, *Disturbing Revelation*, 190.

46. "The reason Girard prefers the term *mimesis* to *imitation* is that it avoids the connotation associated with the latter term as designating mere copying." Ibid., 188.

47. "And yet there is nothing, or next to nothing, in human behaviour that is not learned, and all learning is based on imitation. If human beings suddenly ceased imitating, all forms of culture would vanish." Girard, *Things Hidden*, 7.

48. See Fleming, *Violence and Mimesis*, 10–12, for a clear overview of desire and mimesis—although Girard notes, "Simplicity and clarity are not in fashion at the moment." Girard, *Things Hidden*, 9.

49. "The majority of Girard's work can be properly viewed as an exploration of the

three simple questions: what causes social groups and societies to come together and cohere successfully? What causes those groups to disintegrate? What is the function of religion in these two groups?[50]

Mimesis is a phenomenon which evokes desire, the corollary being that this desire then structures *mimesis* which means that human beings are not primarily perceived as individuals who *have* desires, but rather as persons who, in a real sense, *are* their desires.[51] Alison argues that since the "me" of each person is founded by desire, we cannot say that desire is our own, as though it belonged to some pre-existent "me." The "me" is radically dependent on the desires whose imitation formed it and this means, Alison argues, that there is no "real me" at the bottom of it all, after I've scraped away all the things I've learned, all the influences I've undergone.[52] This view is in line with Girard's primary focus which is not ontological; he is in fact more interested in functions and choices as defining factors.

Consequently, Girard argues that if *acquisitive mimesis* divides by leading two or more individuals to converge on one and the same object with a view to appropriating it, *conflictual mimesis* will inevitably unify by leading two or more individuals to converge on one and the same adversary that all wish to strike down.[53] This cause and effect element within mimetic theory is particularly pronounced in terms of the contagious nature of acquisitive mimesis which leads to the multiplication of people polarized around a particular object, ultimately resulting in mimetic frenzy. This inevitably leads to conflictual mimesis when the community unites against an arbitrarily chosen enemy who will be sacrificed, thus facilitating the death of a victim who the community unshakeably holds to be the one and only cause of its trouble.[54]

---

broad—cultural, religious, and philosophical—ramifications of non-conflictual and, especially, conflictual mimesis." Fleming, *Violence and Mimesis*, 6.

50. Kirwan, *Girard and Theology*, 20.

51. Ranieri, *Disturbing Revelation*, 188.

52. Alison, *Joy of Being Wrong*, 12, 30–31.

53. Girard, *Things Hidden*, 26.

54. "Once it is understood that the inversion of the real relation between victim and community occurs in the resolution of the crisis, it is possible to see why the victim is believed to be *sacred*. The victim is held responsible for the renewed calm in the community and for the disorder that preceded this return. It is even believed to have brought about its own death." Ibid., 27.

Violence

There is for Girard nothing inherently bad or destructive about mimetic desire, it only becomes problematic when two or more people desire the same object; until this is activated, mimetic desire lays dormant and passive. When activated the situation rapidly degenerates into violent conflict which, given the mimetic character of desire, is eminently contagious. As the mimetic contagion spreads, the condition of society deteriorates, rent by division and violence; the ensuing chaos can only be curtailed by the group's selection of a victim who is identified as the cause of the present crisis.[55]

It is this new mimesis of "all against one" that unites rather than divides, providing reconciliation and a sense of unity and purpose for the lynch mob as their violence and hatred, previously manifest against one another, can now be unleashed upon a single victim.[56] Girard represents violence as an otherwise overwhelming and unstoppable force which can debilitate or destroy a society once unleashed—barring the intervention of the victimage mechanism.

At this point in Girard's theory the origins of cultural, social, and political distinctions are traced back to fundamental distinctions between "good" sacred violence that brings unity and peace and "bad" profane violence resulting in chaos. Certain kinds of violence are granted legitimacy in the interests of preserving civilization, while illegitimate violence is banned.[57] In this milieu, violence is a primary and necessary cultural force out of which society is formed and framed and also part of the means by which it grows, evolves and is sustained.

Scapegoat

Violence has thus been inherent and central within human culture since its inception and is an intrinsic element of societal and cultural formation and identity. The uniting of the majority against an arbitrary victim is, for Girard, the only available means by which violence can be held in check. It is important to note that, for him, only violence can effect reconciliation and provide the basis on which a culture can ultimately thrive. The cultural and societal beneficial effects of the scapegoating of a single victim are the grounds upon which ritual is instituted and in which the community will

55. Ranieri, *Disturbing Revelation*, 189.

56. In fact, "This victim is the embodiment of all evil, and appears to the mob to be responsible for the crisis." Kirwan, *Discovering Girard*, 49.

57. Ranieri, *Disturbing Revelation*, 190.

engage from that point on. It is the ritual re-enactment of the sacrificial victimage mechanism which safeguards the community from further spontaneous outbursts of violence.[58]

The finding and ritual expulsion or victimhood of a scapegoat does not address the disorder itself; rather it diverts attention long enough to allow the underlying causes to remain in place. DeLay characterizes Girard's theory as a mathematical formula in which: "Person (A) offends another (B) which creates a third element of conflict (X). The surrogate sacrifice (-X) cancels the conflict, but leaves A and B to conflict again later. This equation of $(A + B) = X + -X$ becomes ritualized so that the offense is continually mitigated and the community can survive. The violence against a surrogate is so important to the community that it eventually becomes sacred."[59] The practice of ritual sacrifice therefore reinforces and legitimizes the very disorder which continues to threaten the social order even as its continuance constitutes the *status quo*.[60] The victimage mechanism, therefore, is not a definitive or decisive action but rather an *on-going ritual* which saves the community from the worst excesses of frenzied mimeticism; at the same time perpetuating its own worth as the only means of serving this societal need.[61]

Ellens agrees, noting that, even a superficial consideration of history informs of the fact that violence breeds further violence rather than eradicating it. He concludes:

> The most common and most universally agreed-upon reality of history is the fact that quelling violence and social or intrapsychic dissonance by a violent or physically aggressive action that victimizes a person or a people as scapegoat merely breeds a

58. Hardin, "Violence," 189.

59. Tad Delay, "Violence is the Origin of the Sacred," *God is Unconscious* (blog), April 6, 2012, http://taddelay.com/blog/tag/sacrifice#.T_FmclLtu_I.

60. Burrell, "René Girard," 444.

61. "Polarized by the sacrificial killing, violence is appeased. It subsides. We might say that it is expelled from the community and becomes part of the divine substance, from which it is completely indistinguishable, for each successive sacrifice evokes in diminishing degree the immense calm produced by the act of generative unanimity, by the initial appearance of the god. Just as the human body is a machine for transforming food into flesh and blood, generative unanimity is a process for changing bad violence into stability and fecundity . . . If the god is nothing more nor less than the massive violence that was expelled by the original act of generative unanimity, then ritual sacrifice can indeed be said to offer him portions of his own substance." Girard, *Violence and the Sacred*, 280–81.

festering and irrepressible counter force and ferment. This eventually manifests itself in another revolution.[62]

Violence and its antidote, the scapegoat, are for Girard inextricably linked in a symbiotic relationship—violence requires sacrifice and sacrifice is unnecessary without violence.

Sacrifice

In response to the accusation that he endorses a "non-sacrificial reading of the death of Christ" Girard states his belief in two kinds of sacrifice.[63] Using the story of Solomon's judgment of the two prostitutes and the baby, recounted in the third chapter of 1 Kings (perhaps the only place, he contends, where both kinds of sacrifice are presented), he interprets them as doubles engaging in mimetic rivalry.[64] Solomon offers to split the child between them; one agrees, seeking to triumph over her rival, whilst the other, seeking only the child's well-being, says the other can have it. On the basis of this act of love, the king declares her "the mother."

Girard notes that it does not matter who the biological mother is; the one willing to sacrifice herself for the child's life is, in fact, the mother. Again, he is not primarily concerned with ontology but function, with sacrifice providing the only possible solution to mimetic rivalry whilst also being its foundation. The second woman, he states, is willing to sacrifice everything she wants for the sake of the child's life and this is sacrifice in the sense of the gospel; it is in such manner that Christ is a sacrifice since he gave himself "for the entire world."[65] Conversely, "bad sacrifice" is the kind of sacrifice that prevailed before Christ and which originates because mimetic rivalry threatens the survival of a community. In Christ's death, as the ultimate "scapegoat" he, as the Son of God, and since he is innocent, exposes all the myths of scapegoating and reveals, once and for all, that the victims of scapegoating have all been innocent whilst the communities were guilty.[66]

Admittedly, Girard presents an unorthodox view of sacrifice in the gospel accounts, arguing that they are only spoken of in order to ultimately

62. Ellens, "Religious Metaphors," 269.

63. "All sacrificial rites are based on two substitutions. The first is provided by generative violence, which substitutes a single victim for all the members of the community. The second, the only strictly ritualistic substitution, is that of a victim for the surrogate victim." Girard, *Violence and the Sacred*, 284.

64. McDonald, "Violence and the Lamb Slain," 42.

65. Ibid.

66. Ibid.

be rejected and denied validity.[67] Jesus, for instance, counters the ritualism of the Pharisees, he says, with an anti-sacrificial quotation from Hosea: "Go and learn what this means, 'I desire mercy, and not sacrifice.'" (Matthew 9:13)[68]

Theory Conclusion

In his teachings on Gospel sacrifice, McDonald observes that Girard lost much of his previous acclaim when he dared to assert that the "shackles of sacrificial religion" were broken for a large portion of mankind by the force of the biblical story in which a number of narratives reversed the classical mythological pattern by *exonerating* the scapegoat and showing the *community* to be guilty of gratuitous murder.[69]

Girard places primary emphasis on the acceptance of this volte-face and presents his position that the Gospels express the message that to escape violence it is necessary to love one's brother completely and to thereby abandon the violent mimesis involved in the relationship of doubles. He argues that there is no trace of this outlook in the Father, and therefore all that the Father asks of humans is that they too might likewise refrain from it.[70] Jungel notes that if this reading is followed, the argument can be made that the Father did not, in fact, require the sacrifice of the Son, but only the obedience of love. Violence, like love, he states, can effect reconciliation; unlike love, which is self-giving, violence is life-taking, so whilst violence sacrifices the life of an "innocent other" to prolong the life of the community, love gives its life for the sake of the other.[71]

In his foreword to Girard's *I See Satan Fall Like Lightning*, Williams notes:

> The desire that lives through imitation almost always leads to conflict, and this conflict frequently leads to violence. The Bible

67. He postulates that "the sacrificial interpretation of the Passion must be criticized and exposed as a most enormous and paradoxical misunderstanding—and at the same time as something necessary—and as the most revealing indication of mankind's radical incapacity to understand its own violence, even when that violence is conveyed in the most explicit fashion." Girard, *Things Hidden*, 180–81.

68. Ibid., 180.

69. McDonald, "Violence and the Lamb Slain," 41.

70. "That is indeed why the Son promises men that if they manage to behave as the Father wishes, and to do his will, they will all become sons of God. It is not God who sets up the barriers between himself and mankind, but mankind itself." Girard, *Things Hidden*, 215.

71. Jungel, *Mystery of the World*, 314–15.

unveils this process of imitative desire leading to conflict and violence, and its distinctive narratives reveal at the same time that God takes the part of victims. In the Gospels the process of unveiling or revelation is radicalized: God himself, the Word become flesh in Jesus, *becomes the victim.* The innocent victim who is crucified is vindicated through his resurrection from the dead. The disciples of Jesus finally undergo a complete conversion as they move from being lost in the mimetic desire of the crowd to imitating Christ, which occurs through their experience of Jesus' resurrection. Their conversion and the resurrection of Christ are two aspects of the same event.[72]

For Girard, therefore, the life of Jesus Christ is the life of a nonviolent human being whose "project" was to rid humanity of violence by bringing violence out into the open and exposing its lies.[73]

The hypothesis of Girard in regard to violence is elegantly straightforward and yet belies many layers of depth. Indeed, Hardin observes that Girard has presented a theory which is both disarmingly simple in its structure and yet complex and subtle in its comprehension.[74] Ranieri adds that the test of a theory is its explanatory power and on this count he contends that Girard's theory is particularly strong. His fundamental insights not only discern a comprehensive intelligibility in the biblical text, Ranieri concludes, but they also help to explain an enormously wide range of cultural, social, and political phenomena.[75]

What the theory lacks, however, is an ontological base. Certainly, the idea of Christ overthrowing the sacrificial cultus is suggestive and yet without an ontological force of evil, let alone a "personified" Satan, Girard's argument lacks ultimate substance and foundation. Christ is presented as no more than a moral visionary and a model of resistance and iconoclasm, rather than being perceived as an *actual* victor over an *actual* adversary.[76] In this regard Girard's conclusions are redolent of the MIT; concurrently, they are far removed from the perspective of this thesis which upholds at least a

72. Williams, "Foreword," in Girard, *I See Satan Fall*, x.

73. Hardin, "Violence," 11. Girard states that "Jesus invites all men to devote themselves to the project of getting rid of violence, a project conceived with reference to the true nature of violence, taking into account the illusions it fosters, the methods by which it gains ground, and all the laws which we have verified . . ." Girard, *Things*, 197.

74. Hardin, "Violence," 108.

75. Ranieri, *Disturbing Revelation*, 187–88.

76. McDonald, "Violence and the Lamb Slain," 43. Conversely, Bell contests that "the figure of the devil is central to the New Testament view of redemption and . . . should also be central to Christian dogmatics." Bell, *Deliver Us from Evil*, 6.

personification of evil in the Satan and at most an actual, ontological being standing against and at war with Jesus Christ.

Girard has presented a view of salvation history in which God has used the sacrifice of Jesus on the cross as an ultimate means of expressing the futility of sacrifice. The fact remains for Girard that sacrifice and violence have nonetheless been used by God in order to accomplish his ends prior to their being used to herald the end of divine violence. We conclude, therefore, in agreement with Girard, that divine violence is not part of God's ultimate plan, but that violence has unequivocally been a primary function of God and a key means for him to accomplish the end of facilitating peace amongst humans perhaps through, in Girardian fashion, the scapegoating of the Satan in his being overcome at the cross.

Girard's theories provide interesting and apposite cultural and anthropological insights into societal and biblical violence. What they fail to take account of, however, is any transcendent or spiritual analysis or understanding; Girard actively discounts such talk, claiming that the language of the time must be spoken which, for him, is naturalistic.[77] The setting of arbitrary and inhibiting parameters upon research and understanding is, however, by definition limiting of a fully inclusive and holistic theory.

So, whilst we embrace Girard's criticism of a propitiationary reading of Christ's death, we look beyond him for understanding of the primary reasons for the cross, seeing Girard's conclusions as secondary, or even tertiary, to Christ's ultimate and primary goal of defeating an *actual* Satan and thereby setting humanity free from his authority, grasp and power. Also, whilst we accept Girard's contention that God used the sacrifice of Jesus to show the ultimate futility of sacrifice, we argue that sacrifice and violence had nonetheless been used copiously *prior* to this final denouement in order for God to accomplish his soteriological ends.[78]

We are not arguing that divine violence is God's primary or even ultimate plan. We nevertheless contend that it was, and perhaps still is, at least a primary divine *function* and a means by which God facilitates final and lasting peace—both between humanity in a societal setting and then ultimately and eternally between humans and God through the forceful, irresistible and violent overcoming of humanity's enemy—The Satan.

---

77. McDonald, "Violence and the Lamb Slain," 43.

78. We go further, endorsing the view of Rahner that "power is something to be gradually modified and absorbed by love, like concupiscence and all its consequences. It should be used to bring about its own abrogation, though this is only absolutely possible eschatologically. It should be the agent of its own elimination—which is possible in itself, since it is God's creation and of itself sin, which alone cannot have in itself the power to conquer itself." Rahner, *Theological Investigations*, 4:406.

Nicholas Wolterstorff

Wolterstorff reveals himself as a scholar with a further suggestive argument for the accommodation of divine violence as an unwelcome but necessary accoutrement to God's activity, especially when pertaining to his soteriological purposes. Assessing the consequences of this accommodation he observes that love and justice are not to be seen as conflicting elements, but are actually in harmony;[79] he observes that a love which perpetuates injustice is actually a malformed love.[80] He highlights this perceived conflict between love and justice observing that, in fact, to act out of love is perforce not to treat the recipient as one does because justice requires it; rather, he argues, to treat someone as one does because justice requires it is perforce not to be acting out of love.[81]

Love on God's Own Terms

Wolterstorff claims that agapic love is one not motivated or inspired by that towards which it is aimed; it comes from within and is sourced by the lover him/itself.[82] Since there was and is nothing inherently lovable about humans God, from himself, loved them on his own terms and for his own reasons. He is not beholding to anyone or anything and also has no need to justify the "terms and conditions" of his love. Wolterstorff concludes that it is, quite simply, the love of God and a love which is given only in accordance to his own nature and being as the God who does not just love, but who *is* love.[83]

Lex Talionis

Having established the ontological nature and context of God's love, Wolterstorff asserts that a *lex talionis* interpretation of the Sermon on the Mount is erroneous. In fact he argues that Jesus' message in the Sermon on the Mount is a direct assault upon *lex talionis* and the reciprocity code.[84] He critiques

79. Wolterstorff, *Justice in Love*, 1.

80. Ibid., ix.

81. Ibid., vii.

82. Rahner observes that compared to other forms of power, such as physical force or brute strength, "truth and love, acknowledged, affirmed and offered, are truly more real and nobler forces." Rahner, *Theological Investigations*, 4:393.

83. See Wolterstorff, *Justice in Love*, 127.

84. Ibid., 120. Speaking of this ancient Hebrew biblical ethical principle, Ellens describes it as "the law of the jungle" represented in "barbaric tones." Ellens, "Religious

scholars upholding this hermeneutic[85] and insists that not only do Jesus' words in these passages not lend themselves to a literalistic interpretation but that they go much further. On these Sermon on the Mount precepts Mayhew notes that if they were to be taken literally and were then invariably to be acted on, justice would be flouted, chaos would set in, and evil would come to reign.[86]

Further, Wolterstorff contends that, for instance, when Jesus exhorts people, "Do not resist an evildoer," Jesus is not saying, do not resist an evildoer *with violence*, but, *do not resist an evildoer, period*.[87] Conversely, Neufeld argues that mostly Jesus and the New Testament writers prohibit physical violence and yet, the pervasive presence of warnings of judgment for those who do not live in accordance with the will of God, or who do not confess Jesus as Lord and Messiah, are seen to constitute not just the threat of violence in the future but a form of verbal violence in the present.[88]

It is reasonable to expect that God would then apply these principles to his own dealings with those standing against him; ultimately represented in the cosmic power-encounter between the Satan and God. The Satan is the ultimate, ontological representation of "evildoer" whose existence stands counter to God's purposes. Following this argument and employing Wolterstorff's principle, God would be expected to not repay the Satan in a *lex talionis* fashion and actually not resist him at all—letting him do as he pleases with no consequences whatsoever. Or, if "Satan" is presented as a non-personified "force," then letting evil follow its own chaotic route with no attempt to "rein it in" or to set parameters within which it must operate; for Wolterstorff, therefore, "Evil" must be understood as deprivation of some life-good.[89] This, however, contradicts the purposes behind the incarnation of Jesus as a response to humanity's enslavement to sin and the Satan and ultimately to subdue and defeat him through active engagement and confrontation via God's soteriological purposes and plans.[90]

Metaphors," 255.

85. Including Marion, "Evil in Person"; Stassen, "Fourteen Triads"; and Hays, *Moral Vision*. Ellens argues that "few people in the Western world today would speak in favor of running society or personal life by the ancient barbaric code of the law of the jungle." Ellens, "Religious Metaphors," 255.

86. Mayhew, *Theology of Force*, 2.

87. Wolterstorff, *Justice in Love*, 125.

88. Neufeld, *Subversion of Violence*, 7.

89. Wolterstorff, *Justice in Love*, 123–24.

90. An issue that will be considered in the final chapter.

Diminution of Wellbeing

Wolterstorff also considers the behavior that Jesus demonstrated when faced with his own arrest, countering Hay's interpretation[91] by observing that Jesus' response cannot be cited as a model of mere non-violent resistance in the face of oppression, but rather that of one who did not resist *at all*.[92] Wolterstorff therefore initially appears to have definitively closed the door to any kind of active response from either humans or God in the face of persecution or aggression. On the other hand, Mayhew asserts,

> There are occasions when non-resistance and the acceptance of undeserved suffering may have a converting influence. Nevertheless, the bully and the robber and the rapist will frequently have to be met by the Christian with force. It would normally be quite wrong for the Christian to stand by while the weak are maltreated and to call his attitude an expression of the ethical teaching of Jesus.[93]

Wolterstorff too, however, apparently allows for the possibility that in some circumstances the evildoer might be due to receive some sort of diminution of wellbeing if in so doing it ultimately serves the good.[94] This opens the possibility of presenting God as one who primarily balks at expressing retribution, diminution or violence but who, in extreme circumstances, keeps open the option to negatively affect a person's wellbeing if it is undertaken purposefully and for The Ultimate Good.

This empowers divine action, freeing God from a priori inhibition in regard to the scope and parameters of his response to an abject evildoer and especially when it is not just any evildoer, but the author of chaos and evil himself—the Satan; the enemy of God and all he is seeking to achieve. Wolterstorff's position can be presented as an interpretation of his perception of Jesus' own perspective and intent; that is, if a person is to impose an evil or a harm or injury upon someone it must only be as a means to, or a constituent of, a greater good.[95] It is therefore our extrapolation and proposal

91. Hays argues that "from Matthew to Revelation we find a consistent witness against violence and a calling to the community to follow the example of Jesus in *accepting* suffering rather than *inflicting* it." Hays, *Moral Vision*, 332.

92. Wolterstorff, *Justice in Love*, 125–26. Likewise, Belousek notes that "the ethical teaching of the New Testament is not nonviolence, but non-retaliation—and not non-retaliation only, of course, but also love of enemy and love of the poor." Belousek, *Atonement, Justice and Peace*, 71.

93. Mayhew, *Theology of Force*, 2.

94. Wolterstorff, *Justice in Love*, 126.

95. Ibid., 127.

that if it were to serve the good of humanity as a whole through the defeat of someone or something standing counter to God's soteriological purposes then he would be capable and willing to unleash an ultimate, decisive and irresistible diminution of the Satan. For this to be efficacious in the countering and overthrowing of ontological evil, it would de facto have to be violent in delivery.

Wolterstorff proposes the further possibility of diminishing the flourishing of another in his contention that in the event of someone inflicting evil the person capable of preventing it is, in fact, *morally required* to do so, even if this interference compromises and diminishes the one perpetrating the act.[96] Rahner endorses this position:

> The principle of the absolute renunciation of force would not ... be a Christian principle. It would be a heresy which misunderstood the nature of man, his sinfulness and his existence as the interplay of persons in the *one* space of material being. An order of freedom would be misunderstood, if it were taken to be an order of things in which force was considered reprehensible on principle. A fundamental and universal renunciation of physical force of all kinds is not merely impractical. It is also immoral because it would mean renouncing the exercise of human freedom, which takes place in the material realm, and hence it would mean the self-destruction of the subject who is responsible to God.[97]

Promoting "Life-Goods"

A further extrapolation of this principle from humanity to divinity frees God to exhibit and practice force and thereby violence in order to promote the greater, ultimate life-goods of humans.[98] Further, Wolterstorff posits that such acts are *necessitated* by One who is ontologically love, since love requires justice to be demonstrated when it is within the beholder's potential to do so. As an omnipotent being whose nature is love God *must* impose

96. "If someone is about to inflict serious evil on another person and I am in a position to prevent him from doing so, then, even if my preventing him from doing so requires the diminishing of his flourishing, it is often not only acceptable that I do so but sometimes morally required." Ibid., 129.

97. Rahner, *Theological Investigations*, 4:399–400.

98. Mayhew observes, "There is normally nothing Christian, nothing in tune with the Sermon on the Mount, in facilitating evil by doing nothing." Mayhew, *Theology of Force*, 3.

evil (i.e. diminish the flourishing) on one such as the Satan who is both ontologically evil and diametrically opposed to God's soteriological plans.[99] Such plans represent, in an ultimate sense, the greatest possible "life-goods" imaginable; for God to do other than respond and to do so definitively with violence would suggest either his impotence or the lack of an ontological core of love to his being.

In a caveat to his own rule Wolterstorff includes the addition of an "Attitudinal corollary" which states that, "One is never to take delight in imposing evil (diminution in flourishing) on someone; when necessary to do so, one is to do so with regret."[100] Jantzen laments that "flourishing" is a theological concept increasingly ignored or de-prioritized and often conceptually relegated into the shadow of salvation. She observes that it would be a strange theological dictionary or encyclopedia that did not have substantial entries on "salvation"; whereas few, she contends, carry more than a passing reference to "flourishing."[101] She concedes that the significant exceptions to this emphasis on salvation at the expense of flourishing are the theologians of liberation, whether Latin American, Black, or feminist, all of whom, she argues, see flourishing as far more central to the Christian message than do traditional Eurocentric theologians. In Christian theology in Western modernity, she concludes that "salvation" has been a key term whilst "flourishing" has not.[102]

This focus on the diminution of flourishing, however, is in keeping with the outlook and practices of God who, whilst deeming it necessary to violently and irresistibly oppose an evil, violent and powerful adversary such as the Satan, nonetheless does so with no inherent delight. The act is instead merely the regrettable but entirely necessary means to the essential end of removing that which blocks the fulfillment of his eternal soteriological plans for humankind; flourishing thereby complete—an evil adversary vanquished.

99. This is born out as an application for care that Wolterstorff presents as the natural and necessary corollary of an attitude of love. He states that, "One should never seek to impose some evil on someone (i.e. diminish the person's flourishing) as an end in itself; one should seek to impose some evil only if doing so is an indispensable means to promoting greater goods in the life of that person and/or others, only if one should be promoting those greater life-goods, and never at the cost of wronging someone." Wolterstorff, *Justice in Love*, 130.

100. Ibid.

101. Jantzen, *Violence to Eternity*, 206.

102. Ibid.

5

The Primacy of the
Christus Victor Model

Revisiting Christus Victor

IT WILL NOW BE argued that the corollary of these two perspectives, on
divine violence and the Satan's reality, is that one atonement model, the
Christus Victor, presents itself as the only one capable of conjoining the two
into an explicable framework.[1] It will be argued that the CVM is expansive,
inclusive, and robust enough to explain and express both what occurred and
what was accomplished when Jesus Christ went to the cross to die and be
resurrected as well as providing a lens through which to view and understand divine violence.[2]

To avoid the danger of endorsing only extant theological models and
thereby de facto disregarding historical options such as the CVM, it is essential to consider the original context and application of other atonement
models. The primary locus of theology and Christian understanding and
proclamation is not, for Bultmann, the biblical record but the contempo-
raneous cultural context in which the proclamation is made. He argues
that much of the biblical account of Jesus is mythological talk, easily traced

---

1. This acceptance has its detractors, like Finlan, who critiques the Narrative Christus Victor motif presented in Weaver's *Nonviolent Atonement*, commenting on its paucity of biblical evidence and reference. He further adds that a battle between cosmic
forces of good and evil, whilst characteristic of the worldview of the first and second
centuries, is nonetheless inadequate to answer the philosophic needs of today. Finlan,
Problems with Atonement, 99.

2. Christ's ultimate aim within the CVM is summed up by Aulén, who states, "The
purpose of Christ's coming is to deliver men from all these powers of evil. He descends
from heaven, and becomes subject to the powers of this world, that finally He may
overcome them by His death and resurrection." Aulén, *Christus Victor*, 65.

and linked to the contemporary mythology of Jewish apocalypticism and Gnostic redemption myths. This leads him to conclude that insofar as it is mythological talk it is incredible to men and women today because for them the mythical world picture is a thing of the past.[3] Original context and its modern irrelevance is for Bultmann the deciding factor as to the cogence and credibility of Christian kerygma.

On the contrary, it will be shown that ancient theology, including the CVM, remains relevant, especially in terms of understanding spirituality, cosmic forces and divine violence, at least until there is compelling evidence to suggest otherwise. This rather than simply endorsing a de facto over-dependence upon the modern as preferable over the ancient; Walker, for example, links Christian praxis with acceptance of The Divine Drama in both ancient and modern theology:

> In order to understand how we are to fight the Devil today, we need to realise that our fight is directly related to Christ's own victory over the Evil One. If we push into the background God's warfare with the rebel Lucifer, we are liable to underestimate its importance in our own spiritual lives. Some theories of the atonement do precisely this.[4]

The CVM was, of course, conceived closer to the time and experience of Jesus Christ and his original followers; an era conversant and comfortable in dealing with these, by modern reckoning, overtly violent and spiritual issues. Indeed, as far back as the second century AD Kelly notes of Irenaeus that he is quite clear that Christ redeemed us with his blood and that when using the imagery of our enslavement to the Devil he is prepared to speak of the Savior's blood as a ransom.[5]

Also, in the age of the early Church Fathers, the human predicament was, according to Fiddes, frequently understood as that of being oppressed by hostile spiritual powers; people lived in fear of the baleful influence of astral deities or of demons who inhabited the natural world. The victory of Christ over the Devil and all the powers which threatened the life and health of humankind therefore became, he argues, the most popular way of under-standing atonement.[6] Conversely Girard, as we have seen, contends that what is instead incumbent upon philosophers and theologians is to speak the language of *these* times, which he contends are naturalistic.[7]

3. Bultmann, "New Testament and Mythology," 3.

4. Walker, *Enemy Territory*, 40.

5. Kelly, *Early Christian Doctrines*, 173–74.

6. Fiddes, *Past Event*, 7.

7. McDonald, "Violence and the Lamb Slain," 43. Girard counters the accusation of

According to Wright, however, in the CVM God set a clear precedent for the Christian and the Christian Church in terms of the violent manner of his dealing with spiritual enemies, thus advocating the way in which Christian faith should be understood and practiced. He argues,

> The church of Jesus Christ is the church militant. We are engaged in spiritual conflict and need to be equipped for this task. To be sure, the conflict is like no other form of battle and the weapons quite different from any other weapons. We must re-imagine our notions of warfare. Yet the analogy is valid. It would be a pity if embarrassment at the military language or misplaced political correctness were to deprive us of the challenge.[8]

Walker concurs, claiming that Aulén's attack on the Western development of the doctrine of the atonement is irrefutable.[9] Further, Walker contends that Aulén's portrayal of the early Fathers' understanding of God's war with the Devil has been obscured by rejigging the expansive, cosmic drama of what he calls the Great Battle into a rather more prosaic legalistic framework.[10] In other words, the macro has been jettisoned in favor of the micro; the dramatic in the stead of the juridical and the cosmic and spiritual for the human and earth-bound. This ideological and interpretative paradigm shift has incurred huge theological ramifications, not least in terms of understanding God's nature, especially in regard to any perceived relationship and engagement with violence he might have.

The fear of colluding God with violence intrinsic to his being has perhaps also removed the possibility of considering whether there might at least be violence that is *extrinsic* to God's nature and function. This fear has also inverted the importance of that which would come to be seen as, at best, his rather ethereal and insubstantial "enemy": the Satan. Indeed, starting with Anselm and continuing on into modern representations of PSA

---

reductionism saying he is no more so than Paul who desired to "know nothing whilst I am among you but Christ and him crucified"; Paul, Girard states, "did not mean to say that there was nothing besides the death of Christ, but that all knowledge took place in understanding the crucifixion of Christ. It is from that death and the place of that death that all understanding comes. I believe that it is in that sense that my hypothesis, though I keep repeating it over and over again, is not reductionist." Ibid., 43.

8. Wright, *Theology of the Dark Side*, 183.

9. Aulén, *Christus Victor*.

10. Walker, *Enemy Territory*, 40. He notes, "But from the tenth century onwards this whole strain of soteriology [propitiation, etc.] predominated in the West, and under Anselm of Canterbury became far more systematic and juridical. The love of God, the war with the Devil, and many of the earlier incarnational theories of atonement fell away to be replaced by a story of God's wrath and its appeasement by Christ's death." Ibid., 41.

there has been a down-grading of the Satan's importance; certainly, Anselm was principally concerned, according to James, with the relationship of God and humankind, whereas the ransom theories tend to concentrate on God and the devil.[11]

Breaking with Tradition

A theological paradigm shift of this kind, including the absolute removal of the potential of violence—either intrinsic or extrinsic is, however, out of keeping with a Christian faith that had previously readily embraced and kept continuity with Judaic theological principles; Hurtado argues that in the early Christian Church understanding of Jesus is accepted along broadly Jewish theological lines. He notes that the Christian appropriation of the Jewish divine agency category shows a significant mutation in the tradition and in monotheistic devotion, whilst insisting that there are nonetheless clear marks of the category being appropriated.[12] In this schema, the Christian conception of the exaltation of Christ demonstrates a concern for the uniqueness and supremacy of the one God, as seen in the Jewish evidence dealing with chief agents. Christianity is therefore presented as a mutation of Judaism rather than an evolution; there is not in other words, for Hurtado, a profound schism or divergence between the two.

Conversely, Dunn, having considered examples of Christian and Jewish understanding of intermediate beings between God and man, opines that

> if pre-Christian Judaism was already thinking in terms of divine hypostases and intermediaries then to that extent Judaism's monotheism was already diluted or at least modified, to that extent precedents were being evolved for a Christian doctrine of Jesus as divine mediator, and to that extent room was being made for a Christian doctrine of incarnation, that is of a Jesus Christ who was the incarnation of one of these "intermediary beings."[13]

The transition of theology from Jewish to Christian is for Dunn, therefore, not a mutation but an evolution.

The first Christians also inherited a dual focus providing the basic framework within which Christian thinkers have understood atonement

11. James, "Atonement in Church History," 211.

12. Hurtado, *One God, One Lord*, 99.

13. Dunn, *Christology in the Making*, 130.

through the ages; within Judaism and Christianity, then, atonement involves the establishing of right relationship between God and the world through avert confrontation with evil.[14]

Certainly, such an apparently blatant expression of divine violence is not entirely denied by PSA, but is rather subjugated in favor of a primary emphasis on legalism and juridical transaction. It has the corollary loss, however, of cogent understanding and engagement with both the *potential* of divine violence, whether intrinsic or extrinsic, or of the primary importance of an ontological enemy of God who would need to be confronted and defeated. Hanson, for example, criticizes PSA for presenting a repulsive view of an incensed, provoked, wrathful and indignant deity whose demand for propitiation should be banished finally from Christianity, regardless of the degree to which it may figure in other religions.[15] PSA therefore certainly acknowledges divine violence but a violence that is destructive and negative casting profoundly unbiblical aspersions upon God's nature. So, instead of a redemptive or soteriologically-based violence it is rather a cruel and vindictive violence that satisfies God's own needs rather than over-coming an enemy or primarily freeing an incarcerated humanity.

The CVM, conversely, provides the required redress of this proposed movement away from God as One who, in a positive sense, is at least extrinsically violent and engaging in a necessary, mortal and cosmic conflict with an actual enemy that had to be forcefully and irrefutably subjugated and defeated. Aulén states, in fact, that a certain double-sidedness is an essential feature of the classic idea of the Atonement. On the one hand, he argues, the drama of redemption has a dualistic background; God in Christ violently combats and prevails over the "tyrants" which hold mankind in bondage. On the other hand, God thereby becomes reconciled with the world, enmity is taken away, and a new relation between God and mankind is established.[16]

This is an ineluctable caveat in understanding God's relationship with violence, both in terms of his character and his soteriological modus operandi. It also safeguards against the inclinations of PSA to present God's character in a manner befitting Western conceptions of jurisprudence which

14. Ray, *Deceiving the Devil*, 1. Further, Grimsrud argues that meaning can be found in Jesus' death in relation to the continuity of his life and teaching with the Old Testament salvation story; Jesus, he contends, lived and taught a vision of Torah in line with Moses and the prophets, he concludes that, "Jesus reiterated the Old Testament message that God loves human beings, that salvation follows from simply trusting in that love, and that the social life that follows from centering life on God's love takes the form of mutual regard and service, not domination and exploitation." Grimsrud, *Instead of Atonement*, 112.

15. Hanson, "Grace and the Wrath of God," 151.

16. Aulén, *Christus Victor*, 55.

have, by definition, no place or regard for positive and necessary violence; not extrinsic and certainly not intrinsic. Hanson counsels, however, that it would be an error to regard God from the perspective of liberal democracy, however strong the temptation to do so.[17] This warning prevents advocates of PSA from a priori rejection of the possibility of positive divine violence, especially in response to the interpretative danger of prioritizing contemporary culture and outlooks above the biblical record, theological tradition and history.

Atonement & Violence

Indeed, after outlining the salient features of the three main atonement motifs Boersma concedes that whilst the three interpretative strands differ in significant ways it is nonetheless essential to note that however God is associated with the cross, whether in terms of a demonstration of his love, of punishing his Son, or battling with the Devil—God somehow is always associated with violence.[18] The corollary of this admission, for Boersma, is that such association with violence potentially undermines any atonement model. In regard to the violence he admits to being naturally inherent in each motif, he nonetheless asserts that each model's respective level of violence is closely assimilated with its claim for validity; the higher the level of violence associated with a view, the more likely that it is either illegitimate or invalid. Boersma argues that penal substitution is, therefore, de facto the worst kind of metaphor, followed by CVM then, seemingly innocuous in terms of violence, the MIT, which though apparently the most hospitable nonetheless, he concedes, still involves God in the violence of the cross.[19]

In regard to sacred violence, or the lack thereof, Finlan considers various approaches to the atonement and in particular, their occurrence in Pauline writings. He observes that both the problematic aspects of atonement *and* the effective answer to those problems are found in the Bible; concluding that the Bible is part of the problem and *most* of the solution.[20] Finlan acknowledges the conundrum of presenting a definitive doctrine of atone-

17. Hanson, "Grace and the Wrath of God," 141.

18. Boersma, *Violence, Hospitality and the Cross*, 40.

19. Ibid., 41.

20. Finlan, *Problems with Atonement*, 96. Aulén acknowledges that perceived absence of rationality and lack of definitiveness can raise problems for the potential acceptance of a doctrine. "When theology," he argues, "sets itself to seek for fully rational explanations of all things, it is only too evident that it must set aside the classic idea, with all its contradictions, as a crude and primitive stage in the attempt to express truth . . ." Aulén, *Christus Victor*, 157.

ment—that such is difficult, if not impossible, to ascribe. The only option, he proposes, is a "working model" acknowledging eclectic, overlapping and aposiopetic elements of this seemingly multifarious doctrine.[21]

Whether dealing with a "working model" or not, deconstruction of the central themes and key characters necessary for a basic soteriological and atonement model presents God, the Satan and humans as essential, non-negotiable constituents.[22] A similar simplification of the PSA and MIT models likewise forces the concession that the Satan has been either side-lined or removed from their doctrines with differing consequences; conversely, to some extent, the CVM de-prioritizes humans. The result of this synthesis presents the latter as both best and preferable model in its ability to make sense of God's endorsement and utilization of positive violence—whether represented as intrinsic to his being or extrinsic to his actions. By such means, it is possible to uphold both divine sovereignty and freedom through a model taking seriously original biblical evidence for the Satan as an ontological being and a dangerous and powerful enemy of both God and humans. As Watt notes,

> Inherent to the gospel narratives is the presence of Satan and evil. None of the gospels can be read without acknowledging the contrasting presence of evil and Satan. The reality of the presence of God in Christ is unfolded in the context of conflict with and eventual victory over evil.[23]

Barth concurs with the primacy of God's right and ability to choose, stating that God initiates the covenant of grace as the beginning of all his works and ways and to destroy the rule of the Satan over mankind, thus opposing the kingdom of Jesus Christ to the Satan in triumphant superiority.[24]

For a particular soteriology to be resonant with the original biblical representation of both the Satan and God's use and endorsement of violence, therefore, particularly in regard to atonement violence, it is theologically necessary to present the imperative of an ontological enemy of God: the Satan. Illustrating this point and further to the biblical quote, "The reason

---

21. Gunton confirms that "rationalism is an inadequate orientation towards the mysteries of our universe, particularly those concerned with the living of life under God." Gunton, "Christus Victor Revisited," 130.

22. It is important to acknowledge that "the soteriological landscape of the New Testament exhibits a rich texture, diverse and powerful. This complex landscape does not lend itself to being diminished into précis form." Watt, "Soteriology in the New Testament," 505.

23. Ibid., 508.

24. Barth, *CD* 2/2:450.

the Son of God appeared was to destroy the works of the devil" (1 John 3:8) Wright asserts that the removal of this element of conflict from the Gospels would lead to a major misunderstanding of the mission of Jesus.[25] This, of course, is also true of the perception of this mission for First Century believers and, more tellingly, for Jesus himself.

We contend, therefore, that the best way for such an understanding to be presented is through the CVM which takes seriously both the original cultural milieu of soteriological theories and their expression in a modern context. However profound the problems are regarding traditional interpretations of atonement and in particular their association with divine violence, it is essential to understand properly and engage thoroughly with the experiences of the earliest Christians; denying this historical context promotes, according to Ray, an untenable ahistoricism.[26]

A Cosmic & Ontological Model

Summarizing the CVM Boyd, for example, argues that the timeless *cosmic* significance of Christ's work is ontologically more fundamental than its *soteriological* significance. He notes that the soteriological significance of the cross is the meaning that is perhaps most important to human beings and should never be minimized and yet concludes that there can only ever be an accurate understanding and appreciation of this significance if it is understood in the context of the cosmic significance of Christ's actual victory.[27] Elsewhere, Boyd notes that biblical understanding of spiritual warfare requires, as a central component, a belief in angels, Satan and demons as real, autonomous, free agents, as well as a belief that the activity of these beings intersects with human affairs, for better or for worse. He accepts, however, that many modern people, including many Christian theists, find this belief inherently implausible.[28]

It is this cosmic, ontological element that, for us, further commends the CVM and its unique ability to link God's nature and purposes and his coalescence with positive divine violence. Rather than speculating about various ethereal outcomes to the atonement in regard to sin and forgiveness, the CVM is instead a model concurrently both metaphorical and yet beyond metaphor. It has previously been noted that McFague describes a metaphor as seeing one thing *as* something else, pretending that, "this" is

25. Wright, *Theology of the Dark Side*, 18.

26. Ray, *Deceiving the Devil*, 102.

27. Boyd, "Christus Victor View," 33.

28. Boyd, *God at War*, 32.

"that" because we do not know how to think or talk about "this," so we use "that" as a way of saying something about it.[29] This leads to the proposition that metaphorical thinking means spotting a thread of similarity between two otherwise dissimilar objects, events, or whatever, one of which is better known than the other, and thereby using the better-known as a means of speaking about the lesser known.[30] Whilst this is the case with other atonement models and metaphors, it is our contention that uniquely in the CVM "that" is not being used to refer to and explain "this"; but in a literal and connected way, "this"—the CVM—is being used to explicate "this"—the death and resurrection of Christ and the consequences thereof. It is therefore unequivocally the only model that represents an explanation and description of what, in both the broadest and most specific theological and cosmological senses, *actually* happened in the atonement in terms of the necessary and violent overcoming of an actual adversary—the Satan.

Gunton disagrees, stating that it would be overly literalistic to construe the metaphorical elements of an understanding of the atonement as a victory as if such language was naturalistic. This, he argues, is the problem with those patristic formulations of the atonement that are linked with the CVM which wrongly, he claims, overlook the metaphorical nature of soteriological language.[31] In fact, Gunton further notes that only the literal-minded would ask the question as to whom was the ransom paid when Christ died on the cross which, he suggests, means that it is usually not the Bible but its interpreters with whom issue ought to be taken.[32]

Conversely, in his consideration of the ransom motif Wright posits that when Jesus sought to prepare his followers for a gigantic and previously unimagined vision that he used many strands to do so including story, symbol and meaning. These, he argues, are woven together so that it becomes difficult to follow a single thread without realizing how tightly it belongs to the others as well. When trying to explain how the powers of this world would be held to account, therefore, Jesus spoke in terms of giving his life as "a ransom for many" (Mark 10:45) which, Wright argues, is a concept so outside their worldview that they could not understand it; he notes that at this point such was their inability to interpret and comprehend that they were not even able to appreciate the fact that when he spoke about his forthcoming death, he meant it in a literal, concrete sense.[33]

29. McFague, *Metaphorical Theology*, 15.

30. Ibid.

31. Gunton, "Christus Victor View," 134.

32. Ibid.

33. Wright, *Simply Jesus*, 175.

Likewise, it might be that other seemingly inexplicable stories and events might also be understood more literally. Specifically, for instance, God irresistibly and violently confronts evil present in the person of the Satan and forcefully and powerfully overcomes him, resulting in the Satan's defeat and the liberation of humans to whom he had previously laid claim, whether legitimately or not. Or, as Neufeld puts it in his assessment of the CVM,

> Humanity is not so much "bad" as "captive," not so much per-petrator as victim. Humanity is thus less in need of punishment than of liberation or salvation. Humanity is not saved from God's wrath but from Satan's hold on it.[34]

As previously acknowledged, Athanasius notes, the air is the sphere of the Devil, the enemy of the human race who, having fallen from heaven, endeavors with the other evil spirits who shared in his disobedience both to keep souls from the truth and to hinder the progress of those who are trying to follow it.[35] In other words, an ontological enemy of God exists and has to be defeated in order for humans to be free and salvation won—in this manner, metaphor and actuality perichoretically intertwine.

This representation of Christ's mission, of atonement and of God's nature, including positive violence—whether intrinsic or extrinsic—and in association with soteriological purposes, finds its culmination and fullest, ontological expression in the CVM. Aulén himself synthesizes his perspective of the model:

> The central idea of Christus Victor is the view of God and the Kingdom of God as fighting against evil powers ravaging in mankind. In this drama Christ has the key rôle, and the title Christus Victor says the decisive word about his rôle.[36]

It is a model that is not, therefore, "once-removed" from spiritual and ontological reality by metaphor or symbol; instead it represents an historical event expressing and marking an historical moment in which a spiritual and theological event was actualized.

This point is illustrated by Placher who observes that Christ is not merely a scapegoat, randomly dragged to the Temple for sacrifice, but is a volunteer in the battle against evil; to be sure, Placher concedes, there is still suffering, which is celebrated—but not because it is good; rather, because it

---

34. Neufeld, *Subversion of Violence*, 84.

35. Athanasius, *On the Incarnation*, 55. He adds, "But the Lord came to overthrow the devil and to purify the air and to make "a way" for us up to heaven . . ." Ibid.

36. Aulén, *Christus Victor*, ix.

is the agent of the transformation of the world.[37] Not only a myth, a symbol or a metaphor of something that "sort of" happened, but that would remain inevitably invisible and impervious to outside observation; but rather a chosen, divine event leading to actual transformation in time, space, history and the cosmos. A real model expressing and representing reality, that God positively and violently overcomes the Satan—or rather that the actual actually exists and does so as an integral part, in fact in symbiosis with, that which it actualizes.

A Violent, Dramatic & Holistic Model

Although the CVM provides an explication of soteriology in the overall life of Jesus, this does not denigrate the on-going centrality of Christ's passion. Aulén is right to note that if the earthly life of Christ as a whole is to be regarded as a continuous process of victorious conflict, it is his death that is the final and decisive battle.[38] It is only the CVM that sees this final event as a battle, or at least presents it in a manner consistent with the normative use of warfare terminology.[39] The CVM presents itself, therefore, as the only model to explain both the ontological and cosmic nature of the atonement whilst also engaging with and integrating the concept of divine violence.

All the atonement models agree that the problem is humankind's radical and complete falling away from God's best purposes; relationship between them is shattered and division engendered, with no possibility of human rectification.[40] A divine paradigm shift had to occur if the way was to be opened for God and humankind to be back in right relations—a new epoch had to be heralded. Indeed, the mark of this new era is, according to Moltmann, the crucified Christ, or as he calls this event, the specific thing about Christian theology, both as regards its identity and as regards its relevance. For Moltmann, Jesus Christ on the cross does not merely stamp its content, but rather gives Christian theology its form and its *Sitz im*

---

37. Placher, "Christ Takes Our Place," 16.

38. Aulén, *Christus Victor*, 30.

39. "battle > *n*. 1. a sustained fight between organized armed forces. 2. a lengthy and difficult conflict or struggle. > *v.* fight or struggle tenaciously with an opponent or to achieve something." "Battle," in *Concise Oxford English Dictionary*, 115.

40. "Creation involves risk, and this risk in turn issues in sin and evil which threaten the creatures with dissolution and distortion." Macquarrie, *Principles*, 268. Fiddes notes that the backdrop to a universally comprehensible concept of salvation is the assumption that "the life of human beings and that of the wider natural world is distorted, self-destructive, or failing to reach its true potential." Fiddes, "Salvation," 176.

Leben.[41] The theological and historical paradigm shift was brought about, for Moltmann, through this particular Christ-event and so in regard to an authentically Christian future and sense of hope the starting point lies in faith's fundamental recognition that the anticipation of the divine future took place in the crucified Christ.[42]

In a similar vein, Boyd notes that humans are reconciled because the cosmos has been reconciled and this because the rebel powers have been put in their place in order that humans can once again be presented "holy and blameless" before God.[43] This emphasizes the spiritual and cosmic nature of the problem and its solution—a situation that only God could rectify and then only with the exercise of positive violence, albeit reluctantly and in a primarily spiritual context; for God alone can atone, because only God can bear the cost of atonement.[44]

In his explication of what happened in this "spiritual context" Wright notes that when Jesus explained the meaning of his forthcoming death, he did not give his followers a theory, neither did he give them a set of scriptural texts; instead, he gave them a meal.[45] This Passover meal, Wright contends, was not one in which they only looked *backwards* to the miracles by which God had released the Jews from Egypt; but rather it was a meal which also pointed *forwards* to the great sacrifice by which God would rescue his people from the bonds of their ultimate slavery. This, he argues, would be the real Exodus and one in which the tyrant defeated would not be Rome, but rather the dark power standing behind that great, cruel empire.[46]

Wright further delineates what, or rather *whom*, this "dark power" would be, arguing that somehow, Jesus' forthcoming death will constitute his victory, or rather God's victory, over "this world's ruler," who is not merely the Caesar, but rather the power that stands behind the Caesar, using him for its dark, destructive purposes.[47] Likewise, in assessing salvation in the book of Revelation Grimrud observes that the veneer of respectability and claim for divine support for the way of empire is torn away and that John's intent is to reveal the "beastly" nature of Rome and thereby to lay

41. Moltmann, *Future of Creation*, 60.

42. Ibid., 57.

43. Boyd, "Christus Victor View," 33.

44. Hanson, "Grace and the Wrath of God," 154.

45. Wright, *Simply Jesus*, 176.

46. Ibid., 176–77.

47. Ibid., 178.

bare the actual source of Rome's power—not God at all but the Dragon, the Satan, himself.[48]

Whereas other atonement theories are by their own definition and understanding metaphorical the CVM is instead, we again assert, simultaneously both a metaphor and an actual representation of the ontological, cosmic and spiritual reality that there is a Devil who reigns and rules over a dark kingdom. On the other hand, Wink, in his consideration of the eventual overthrow of various systems, such as Eastern Europe and China, by means of their new desire to embrace democracy, compares them to a time when God's system will replace the Domination System, a term which he has previously closely associated with Satan—and by "Satan" he is referring to the world-encompassing spirit of the Domination System.[49]

This will be a "replacement," Wink argues, not achieved by violent confrontation, but rather by means of a movement whereby increasing numbers of people find themselves drawn towards the values of "God's system."[50] This optimistic, humanistic and profoundly metaphorical perspective finds a parallel with MIT and is a representation of a means by which God will "overcome" a conceptual evil via a bloodless and peaceful "coup"; there is, of course, no ontological enemy for Wink and therefore no need to confront and defeat this "adversary" in anything other than a metaphorical sense.

Conversely, we assert that in his Virgin Birth, life, teaching, example, death and resurrection and not at the cross as an isolated event, Christ actually overcame and defeated this being, the Satan, literally and violently wresting back from him the humans that he had previously owned through their conscious disobedience and concomitant slavery. This macro-narrative element represents another key constituent of the CVM which differentiates it from other atonement models in that it is not only concerned with the events of Jesus' passion, crucifixion and resurrection.[51] Instead, the CVM acknowledges and expresses every single aspect of Christ's life—from incarnation to resurrection—and presents them as being fundamentally *about one thing*: victoriously manifesting the loving kingdom of God over and against the destructive, oppressive kingdom of the Satan.[52]

---

48. Grimsrud, *Instead of Atonement*, 222.

49. Wink, *Engaging the Powers*, 9.

50. Ibid., 58.

51. In fact, the CVM is perceived as the divine victory over certain powers of evil and "reconciliation is achieved because after the incarnation and death of Christ their power to do harm is taken away by God." Gunton, *Actuality of Atonement*, 55. Incarnation and death are here referenced in one doctrine, integrally and inherently linked.

52. Boyd, "Christus Victor View," 40.

It is, therefore, not a doctrine of a moment or of a singular event, a mere time-specific theological proposition; rather it is a dramatic, dynamic and all-encompassing narrative of a seen life and an unseen spiritual reality[53]—the human and the divine realms conjoined and symbiotically linked in an expression of ultimate duality. This rather than the cosmology claimed by Bultmann who contends that the cosmology of the New Testament is essentially mythical in character and that the world is presented there as a three-storied structure, with the earth in the center, the heaven above, and the underworld below.[54]

This "structure" is populated, according to Bultmann, with various celestial beings, the angels above and hell below as a place of torment. Even the earth, he states, is not merely a place of natural, everyday events but is rather the scene of supernatural activity. His simplification of New Testament cosmology is an overstatement of extant views illustrating his thesis that first century understanding of the universe was at best naïve and at worst abjectly erroneous in correctly understanding the world as it really is; in other words, how secular people and liberal Christians perceive it today.

The CVM, therefore, presents a compelling and dramatic account of God and his character, including his use and expression of violence, as well as his purposes and in a manner which surpasses the theological scope of any other atonement model. It is this holistic quality, in fact, that commends it in regard to its expression of the full sweep of salvation history, interrelated and inter-dependent as part of a holistic soteriological picture and not one which limits atonement to a momentary theological "snap-shot."

Further, it also makes sense of salvation as a narrative, a story with a symbiotic beginning, middle and conclusion, re-affirming the theological truth of the unity of otherwise seemingly separate, disparate and supposedly unrelated elements of Christ's life, ministry, death, resurrection and purposes.[55] Thusly, Gregory of Nazianzus's comment on the purpose of the incarnation—that God, by forcefully overcoming the tyrant, might set us free and reconcile us with himself through his Son—can be contextually understood, both in its original setting and its modern representation.[56]

---

53. Speaking of the CVM Rieger notes "the dramatic form this view takes; it is a story as much as a set of propositions." Rieger, "Good News," 381.

54. Bultmann, "New Testament and Mythology," 1.

55. See Walker, *Telling the Story*, 13–14, for a nine-point overview of the gospel's elements in "grand narrative" form.

56. "Holiness had to be brought to man by the humanity assumed by one who was God, so that God might overcome the tyrant by force and so deliver us and lead us back to himself through the mediation of his Son." Gregory of Nazianzus, *Oration 45*, 9, 26.

The CVM therefore does more than merely provide understanding and insight into the atonement; like one of its descriptors, the Dramatic Model, it presents the atonement of Christ as more than something which occurred only in the last week of his life on earth. Instead the CVM is an atonement model which focuses upon God—what he set up, what he won back and how his purposes are always fulfilled regardless of what the Satan or humanity does to oppose him. The fulfilling of these purposes will be accomplished by whatever means are necessary, even when these means run counter to God's own, expressed ideals in terms of his character and predicates. This is the case in terms of the atonement when, against his own ontology of love, he nonetheless utilizes positive violence as not merely the best, but the *only*, means by which humans can be set free from the Satan's ownership and grasp, whether legitimate or not.

We conclude, therefore, that the CVM is the only interpretation of Jesus Christ's crucifixion which holds together and explicates the full interpretative weight and otherwise divergent and mutually exclusive elements of God's character in regard to positive divine violence and the existence and necessary defeat of an actual enemy. It is not merely the best or primary means of interpreting the atonement; it is, in fact, the only way the atonement can be expressed ontologically and without the concurrent disacknowledgement, denial or loss of both positive divine violence and of an ontological, evil enemy of God in the Satan.[57]

---

57. Considering the role of theology, Bell observes that, important though it is for it to engage with the narrated world and the *telling* of myths, it also needs to do *work* on myths; thereby engaging with the discussed world in which it is necessary for theology to articulate the ontological status of the Satan. In this manner, theology will be able to form a bridge across from mythology to metaphysics. Bell, *Deliver Us from Evil*, 116. We contend that the CVM and the manner of its understanding and engagement with the Satan is an important element in building this "bridge."

Conclusion

WE HAVE DEMONSTRATED THROUGHOUT this thesis that the theological task of ascertaining the degree to which God is associated with, or utilizes force and violence is, of course, fraught with controversy and difficulties. In order to reach a position from the evidence rather than prior to it, however, it has been shown that it is essential to be free of presupposition and agenda that might otherwise color or influence the parameters and context of theological reflection and exploration. Hart notes,

> As in christology we cannot simply construct a portrait of the human Jesus rooted in our own perceptions of empirical human-ity, but must always reckon with those things which differentiate his humanity from ours, precisely because it is in these very ele-ments that his revelatory and salvific significance resides, so too in this matter of theological definition, while our starting point must inevitably be with our own creaturely and sinful percep-tions and experience of love, fatherhood, righteousness and the rest, we must expect and allow the limits of these perceptions to be ruptured and their content to be transformed as they refer us beyond the ordinary and familiar to the humanity of God, and beyond still, to God's own life and being.[1]

It is this endeavor to understand and explicate God's "own life and being," rather than the projection of human mores and post-modern per-spectives and sensibilities upon God, in regard to force and violence, that is central to this thesis.

All too often the proposition that God is love negates even the pos-sibility of entertaining divine violence whether intrinsically, extrinsically, ontologically, functionally or as an attribute.[2] This position, however, repu-

---

1. Hart, *Regarding Karl Barth*, 179–80.
2. This position is characterized by Cremer who argued that the divine action as

diates a full and thorough understanding of God and the complexity of his nature and how he has revealed himself historically through the Scriptures. Barth, for instance, upholds the biblical tension between freedom and love as the basic and foundational concept in the doctrine of the divine essence and attributes, not the thought of love alone.[3]

This freedom can be exercised by God in any manner he sees fit, including his divine right to freely choose to manifest power, force, violence and perhaps, as we considered, even abuse, in order to fulfill his soteriological purposes. This freedom is essential for the accomplishment of God's plans and as Rahner notes, the exercise of freely chosen divine power is not irrelevant to salvation—rather, it is a process either of *salvation* or *perdition*.[4] Rahner observes that since might is a real characteristic and natural creation of God it is not, in and of itself, simply sinful and anti-god. Rather, he notes, it is because it is a natural divine creation that it can be used for good ends as well as being perverted to serve sinful ones.[5] Finally, because it is a characteristic creation of God's it is also one that cannot be suppressed whilst this world lasts—it cannot ever be eliminated.[6] Might, force and violence are here to stay—how they might be utilized by God and humans is beyond the scope of this thesis—what is clear is that they will not cease to be associated with God and his activity simply by theological denial.

---

presented in the New Testament witness demonstrates the love of God as it is manifested in Jesus Christ. For him, to speak of the love of God is to say that God puts his whole being and self into willing to be, and actually being, for humanity and in fellowship with humanity. In such a revelation of God's love is seen the epitome of God's essence and the means by which this essence is revealed and known, so that the qualities of his loving action are in fact qualities of God's essence. Cremer, *Christliche*, 18–19. In this manner, for Cremer, the most profound truth about God is revealed, that he is love and this is not merely God's central attribute but one that overshadows and influences all others, thus negating other potential attributes such as force and violence.

3. Barth objected to Cremer's argument, stating that it takes too little account of the freedom of God in his love and thereby ascertains the being and function of God too exclusively in his dealings with humanity. The fact remains, Barth concludes, "that God is He who gives everything life and breath and all things and who therefore does not need the service of men's hands to be who He is . . ." Barth, *CD* 2/1:282–83.

4. Rahner, *Theological Investigations,* 4:402. He also states that "power is not *just any* element in human life. It is . . . along with sexuality, indeed even more than this, perhaps one of the most fundamental forces in our existence. And it is not just something of limited and localized importance in human life: it pervades the whole; it is not in a very special way, which man cannot properly perform in the present order of sin and of Christ, without the holy and elevating grace of Christ, without faith and love. It is one of the acts in which salvation or damnation is decisively achieved." Ibid., 403–4.

5. Ibid., 404–10.

6. Ibid., 402.

Throughout this thesis, therefore, it has been demonstrated that atonement, understood as the reconciling, redeeming, liberating activity of God in Christ, is an essential Christian belief.[7] Further, and more pertinently, the subject of the atonement is absolutely central to Christian *theology*; directly related to the perception of God's nature and, in our case, to what degree violence, whether intrinsic or extrinsic, is evident.[8]

In regard to the current theological milieu and in particular the practice of selectively accepting particular Scriptures to the exclusion of others, with their perceived erroneous concomitant theologies and perspectives, Marcion provides a helpful illumination to our thesis.[9] It is our contention that, in one form or another, Christian theology risks falling into various manifestations of conscious or unconscious neo-Marcionitism.[10] This is not to say that an individual theologian would be actively pursuing a Marcionite perspective; instead it is that whether or not they were consciously advocating Marcionite hermeneutics they would nonetheless be following a similarly selective methodology. The impending danger is the rejection or at least reinterpretation of those parts of Scripture, in a Marcionite manner, that present a view of God that is thought to be unpalatable or does not fit into a pre-ordained theological perspective. Enslin notes of Marcion, for instance, that he made a choice between a God he liked and one he did not; then simply choosing to accept and worship the one that met his own sensibilities whilst vilifying and rejecting the one that did not. For Marcion, therefore,

> the true God, the hitherto undivulged God of love, who is himself goodness and love and who desires love and faith from men, was thus totally other than the wrathful, jealous, and capricious God of the Jewish Scriptures, who demanded from his worshipers not love and faith but fear and obedience couched in terms of outward righteousness.[11]

Such an outlook, of course, could include consideration and acceptance of divine violence.

---

7. Ray, *Deceiving the Devil*, 5.

8. Aulén, *Christus Victor*, 12.

9. "Marcion erred not just in the breadth of his de-canonization of the entire Old Testament but in his de-canonization of any of it." Bruce, *Spreading Flame*, 224.

10. It has already been noted, for example, how the teachings of Feuerbach in regard to "projecting one's image onto God" are a case in point. See Feuerbach, *Essence of Christianity*, 12.

11. Enslin, "Pontic Mouse," 9.

We have rejected such neo-Marcionite perspectives and instead, when encountering compelling but challenging notions of God's nature, such as intrinsic or extrinsic violence, we have, at the very least, been open to its consideration and thereby its potential incorporation into a broader schema. This has facilitated a more textured and nuanced view of God, including his extrinsic use of violence, as revealed in the Judeo-Christian canonical Scriptures. It has been a demanding methodology and yet one inclined to present a robust and authentically biblical account of God in whose image humans are made. This chosen route is posited as opposed to one in which there is a deconstruction and subsequent reconstruction of a god made in the image of humans according to their era, denomination, outlook, predispositions, sensibilities and preferences.

As we have shown, in fact, every atonement theory, model or motif has inevitably leant upon and drawn from its extant social structure so that, for instance, in the eleventh century Anselm's view of debt payment was set in the historical milieu of medieval feudalism.[12] In a similar vein, Gorringe adds that Anselm witnessed the birth of a new world that was reflected in his work and that the field of law, in particular had an obvious bearing on his theology.[13] Gunton, on the other hand, notes that not only was this not actually the case but, in fact, exactly the opposite is true in that the feudal rulers duty was to maintain the order of rights and obligations without which society would collapse and, Gunton argues, Anselm's God is understood to operate *analogously* for the universe as a whole: as the upholder of universal justice.[14]

For Ray, however, the Anselmian model includes a purely juridical notion of justice and one, she asserts, that is untempered by love or compassion; indeed, as a result of the original rebellion, obedience becomes the prerequisite of love.[15] Southern accepts that Anselm's thesis could stand on its own with every trace of feudal imagery removed whilst also conceding that his arguments were nonetheless clearly colored by the social arrangements that surrounded him.[16] The point is that every theologian and every theology is de facto subject to environment, culture and worldview, with

---

12. Weaver, *Nonviolent Atonement*, 192.

13. Gorringe, *God's Just Vengeance*, 87.

14. Gunton, *Actuality of Atonement*, 89.

15. Ray, *Deceiving the Devil*, 35.

16. Southern, *Saint Anselm*, 221–22. He concludes that "the *Cur Deus Homo* was the product of a feudal and monastic world on the eve of a great transformation." Ibid., 222.

the corollary that each current atonement model is invariably adjudged by some in the following era to be defunct, redundant or worse.[17]

Consequentially, both subliminally and overtly the culturally extant, socially and theologically acceptable parameters within which understanding God's nature occurs inevitably take center-stage; necessarily dominating and subjugating all other modes of perception and interpretation. Belousek, for example, argues that the overriding paradigm in post-modern culture is that of retribution. It is this principle, he argues, that provides the rationale for an understanding of justice, capital punishment, just war and, theologically, for PSA.[18]

Rather, therefore, than endorsing a particular perspective on the atonement (or indeed on *any* theological position) because of a pre-held tradition or stance there must instead be awareness and engagement with the relevant issues and the context in which each era does its theology coupled with close consideration of what the theology is responding *to*. Certainly, the history of dogma and doctrine is not one without nuance and texture. In regard to the "Arian Controversy" of the fourth century, for example, Hanson concedes that this term itself is flawed and represents an over-simplification of both the theological debates and the historical context of the time. These caveats aside, he nonetheless acknowledges that the ideas of Arius, whether or not they explicitly found their genesis with him or not, forced the Christian Church and its theologians to address issues on both monotheism and the worship of Jesus as divine being, which might otherwise have remained unresolved.

> The theologians of the Christian Church were slowly driven to a realization that the deepest questions which face Christianity cannot be answered in purely biblical language, because the questions are about the meaning of the biblical language itself. In the course of this search the Church was impelled reluctantly to form dogma.[19]

Only when these concerns are properly acknowledged and addressed will it be possible to avoid jettisoning, in a wholesale manner, all that has gone before, wrongly ascribing all ancient theology to be terminally culture-bound and therefore redundant to a postmodern world, its sensibilities, and

17. Before presenting his ideas for the MIT Rashdall sets out his prolegomena, asserting that "it is, indeed, impossible that any educated person at the present day can really think of God and the universe exactly as was done by the men of the fourth century or of the thirteenth or of the sixteenth." Rashdall, *Idea of the Atonement*, vii.

18. Belousek, *Atonement, Justice and Peace*, 24–58.

19. Hanson, *Christian Doctrine*, xxi.

its worldview.[20] Even by the time Christianity was introduced into Black Africa in the fourth decade of the nineteenth century, for instance, the worldview of the Christian theologian retained only a veneer of the biblical worldview. It had become, according to Imasogie, a "quasi-scientific world-view" and whilst the Christian missionary might still mouth references to demon possession, angels and spiritual forces they did so with diminished emotional overtones.[21]

Instead of embracing such an unqualified bias for that which is perceived to be the new at the expense of the "old," acknowledgement must be made that history might, in fact, turn full circle in its perceptions; in this case—of the metaphysical. Consequently, older theological models might yet maintain relevance today in their means of understanding and expressing the atonement. More pertinently for our thesis is the further issue of God's nature and in particular the place of extrinsic violence in the divine economy; it might transpire to be that these "older models" have as much or even more theological and praxeological insight than when first posited. Boyd, for example, argues that in the majority of global cultures there is now an increasing appreciation and validation of what he calls the "commonsense" assumption that the world is not simply physical. There are now instead, he notes, fresh attempts at giving nonreductionistic interpretations to the nearly universal conviction that reality is both physical and spiritual, visible and invisible, and that these two dimensions are two sides of the same coin.[22]

So, theology has always necessarily been produced within an extant cultural context and worldview and also often appears in *response* to a particular party, perspective, issue or group of its day. Ferdinando, notes for example:

> Many Western interpreters have responded to Biblical demon-ology with attempts to contextualise it in such a way that it still has something to say within the rationalistic worldview. Such hermeneutical manoeuvres normally entail a reinterpretation of the language of demons such that its referents are understood in terms of tangible realities in the material world.[23]

20. As we have already considered in this thesis amongst various theologians and scholars including, for instance, Bultmann, Wink, and Girard.

21. Further, he notes that "on the intellectual level the theologian found it necessary to reinterpret them, at best, as symbols without ontic content or, at worst, as the figment of the imagination of a primitive age under the influence of an ancient world view." Imasogie, *Christian Theology in Africa*, 52.

22. Boyd, *God at War*, 63–64.

23. Ferdinando, "Screwtape Revisited," 105.

Rare, therefore, is the theological dictum that comes about in an initiating manner, merely through the desire of a particular theologian to embark upon theological speculation for its own sake. Instead, most, if not all, historic, orthodox Christian theology has emerged because of a pre-existing heterodoxy or worldview that required countering. There have, of course, been multifarious instances of this phenomenon; suffice it to allude to one representative case in the form of Newbigin's response to the secularism, pluralism and humanism he encountered in England on his return from cross-cultural missionary work in India. In delineating his method for engaging with these societal elements he asserts that "it is quite certain that long-established dogma only gives way to critical attack when that attack is based on some other beliefs. Criticism does not come out of a vacant mind."[24] This being the case, one of the pressing issues for Christian theology becomes the quest to ascertain what the current heterodoxy, worldview or issue is that must be engaged with, responded to and answered.

Each era or group of course has a natural, contextual propensity towards particular outlooks and outcomes, for instance, Twenty First Century America's favor of Capitalism and a Star Trek fan's preference for science fiction as a literary genre. In the same manner theologians, who are predominantly and stereotypically stylized as conservative, intelligent, literate, logical, male, academic, diligent, white and middle class (to name but a few generalizing traits) tend to favor a theological schema perceived as logical, consistent and juridical.

Gorringe argues, in fact, that from Anselm onwards satisfaction and sacrifice have been read together, and sacrifice has therefore been understood as propitiation. Even today, he contends, such a connection is felt by many Christians to be self-evident and thereby a testament to the power of the intellectual and emotional structures which have reinforced retributive theory.[25] Further, Ray notes in her panegyric to feminist thought and ideology that traditional Christian theology has been revealed to be androcentric and that

> beginning with the recognition that theological doctrines and
> traditions have been shaped almost exclusively by men, whose
> ideas and interpretations have been erroneously promoted
> as value-free and universally applicable, feminists and other
> contextual theologians have further noted that these ideas and
> interpretations inevitably reflect the experiences and interests

24. Newbigin, *Pluralist Society*, 1.
25. Gorringe, *God's Just Vengeance*, 29.

of their authors, who tend to be members of society's educated elite.[26]

Conversely, followers of the more metaphysical and, by implication, less academic Christus Victor model might equally then be characterized by said theologians as at best old-fashioned and caught in a long-distant worldview and at worst as subjective, sensual, non-theologians who are more interested in feelings, drama and subjective experiences than theological facts and theories. In his assessment of Aulén's understanding of New Testament language for that which holds humans in bondage and about the demonic in general Gunton, for example, concludes that the texts present the reader not with superhuman hypostases "trotting about the world," but rather with what he calls the metaphorical characterization of moral and cosmic realities which would otherwise defy expression.[27]

To counter such negative ascriptions, more credence should be given to those eras and theologians, both Jewish and Christian, who risked bloodshed and pain for their beliefs, thus forging their theology in a crucible of suffering, in response to victimization and attempted subjugation. Volf argues that it is slightly too arrogant to presume that contemporary sensibilities about what is compatible with God's love are so much healthier than those of the people of God throughout the whole history of Judaism and Christianity. He further contends that in a world of violence it would, in fact, not be worthy of God *not to wield* the sword; if God were *not angry* at injustice and deception and *did not* make the final end to violence, Volf concludes, God would not be worthy of human worship.[28] Volf's self-stated intention is not, therefore, to demonstrate that God's violence is unworthy of God, but rather that it is *beneficial* to humans.

Having a theology set in antiquity and forged in suffering does not, of course, in itself guarantee theological orthodoxy and yet it should at least earn the respect of an undoubtedly more privileged era of academic theologians. This might equate, quite simply, to the acceptance that it is arrogant to de facto cast historical theology aside in preference for contemporary theology with its distinct agendas and a primary desire to protect its denominational base. For example, some modern outlooks lead to predetermined representations of God and the atonement from the theological setting of predominantly non-violent and pacifistic frameworks.[29] Blumenthal notes

26. Ray, *Deceiving the Devil,* 19–20.

27. Gunton, *Actuality of Atonement,* 66.

28. Volf, *Exclusion and Embrace,* 303.

29. For example, it could be argued that it is more than coincidence that causes various contemporary Mennonite and Anabaptist theologians writing on the atonement

that the choice to erase certain biblical themes is, however, both necessary and inevitable for certain groups on what they see as "spiritual grounds." He cites the instance of the Quaker, Ellwood[30], who after compiling a group of violent biblical passages disavows them in an act of piety, claiming that ultimately for the Friends it is not the written page but the Light within that provides final authority on God and theology.[31] Such methodology, claiming that unpalatable actions cannot represent the true God or be scriptural is unsophisticated, suppressing the difficult side of both human and divine being and thereby the personalist image which, Blumenthal concludes, is the bond between God and humanity.[32]

On the contrary, instead of allowing any consideration to predetermine theological perspective and understanding it is our contention, especially in the context of such a contentious issue, that theology must let God be the God that the canonical Scriptures reveal regardless of any fallout or controversies engendered. An extreme representation of this methodology is proposed by Atlan who, in his consideration of referring to God in relation to the struggle against violence, concludes that it is perhaps more economical, indeed more effective and less dangerous, to refer to the God of violence rather than the God of love.[33] In stating the stark contrast between "the God of violence" and "the God of love" Atlan does not oppose the two, but rather uses the phrase "the God of violence" to refer to a God who takes upon himself what he calls the "founding violence" and is therefore not "entirely love" in relation to the world.[34]

In a similar, but less stark assertion, we therefore present God as One who is ontologically love, but crucially is both capable and willing to use and utilize extrinsic violence, even when this is against his best intention and desire when this is required; in the majority of biblical instances this will especially be manifest for his soteriological purposes. Boersma illustrates our contention:

> Violence can be a positive expression of love. But this is not
> to say that violence is so pervasive as to lie at the heart of the
> created order or of human culture. Human (as well as divine)

---

to arrive at non-violent conclusions. See, Belousek, *Atonement, Justice and Peace*; Grimsrud, *Instead of Atonement*; Neufeld, *Subversion of Violence*; Weaver, *Nonviolent Atonement*.

30. Ellwood, *Batter My Heart*.
31. Ibid., 13.
32. Blumenthal, *Facing the Abusing God*, 243.
33. Atlan, "Founding Violence," 206.
34. Ibid.

acts of hospitality may be characterized by the presence of some degree of violence, but these acts are still acts of hospitality as long as the violence is limited to that which is justifiable in the interest of the absolute hospitality of the eschatological future.[35]

The ends for Boersma, therefore, justify the means; whilst another attempt to square this theological circle of God's ontology of love and his use of extrinsic violence has come from feminist theologians who oppose traditional atonement models as being both male-orientated and supportive of abuse.[36] Critiquing this perspective it has been observed that their argument is not expanded with biblical scholarship, background in cultic theology, metaphorical appropriation of cultic images or any history of the phases of doctrinal development.[37] Feminist appeals of this kind, it is contended, are thereby not enough on their own to provide grounds for a new theology; it is instead necessary to give a sustained account of how and why these doctrines originally emerged. Strong biblical scholarship is therefore needed and the case against traditional atonement cannot be argued with ethical instincts alone, otherwise there is little mooring or depth to the new theologizing.[38]

Ironically, in his judgments Finlan utilizes the very methods he condemns, pre-concluding that the RCVM is a "crazy-making" theology leading to a false representation of God's "true" character whilst producing suicidal saints and rage-dominated parental figures who think they are helping their children by beating them.[39] Any theologian claiming to be consistent to a clarion call to Good Theology, however, needs to be cautious about ascribing any atonement model as "unpalatable" in such an a priori manner. Instead, it is irrelevant whether a particular theology or doctrine is perceived to be unpalatable or difficult; Christian theology does not have to pass human tests of acceptability in order to be deemed orthodox. Rather, as argued against some feminist theologians, what is required is a vigorous process of appropriate research and an unwillingness to give in to emotional agendas or a priori positions.

Perhaps both of these charges can be made against Spence who, in his critique of a soteriological model based on victory and power, as seen in CVM, concludes that conversely the notion of biblical peace has to do

---

35. Boersma, *Violence, Hospitality and the Cross*, 144–45.

36. Brown and Parker, "God So Loved," 1–30.

37. Finlan, *Problems with Atonement*, 104.

38. Ibid.

39. Further, such an outlook, Finlan argues, makes God "either weak or cruel, either easily manipulated or corrupt." Finlan, *Options on Atonement*, 87.

with reconciliation with God, between humans and with creation. His own understanding of the biblical evidence facilitates what he argues to be the sort of peace that is brought about by a mediator not a SWAT team, or rather one whose holocaust has the fragrance of a lamb-offering rather than the smell of cordite.[40]

A process of this kind, however, does not and must not de facto disallow linking extrinsic violence with a God who has, as we have demonstrated, long endorsed, embraced and utilized it, both in a cosmic and historical context. A corollary of this perspective, which has in fact become the prolegomena, is the focus not on whether God has extrinsic violence as an element of his being, but rather what consequences might follow for humans who, as a result of their view of divine violence, seek to thereby endorse violence or use it themselves. In a modern representation of this argument, Northey makes a claim against Boersma's argument.[41] Boersma, Northey contends, introduces into his reading of the atonement a concept of "violence at the boundaries" which, Northey argues, is simply not evident in the founding texts.[42] Northey then concludes:

> If violence is the ultimate addiction of the human race, Boersma with most of his Reformed and Western theological colleagues would not join Violence Anonymous—or the church!—to learn the ways and practices of abstention from it.[43]

This concern that an advocation of divine violence will potentially cause human violence and perhaps especially Christian violence, has been prevalent for many centuries. It has, in fact, caused some to jettison the notion or potential of divine violence for fear of the praxeological ramifications that might be incurred. In his assessment of the Church in relation to Knights and chivalry in the medieval period Kaeuper notes that it was both sheer necessity as well as intellectual heritage which gave the medieval Church a tradition of ideas which opposed some but not all violence; further, he claims, even within Christendom none could doubt that the evils inherent in an imperfect world would require the use of armed force in their solution, as they always had.[44] Certainly a Church which embraces, to one degree or another, the notion and potential advocation of violence is poten-

---

40. Spence, *Promise of Peace*, 115. His conclusion is that an advocation of the CVM will leave humanity "with a somewhat bleak prospect, reminiscent of one that is forever winter and never Christmas." Ibid., 116.

41. As presented in his *Violence, Hospitality and the Cross*.

42. Northey, "God's Peace Work," 366.

43. Ibid., 370.

44. Kaeuper, *Chivalry and Violence*, 63.

tially open to being used as a wing of the secular state in its desire to resolve difficult issues. Kaeuper concedes that whilst clerical theory accepted violence for right causes and not for wrong it remains a distinction that is tricky to make at the best of times, and especially so in an imperfect world.[45]

This is undoubtedly a controversial theological issue and a conclusion is not to be entered into lightly or without due diligence to biblical and historical evidence; remaining conscious, but not led by, potential praxeological consequences that such opinions might incur. The biblical witness to a violent God, albeit extrinsic violence, has nonetheless often been used to encourage and justify innumerable human acts of violence not least, for instance, that perpetrated in the current so-called "war on terror."[46] This corollary cannot be overlooked and yet neither can it be allowed to hold primary influence, thereby adversely affecting the formulation and structure of a theological position—especially not in an a priori manner.

Indeed, in regard to an adherent's praxeology the three primary monotheistic world religions (Christianity, Islam and Judaism) have at their core a religious metaphor grown into a psychological archetype that legitimates violence in the grossest imaginable forms, justifying it on the grounds of divine order and behavior.[47] Nelson-Pallmeyer observes that violence-of-God traditions are, in fact, the very heart of the Bible, representing an "elephant in the room" of which nobody dares speak.[48] For there to be progress in understanding the truth of such a controversial issue the Church and theology have to be forthright,[49] battles of old re-examined and perhaps re-fought, especially in regard to the atonement and God's nature, including violence and the purpose and perception of a dualistic worldview.

Once theology has re-presented its beliefs on Jesus Christ, the man from Nazareth, crucified under Pontius Pilate and the cornerstone of Christian faith it must demonstrate the praxeological consequences of these outlooks. Moltmann asserts that throughout history the crucified Christ challenges Christian theology and the Church which dares to call itself by his name.[50] In re-considering ancient atonement theories, divine violence and the reappraisal of the ontological nature of evil and the demonic realm, the challenge for theology is all-encompassing and culturally pertinent.

45. Ibid., 91

46. Young, *Violence of God*, 1.

47. Ellens, "Religious Metaphors," 270.

48. Nelson-Pallmeyer, *Is Religion Killing Us?*, xiv.

49. In the face of such challenges Moltmann believes that the Church must come out from "behind an alien mask drawn from history and the present time." Moltmann, *Crucified God*, 3.

50. Ibid.

The Church and its theology therefore continually face choices as to whether their perspectives will be defined primarily by modern sensibilities or by the biblical record and historical theology. So, it should be noted that whilst modern sensibilities might baulk at affirming the ontological reality of the Satan and the demonic realm the New Testament does not share these concerns. Indeed, Bell claims that the New Testament assumes that the devil "exists" every bit as much as it assumes that God "exists."[51] More in keeping with the extant "received wisdom" of Western Christian theology, however, Cupitt, in an open letter to the Archbishops, Bishops and members of the General Synod of the Church of England celebrates what he calls the "liberation of mankind" from demonological and similar beliefs, which since the Reformation and the rise of modern science has been a great blessing.[52]

In such a theological context, non-violent doctrines can de facto appear more appealing than violent ones and are thereby pursued as a "best choice" to avoid the kind of "challenges" that Moltmann regales.[53] An a priori irenic and non-violent route therefore prioritizes palatability and accessibility above the content of a doctrine. Finlan argues, for instance, that if the Gospel could be communicated without violent metaphors, there may be people who will receive this message with joy, whose faith will be reborn.[54] Undoubtedly, some would embrace such a Gospel—conversely others, however, would reject it on the same terms. The issue, therefore, must not primarily be one of popularity, presentation and palatability, but of actuality.

In his consideration of the quest to achieve an attractive and plausible rationale of human interaction with the world in language and to avoid the choice between "objectivist" and "subjectivist" epistemologies, Gunton concludes:

> That is not to deny, however, that a choice of some kind is required, for it must be true that, finally, we are either talking about something beyond the structures of the human mind or we are not. We may see the world through such structures and with their assistance, but unless it is *the world* we see, our position is finally completely subjectivist or even solipsist.[55]

51. Bell, *Deliver Us from Evil*, 2.

52. Cupitt, *Explorations in Theology*, 6, p. 51.

53. Belousek argues that the cross of Christ demonstrates "not simply nonviolence, but God's retribution-transcending, sinner-redeeming, enemy-reconciling love, justice, and peace." Belousek, *Atonement, Justice and Peace*, 73.

54. Finlan, *Problems with Atonement*, 120.

55. Gunton, *Actuality of Atonement*, 40–41.

Therefore, whether people will be better disposed towards the message should never be the defining concern as to how theology is approached in terms of understanding and defining the Gospel. There is always a danger in "letting go" of certain doctrines and beliefs[56] but there is the further hazard of redefining theology or the biblical record in order to match and appeal to extant cultural liberal sensibilities.

Another problem causing interpretative labors to explain away the characterization of God as a divine being linked with extrinsic violence is the increasing awareness of the abusive character of religion itself in the name of God.[57] This is an understandable consideration and yet one that ultimately remains irrelevant to the ascription of attributes to God; it is primarily concerned with modern cultural mores and of their being erroneously and anachronistically placed into ancient biblical perspectives.

Žižek challenges this kind of practice in his observations on the contemporary perception of mercy, turning the argument of anti-death penalty advocates around who claim that it is an act of arrogance to punish or kill other human beings. Instead, he argues that what is truly arrogant and sinful is to assume the prerogative of mercy. Who amongst ordinary mortals, he reflects, especially those who are not the culprit's immediate victim, has the right to erase another's crime or to treat it with leniency. He contends that such a role can only be fulfilled by God and that only he can erase another's guilt, concluding that the duty of humans is to act according to the logic of justice and to punish crime. In fact, *not* to do so entails what he calls the true blasphemy of elevating oneself to the level of God, of being seen to act with his authority.[58] Žižek therefore ignores current social perceptions and mores, instead reaffirming the primacy of God's timeless authority over contemporary human concerns, issues and cultural outlooks.

In response to this argument that there might be a correspondence between divine action and human behavior Volf counters that the thesis has one small but fatal flaw: humans are not God; he further notes,

> There is a duty prior to the duty of imitating God, and that is the duty of *not wanting to be God*, of letting God be God and humans be humans. Without such a duty guarding the divinity of God the duty to imitate God would be empty because our concept of God would be nothing more than the mirror image of ourselves.[59]

---

56. See Finlan, *Problems with Atonement*, 120–21.

57. Brueggemann, *Divine Presence*, 12–13.

58. Žižek, *Violence*, 193–94.

59. Volf, *Exclusion and Embrace*, 301.

The proposition that God entertains or utilizes power, force and extrinsic violence certainly has profound and far-reaching praxeological implications for Christian and Church.[60] It is important to recognize with Turner therefore the difference between Christian passivism and Christian pacifism.[61] This is also true of God, who on innumerable occasions intervenes in history in a demonstrative and sometimes violent manner, to protect those who cannot protect themselves. Turner therefore concurs with Žižek when concluding that "to surrender our rights is one thing, to surrender the rights of others is to surrender what it is not ours to give."[62] Mayhew further observes that force may indeed lead to violence, neither of which will, themselves, build up the kingdom of God. On the other hand, he argues that a failure to use force may lead to cruel repression rather than to God's kingdom; the great offence against human and Christian values, according to Mayhew, and which may require Christians and others to employ force is therefore injustice.[63]

Whether a particular theological position might or might not lead to negative praxeology has, however, no bearing whatsoever on the search for God's nature and functions. This remains a concern, however, for Juergensmeyer who addresses the affect that theological perspectives have on those with an agenda of violence. He asserts that for those ascribing violence to God there is no need to compromise an individual's goals in a struggle that has been waged in divine time and with the promise of heaven's rewards. There is also no need, he argues, to contend with society's laws and limitations when one is obeying a higher authority; in spiritualizing violence, he concludes, religion has given terrorism a remarkable power.[64]

60. "The Christian cannot simply accept power naively as merely an obvious existential of human existence. For it exists *either* as the embodiment of sin, egoism, rebellion against God and the worldly impatience of unbelief, which refuses to accept the promised glory simply as eschatological gift of the power of God, but uses its own might—and hence inevitably brutality and cruelty—to try to force that glory down into this aeon itself and bring it under its laws; *or* it exists as the effort of faith which knows that power is always unreliable and unrewarding, but accepts it obediently as a task from God, as long as he wills." Rahner, *Theological Investigations*, 4:409.

61. He adds a caveat to the subject of non-resistance to evil, observing that, "Christians should always seek to do something better than force. They are not entitled to do nothing at all in the presence of giant evils. If they cannot see any better solution at a given moment than the use of force, then they must use this in shame and penitence rather than contract out of doing something. To contract out of situations is not to obey the law of love. Pacifism may be one thing, passivism is quite another." Turner, *Jesus Master and Lord*, 326.

62. Ibid., 325–26.

63. Mayhew, *Theology of Force*, 7.

64. Juergensmeyer, *Terror in the Mind of God*, 221.

Whilst these concerns are real we nonetheless contend that a theology primarily born out of extant human outlooks, concerns and considerations would be a great deal worse than worthless, defined by emotions rather than biblical evidence, by feelings and fears rather than by theological outlooks and evidence. If it is therefore concluded that God's nature incorporates violence this must be expressed with no attendant attempt to re-define him and his character in a manner more acceptable or palatable for those preferring a gentler, kinder and more "safe" God. Instead, theology must be articulated in terms of what is *found* and not led by any a priori agendas and perspectives that are *brought*. This will curtail the current desire or inclination to re-model him, his character or his purposes in terms which might be perceived to be more pleasant, expedient and comfortable for a post-modern audience.

In a chapter entitled "Defending God's Behavior in the Old Testament," Siebert notes, before assessing the various means that have been presented, that one of the primary reasons so many people find God's behavior in the Old Testament unsettling is because it does not conform to their fundamental beliefs about God as being good, loving and fair; going on to ask whether these beliefs about God are actually unwarranted or, at least, overstated—concluding that it might actually be the case that God is both good *and* bad, just *and* unjust, loving *and* abusive.[65]

On another issue that might be difficult for some to consider, let alone accept, Boyd asks whether such a modern audience might find it too much to consider the possibility that angels and one fallen angel in particular might be centrally relevant to understanding evil in the world. He argues that, in fact, it is not asking too much and neither is it apologetically disastrous.

> To the contrary, in this present climate such a postmodern (and yet biblical) approach will, if anything, be prima facie judged by many as inherently compelling. Far from being a liability, the supernatural dimension within the warfare worldview may increasingly be one of its strongest apologetic features. Indeed, it is likely that future theologies and theodicies that persist in operating within the narrow structures of modern Western naturalistic categories will increasingly find themselves irrelevant to Western minds.[66]

Our conclusion is that God is and has always been embroiled in extrinsic violence and necessarily so, since without it there would be no possibility of him overcoming a definitively, and perhaps even ontologically,

---

65. Siebert, *Disturbing Divine Behavior*, 60–71.

66. Boyd, *God at War*, 63.

violent adversary in the Satan.[67] Just as Adolf Hitler and the Third Reich[68] would not have been placated and defeated by love, good will and committees, so the Satan would not be defeated by love alone, but only by a forceful, robust and irresistible love that manifests itself in the bloody, gory, violent and victorious death of Jesus Christ.[69]

We have shown it to be incontrovertible that God has, throughout history, demonstrated his reluctant willingness to do whatever is necessary, culturally intelligible and appropriate in order to fulfill his purposes. In the Old Testament this meant responding with explicit but extrinsic violence in a culture drenched in blood and inculcated in war. Indeed, in his assessment of God's activities in the Old Testament, Gibson notes of the examples he cites of God behaving "very unpleasantly indeed," that he has simply spelt out what the text itself says. He claims to have not read anything into the stories that is not already there; concluding that the only way to make these Scriptures acceptable to modern perceptions of God is to do "quite a bit of doctoring."[70]

Further, in the New Testament Jesus is seen to overtly and violently confront both religious authorities and spiritual powers and principalities. The same word is used to both expel demons and to expel those in the Temple, Hauck observing that when ἐκβάλλειν is used in the New Testament it has the sense of "to expel" or "to repel," especially in the case of demons, who have settled in men as in a house into which they have unlawfully penetrated.[71] Jesus' confrontation with demonic forces was, therefore, a direct power-encounter; ultimately between God and the Satan constituting, by definition, an act of warfare and therefore violence.

In a similar fashion, Jesus' act in expelling, or throwing out, those in the Temple who would otherwise have wanted to stay, is an expulsion which, as we have demonstrated, was directly against their best interests and, tellingly, also against their volition. It should therefore be considered de facto as a

67. In the context of the biblical quote that "the reason the Son of God appeared was to destroy the devil's work" (1 John 3:8), Green states, "I believe the Christian doctrines of God, of man and of salvation are utterly untenable without the existence of Satan. You simply cannot write him out of the story and then imagine that the story is basically unchanged." Green, *Satan's Downfall*, 20.

68. In fact, Gunton notes, "There have been times in history when it appears that whole societies have been in a kind of moral slavery, as is often said to have been the case with Hitler's Germany." Gunton, *Actuality*, 73.

69. "Divine violence is not always opposed to divine hospitality but may well be a suitable instrument in ascertaining the hope of the entire cosmos being embraced by the hospitable love of God." Boersma, *Violence, Hospitality and the Cross*, 201.

70. Gibson, *Language and Imagery*, 24.

71. Hauck, "βαλλω," 527.

violent act. If indeed Jesus' encounters with the Satan are violent, so are his actions in the Temple Incident; both of which find their ultimate conclusion in God's violent overcoming and defeat of the Satan at the cross.[72]

This thesis has argued that it would be both futile and impossible to overcome an ontologically violent and evil being with anything less than irresistible force. Further, in the eschaton Jesus the Messiah will return, framed in violent concepts and imagery, to herald an eternity of peace, love and non-violence. Indeed, in answer to the question as to who should be engaged in separating the darkness from the light and who should finally exercise violence against the "beast" and the "false prophet" Volf posits that echoing the whole New Testament, the Apocalypse mentions only God.[73] Certainly this theme of holy war plays a prominent role in Jewish eschatological expectation with the future bringing the final victory of the divine Warrior over his enemies and over the enemies of his people. The tradition of an eschatological or messianic holy war, according to Bauckham, can be divided into two forms, one in which the victory is won by God alone or by God and his heavenly armies and another in which God's people play an active part in physical warfare against their enemies.[74] Either way it is, to say the least, rather a violent prospect.

Until then, violence continues to exist, exerting and manifesting itself through sin, the flesh and the Satan as a means of power, protection and of achieving desired ends; a non-violent God seeking to confound and still such violence would have been doomed to failure. Instead, a God with an element of severity is required, a concept often neglected but which prevents thinking of God in a manner akin to a doting grandparent or a celestial Santa Claus figure. Volf critiques such an outlook noting that many people think of God in this way, as merely a Santa Claus conveniently enlarged to divine proportions. He concludes that such a "Santa Claus God" demands nothing from us; a divine Santa is the indiscriminately giving and inexhaustibly fertile source of everything that is, and everything that is to come our way.[75] On the other hand, the idea of a necessary divine severity rightly preserves genuine moral *gravitas*, particularly righteousness, in God and in God's vigorous dealings with humans.[76]

---

72. "A biblical perspective requires a relative cosmic dualism that affirms real warfare, both in Christ's life and in ours, while at the same time insisting on ultimate divine sovereignty." Boersma, *Violence, Hospitality and the Cross*, 200.

73. Volf, *Exclusion and Embrace*, 301.

74. Bauckham, *Climax of Prophecy*, 210.

75. Volf, *Free of Charge*, 27.

76. Moser, *Severity*, 38.

An element of these "vigorous dealings" is seen in several strands of first-century Judaism where Israel expected either to fight a crucial war or battle, or perhaps to have her God fight it on her behalf—or perhaps, in some traditions, to have the Messiah fight it for her.[77] Anyone telling a new story about this kingdom has to include this as one element, whether in the form of the battle for the "human" to stay alive under the tyranny of the "beasts" (which story could be translated into other imagery, such as the lion waging war against the eagle), the struggle for Yahweh's righteous victory to be won against the evil hordes that ranged themselves against him and his people or the war of the children of light against the children of darkness, or in some other form.[78]

Further, in Patristic atonement models, the Divine Drama is pulsating with the tension and conflict of the Great Battle; it is ironic that when soteriology was put on the map in the eleventh century much of this drama was lost.[79] The newly-adopted PSA view brought with it an almost exclusive focus on Jesus' death on the cross as the substitutionary means. It should be noted, however, that Anselm himself, in the delineation of his theological position on atonement does not highlight substitution but rather satisfaction. This is seen explicitly in *Cur Deus Homo* where, for example, chapter 20 is entitled, "That the Satisfaction should be Proportionate to the Transgression, Nor can Man Make it for himself."[80]

The PSA position, however, represents a means by which God exercised his soteriological purposes with the central doctrine of the atonement, according to Nicole, being in the substitutionary interposition of a sin-bearer who absorbs in himself the fearful burden of the divine wrath against human sin and secures a renewal of access to God and of the reception of his grace. This is a process which, he argues, was figuratively foreshadowed in the Old Testament sacrifices and was then factually accomplished in one all-sufficient and effective sacrifice of the God-man, Jesus Christ, on Calvary; Nicole concludes that substitutionary sacrifice is therefore the fundamental basis of the whole process of salvation according to Scripture.[81]

The CVM, on the other hand, whilst incorporating the cross into its schema, does so in the broader context of the whole birth, life, teachings,

---

77. In the crucifixion, according to Wright, what occurs "is the extraordinary story of Israel's Messiah taking upon himself the Accuser's sharpest arrow and, dying under its force, robbing the Accuser of any further real power." Wright, *Simply Jesus*, 185.

78. Wright, *Victory of God*, 448–49.

79. Walker, *Enemy Territory*, 40.

80. Anselm, *Cur Deus Homo*, 47.

81. Nicole, "Penal Substitution," 446.

death and resurrection of Jesus.[82] The corollary of this more expansive position is that instead of abstract juridical propositions about Jesus as seen in PSA and, indeed, in many if not most of the ancient creeds which leave out huge swathes of Jesus' life and ministry in their proclamation of theological "truth." It is noted of the Apostle's Creed, for instance, that in the teaching of the Christian faith it is used as the *framework* for the teacher's exposition; when used in this way, according to Wiles, it is however more like a syllabus to be worked at than a set of propositions known to be true and calling only for expansion and clarification.[83] The CVM, on the other hand, incorporates the *whole* of the story and the *whole* of the drama.[84] It represents, therefore, a more inclusive and less esoteric understanding of both ontology and soteriology and thereby a more dramatic and expansive view of God, his nature, character, purposes and desires.

Therefore, according to Aulén, not only is Christ's work not limited to the cross but it is rather an event that continues to have an effect, even to the present day. Aulén asserts that the note of triumph which rings through what he calls this "Greek theology" depends not only on the victory of Christ over death accomplished once and for all, but also on the fact that his victory is the starting-point for his present work in the world of men, where He, through his Spirit, ever triumphantly continues to break down sin's power and "deifies" men.[85] In addition, Küng describes Jesus as one not concerned with observing the Torah for its own sake but one who was rather interested in the ongoing well-being of actual individuals. It was, in fact, this freer attitude to the law and his dealings with those who were ignorant of it, or who indeed broke it, Küng argues, which led to such serious confrontations.[86] The point is that Jesus is here portrayed as the very antithesis of one who is intent on primarily upholding or promulgating a juridical doctrine.

82. "As far as Christian faith is concerned, everything depends on the actualisation of divine love in the work of atonement and salvation. Or, in other words, Christ has brought the divine love into the world through his life, suffering, sacrifice, and victory." Aulén, *Christian Church*, 221. Aulén concludes that "the incarnation is perfected on the cross." Ibid., 221.

83. Wiles, "Creeds," 146.

84. For Boyd, "Jesus' life, death and resurrection cannot be separated from each other, not even theoretically. Whereas other models of the atonement," he argues, "tend to isolate the meaning of Jesus' death from other aspects of his life, the Christus Victor model . . . sees every aspect of Christ life [sic]—from his incarnation to his resurrection—as being most fundamentally *about one thing*: victoriously manifesting the loving kingdom of God over and against the destructive, oppressive kingdom of Satan." Boyd, "Christus Victor View," 39–40.

85. Aulén, *Christus Victor*, 44.

86. Küng, *Apostle's Creed*, 77.

When Jesus, for example, prepared his followers for the final, previously unimagined, vision of the crucifixion, the many strands of story, symbol and meaning are woven together so that it is difficult to follow a single thread without acknowledging how tightly it concurrently belongs to all the others.[87] The importance of recognizing the character of each of the interpretative options as metaphorical assertions and the danger of promoting any one at the expense of another has been noted. The metaphor, after all, is not the thing but an essential means of expressing the thing's meaning, which can be extrapolated to the proposition that pushing metaphors too far leads to the unhelpful practice of translating them into literal facts.[88]

The issue remains, however, that unless a metaphor is linked to the reality it represents in a meaningful manner it will be of no final, definitive worth.[89] In addition, without a critical mass of correspondence the metaphor itself is open to laissez-faire, subjective, and existentialist metaphorical construction that ignores the limits or parameters as to the metaphor's suitability of use in a particular situation.

> Our understanding of metaphor depends on our knowledge of the presupposition pool of the creator of the metaphor, and is further enhanced by the availability of a cotext from which the purpose of the metaphor might be deduced. Metaphorical language is like any other manifestation of real language in that it is to be understood only in a context.[90]

In other words, whilst the metaphor is, indeed, not the thing being represented it remains, by definition, the only means by which finite language and image-bound humans can even begin to express transcendent reality.[91] As such, the metaphor, as we have seen, becomes a great deal more than "mere" and instead takes on an ontological link with that which it is expressing. So, until the thing can be "grasped" in any kind of literal sense, then the metaphor is not only the next best thing available, but it is rather the *only* thing available. Indeed, for Urban, reality is, in a sense, doubtless

87. Wright, *Simply Jesus*, 175.

88. Dunn, *Theology of Paul*, 231.

89. "Human language may be inherently metaphorical and may thus require a humble epistemology, but this does not mean that there is no objective world that can, in some indirect fashion, be interpreted. In other words, while our language and interpretative process are necessarily metaphorical, the created order itself is not." Boersma, *Violence, Hospitality and the Cross*, 106.

90. Cotterell and Turner, *Linguistics*, 301.

91. "It is perhaps conceivable that we may have a direct apprehension or intuition of life, but the meaning of life can be neither apprehended nor expressed except in language of some kind." Urban, *Language and Reality*, 21.

beyond language, as he argues that Plato felt so deeply, and yet he nonetheless contends that whilst reality cannot be wholly grasped in its forms, it remains unwise to seek to abandon linguistic forms, because then, he concludes, reality, much like quicksilver, will run through our fingers.[92]

Gunton notes,

> The key to the relation between language and world is something we have met already, its *indirectness*. The world can be known only indirectly, and therefore metaphor, being indirect, is the most appropriate form that a duly humble and listening language should take. In all this, there is a combination of openness and mystery, speech and silence, which makes the clarity and distinctness aimed at by the rationalist tradition positively hostile to the truth. Thus the tables are turned: metaphor, rather than being the Cinderella of cognitive language, becomes the most, rather than the least, appropriate means of expressing the truth. If, then, we are to be true to the way things are in our world we must see metaphor as the most, not the least, significant part of our language.[93]

If priority is to be given to a particular atonement model, a viable way of doing so might be in regard to how the metaphor explicates, amongst other issues, an overarching image and understanding of God, his purposes and character, of humanity and its specific situation and needs and of the Satan, his role and plans and of the cosmos as a whole in the eternal, metaphysical realm. This said, we choose the CVM as the one which most effectively addresses and answers the greatest number of them; atonement has always been a vehicle for conveying information about salvation and the Incarnation but there are, of course, many other vehicles, the best of which, as Finlan has already noted, might yet be a very old one.[94]

A key area of emphasis in comparing the most ancient with the relatively newer atonement models is that a central characteristic of the so-called objective models is their "Godward" focus.[95] Alternatively, there is a marked "Satanward" thrust in the CVM which might, at first glance, present the PSA view as more appropriate and desirable in its explicit theocentricity; exactly opposite, however, is the case. Whilst it is true that the "objective" models place God at their center this importance is focused

92. Ibid., 49.

93. Gunton, *Actuality of Atonement*, 37–38.

94. Finlan, *Problems with Atonement*, 120.

95. Boyd, "Christus Victor View," 14.

on perceived needs within Godself for appeasement or satisfaction.[96] Put
crudely: a needy God demands his due before he can deal with wayward humans. For Weaver, this means that regardless of how the satisfaction theory
of atonement is defended there is, in fact, no consensus amongst scholars
on how to do so. Instead he argues that amidst their "diverse and mutually
contradictory strategies," is the indication that the preeminent concern of
such writers is more to defend satisfaction by any means available than to
ask whether satisfaction atonement truly reflects biblical understandings of
the life and work of Christ.[97] This is the case even when the view of God's
nature engendered by such a defense is almost entirely at odds with their
previously perceived notions of God's love and mercy.

In the CVM, however, whilst the thrust is nominally towards the Devil
it nonetheless leads to a rather different perception of God as One who is so
desperate to win back and to win over lost humans that he will do whatever
it takes to achieve this end.[98] In this sense, in both the RCVM and the later
CVM the central focus and thrust is neither God nor the Satan but is instead
towards an otherwise helpless and captive Humankind. It would, however,
according to Wright, require conflict to overcome humanity's gaoler—a
battle to defeat a powerful enemy.

So whether it is the Sermon on the Mount in Matthew 5–7 or the
Nazareth Manifesto in Luke 4; or a consideration of what Wright calls the
strange language about "binding the strong man" in Matthew 12 or the even
stranger language about the "coming of the son of man"; wherever we look,
he argues, it appears that Jesus was aware of a great battle in which he was
already involved and that would, before too long, reach some kind of climax.[99] Wright concludes that whilst the Bible is never precise about the
exact identity of this figure, this enemy of God, it was "the Satan" whom the
biblical writers had in mind as the one Jesus was ultimately fighting against.

Not primarily, therefore, a God needing reparation, nor a Devil requiring payment but a Humanity requiring saving *from* an Evil Enemy and a
God willing to pay ANY price imaginable to secure them, including the

96. "God is revealed by the cross as one who bears the power of the demonic rather
than punishes those who have fallen into its power." Gunton, *Actuality of Atonement*,
84.

97. Weaver, *Nonviolent Atonement*, 195.

98. In his overview of atonement models Neufeld concedes that in the biblical account "there are clear instances where being saved or liberated means being freed from
the captivity to sin, or of death, or of the 'evil one' or the devil. However the captor is
identified, such captivity is envisioned as humanity being both culpable and helpless in
captivity, and thus in need of rescue." Neufeld, *Subversion of Violence*, 88.

99. Wright, *Simply Jesus*, 117.

endorsement and use of extrinsic violence—a message, in fact, of sacrificial Good News. For Aulén therefore, the point of emphasis is clear:

> In the classic type the work of the Atonement is accomplished by God Himself in Christ . . . He is reconciled only because He Himself reconciles the world with Himself and Himself with the world. The safeguard of the continuity of God's operation is the dualistic outlook, the Divine warfare against the evil that holds mankind in bondage, and the triumph of Christ. But this necessitates a discontinuity of the legal order: there is no satisfaction of God's justice, for the relation of man to God is viewed in the light, not of merit and justice, but of grace.[100]

The point to reiterate with this conclusion, however, is that God is not an angry or violent God per se and therefore certainly does not have or use violence in a manner intrinsic to his being. Rather both his wrath and punishment are extrinsic and reserved for those who actually deserve it—not for those, like his innocent Son, who do not. Ellens, for example, whilst noting that defenders of PSA utilize "sentimental and well-frosted theological terms" in order to turn substitutionary atonement into a "remarkable act of grace," concludes that within such a model, the only way for God to "get his head screwed back on right" is to kill somebody, whether humans or Christ.[101] Further, as Hanson notes, God's punishment is not retributory, but it is reformatory, remedial and deterrent. God does not therefore, according to Hanson, punish in anger and he is never angry with anyone. In fact, Hanson asserts that what he calls the "nightmare" of such an angry God should be exorcised from our thinking.[102]

So, God does exhibit extrinsic, functional violence and confrontation, battle and the ultimate defeat of any who stand against him and against those he loves, this violence is manifest, in particular, against the Satan and on behalf of humans—in other words, those who truly and eternally deserve God's wrath, violence and anger get it in order to implement the liberation of those who are the center of his affection and purposes—human beings.[103]

The PSA model should, then, be caricatured as an inherently "Religious View" upholding, as it does, central notions of the Old Testament and the Judaic Cultus, indeed in large measure fulfilling and completing them.

100. Aulén, *Christus Victor*, 145–46.
101. Ellens, "Religious Metaphors," 263.
102. Hanson, "Grace and the Wrath of God," 151.
103. For those endorsing the CVM, "clearly the issues of violence take on a very different hue. It is the 'violence' of the divine response to the primal violence of the powers holding humanity in their grip." Neufeld, *Subversion of Violence*, 84.

Whatever atonement symbol is preferred it must have original relevance, application and meaning to those who first witnessed and sought to apply the truths of Christ's death and resurrection. Marshall, whilst looking at Paul's interpretative methodology, considers the "atoning deaths" of Israelites in 4 Maccabees and notes that Paul interprets the sin-bearing death of Jesus in terms of the Jewish cult, in the same kind of way as martyrdom was interpreted as sacrificial; there is, he concludes, nothing incongruous about the apparent shift from forensic imagery to sacrificial imagery.[104]

Conversely, the CVM is a grand, sweeping meta-narrative favoring a comparatively "non-religious" view of God and humanity—spiritual yes, religious no.[105] The God of PSA is stiff, angular, officious, unyielding, interested in the minutiae of law and its application rather than the spirit which the law embodies, he is fascinated by, endorses and encourages religion and personal satisfaction at all costs. Green has further concerns with the penal substitution theory and after flagging the potential breakdown in God's perichoretic union he states that he is unsure how the model generates transformed life as it is focused, he argues, on the individual, on forensic judgment and on the moment of justification. He also speculates as to how such a model can keep from undermining any emphasis on salvation as transformation as well as obscuring the social and cosmological dimensions of salvation.[106]

The God of Christus Victor, on the other hand, is presented as One who is accessible, powerful, purposeful and interested more in people than in elements of law. Overall, we contend that the God revealed in the Old Testament is represented as One who can be more closely and readily aligned with Penal Substitution while the God of Christus Victor better represents the God found in the New Testament, manifest in the person of Jesus Christ.[107]

---

104. Marshall, *Aspects of Atonement*, 44. Conversely, Girard contends that "there is nothing in the Gospels to suggest that the death of Jesus is a sacrifice, whatever definition (expiation, substitution, etc.) we may give for that sacrifice. At no point in the Gospels is the death of Jesus defined as a sacrifice. The passages that are invoked to justify a sacrificial conception of the Passion both can and should be interpreted with no reference to sacrifice in any of the accepted meanings." Girard, *Things Hidden*, 180.

105. "This view of the atonement is both highly supernaturalistic while at the same time maintaining that the drama of the atonement was played out on a historical plane. In this cosmology, there is inter-penetration between the levels of the cosmos." Rieger, "Good News," 381.

106. Green, "Kaleidoscopic Response," 114.

107. On whether God has to keep his own commands and is a supporter or enemy of the sacrificial system, see Finlan, *Problems with Atonement*, 94–96. He asks, "Is it not bitterly ironic and contradictory to have God opposing sacrifice all along but utilizing

Each atonement model, as we have shown, leads to particular praxe-ological consequences, imperatives and outlooks both for those embracing them and for those receiving the message. In fact, Ray argues that what is at stake in the endeavor to understand atonement is the moral authority of Christianity itself. She argues that unless Christians can find ways to effec-tively articulate in this day and age their faith in a God who liberates from evil then they will, in fact, have no good news for today's world.[108]

To illustrate this expression of good news and its praxeological cor-ollary, in the theatre, *methexis* is presented and understood as a form of "group sharing" in which the audience participates, creates and improvises the action of the ritual; traditionally it is concerned with a sharing of be-ing and knowledge in the Divine.[109] This posits an intriguing notion of the *involvement* required in salvation—an involvement that finds its supreme expression in the CVM as an integral element of an overall *heilsgeschichte* in which, by definition, the subject is inclusive and *active* in the over-arching "narrative curve" of God's unfolding salvation story and purposes.[110]

Not the witnesses and recipients of an ancient judicial transaction but players and participants in which the subjects transcend the role of "making up an audience." Rather, this is how Jesus puts his kingdom-achievement into operation:

> . . . through the humans he has rescued. That is why, right at
> the start of his public career, he called associates to share his
> work and then to carry it on after he had laid the foundations,
> particularly in his saving death. It has been all too easy for us
> to suppose that, if Jesus really was king of the world, he would,
> as it were, do the whole thing by himself. But that was never
> his way—because it was never God's way. It wasn't how creation
> itself was supposed to work. And Jesus' kingdom-project is
> nothing if not the rescue and renewal of God's creation-project.[111]

---

the death of Jesus *as a sacrifice*?" Finlan, *Problems with Atonement*, 95.

108. Ray, *Deceiving the Devil*, 7.

109. Milbank, *Being Reconciled*, ix.

110. Describing salvation in the context of CVM, Ray notes, "We are saved not from the vicissitudes, vulnerabilities, and inevitable suffering of finite existence, but for a par-ticular way of responding to those inevitabilities, a way that . . . Jesus exemplified in his life and death. Redemption, then, is a profoundly this-worldly affair, though it implies a radical transformation of our conception of and place in the world." Ray, *Deceiving the Devil*, 132. Boyd also concludes that "*our* personal and social victories participate in *Christ's* cosmic victory." Boyd, "Christus Victor View," 34.

111. Wright, *Simply Jesus*, 210. Further, Wright notes that "deeply mysterious though it remains, we should recognize that when Jesus announced his intention to launch God's kingdom at last, he did it in a way that involved other human beings. God

Instead of mere "audience participation," therefore, the players instead find themselves fully embroiled in the story, essential elements in an ongoing *dramatis Dei*, caught up inexplicably in God's immediate and eternal plans for Divine-human unification. McKnight argues, in fact, that the gospel is all about the Story of Israel coming to its resolution in the Story of Jesus—the believer, he contends, needs to let that story become their story. In order to come to terms with this "story-shaped gospel" McKnight concludes that believers will have to become People of the Story.[112]

Simply put and in conclusion, humans, even Christian ones, have never embraced and practiced a love like God's and should likewise never attempt to utilize violence unless it is in anything like the kind of purposeful, righteous and redemptive way that God does. This comparison focuses on human frailties and sinful incapabilities rather than on God, who he is and what he does. Put another way, just because humans mess up love it does not follow that God is not ontologically love. Further, because violence has been the bane of human history it does not follow that God does not have the ability either to endorse or even utilize extrinsic violence as a means of accomplishing *his* goals. Volf notes that it is important to preserve the fundamental difference between God and nonGod, because the biblical tradition insists that there are things which only God may do—one of them, he insists, is to use violence.[113]

Christians nonetheless find themselves paradoxically embroiled in a metaphysical conflict and so, after questioning the portrayal of Christianity in this war with the Satan as one in which it is a "big outfit" or even "well equipped," Walker states that,

> I believe it is both more biblical and closer to the reality of our present historical situation to realize that we are the despised irregular soldiers of Christ—hit-and-run guerrillas, resistance fighters—and that at our strongest we are commando units behind enemy lines.[114]

Walker acknowledges that these images are distasteful to moral-majority America or middle-class Britain as such sentiments are more usually associated with terrorism and anarchy. The crucial point, however, is that until God's invasion of the world, in his final campaign in the Great Battle

---

works through Jesus; Jesus works through his followers. This is not accidental." Ibid., 211.

112. McKnight, *King Jesus Gospel*, 153.

113. Volf, *Exclusion and Embrace*, 301.

114. Walker, *Enemy Territory*, 18.

when the Devil will be finally and ultimately defeated, Christians remain God's militants in enemy-occupied territory.[115]

We conclude that the best way to understand and represent this scenario is to acknowledge God's irresistibly forceful power, his extrinsic violence, and his willingness to use it, albeit reticently, in his actual battle with and eventual, definitive overcoming of the Satan. God, therefore, has always been willing to reluctantly exert extrinsic violence, especially for soteriological purposes. Certainly this doctrine has, according to Boyd, praxeological implications for the Christian, drawing the believer's personal and social victories into participation in *Christ's* cosmic victory, because everything the New Testament says about the soteriological significance of Christ's work is predicated on the cosmic significance of his work. Only the CVM, he concludes, captures the centrality of this cosmic, warfare significance; thus properly expressing the soteriological significance of Christ's work.[116]

In Aquinas's *Summa*, after giving arguments for God's existence, Aquinas views what God is (*quid sit*) primarily from the standpoint of what he is not—excluding things that are not compatible.[117] Whilst it might be argued, using Aquinas' perspective, that a God who is ontologically love is definitely not evil, we conclude that it is not possible, having considered the evidence, to likewise definitively maintain that God is categorically not extrinsically *violent*.

In engaging with such a God we argue that salvation is not, therefore, merely the emulation of Christ's example or the abstract and passive observation of a divine, juridical transaction. Indeed, in his reflection upon Yahweh's dealings with Israel in the Old Testament Brueggemann observes that the relationship is redolent of a marriage, but a marriage between a loving, passionate and demanding husband and an unfaithful wife. In one instance Yahweh admits to an "overflowing wrath for a moment" (Isaiah 54:8) which culminates in his massive act of destroying Jerusalem; Brueggemann concludes that this appears to be the work of a wronged lover who determines to humiliate, and finally destroy, the erstwhile object of his love.[118] When God chose Israel he did so not with a binding, legal contract, but with an exclamation of love (Deuteronomy 10:15), Brueggemann concludes that,

> This is no casual, formal, or juridical commitment. This is *a passion that lives in the "loins" of Yahweh*, who will risk everything for Israel and, having risked everything, will expect everything

115. Ibid.

116. Boyd, "Christus Victor View," 34.

117. Aquinas, *Summa Theologica*, 1.3.

118. Brueggemann, *Theology of the Old Testament*, 384.

and will be vigilant not to share the beloved with any other. This is no open marriage. The outcome of passion so intensely initiated has within it the seeds of intolerance, culminating in violence. There is indeed a profound awkwardness in this presentation of Yahweh, but Israel does not flinch in its testimony. The God who has been madly in love becomes insanely jealous, which is Israel's deepest threat and most profound hope.[119]

Neither should modern believers flinch in their testimony of engagement with this extrinsically violent God which entails the mixed-metaphor of being caught up concurrently in a passionate love affair with a demanding partner, conjoined with enlistment in an army headed by a mighty, demanding and capable "general."[120] This army remains at war and new "recruits," whilst loved, nonetheless have to work with each other and their Leader, their lover, in order to secure their ultimate liberation through a final, decisive victory against an evil, powerful adversary who can only be subjugated and given over to ḥērem by this God of insurmountable love and irresistible force.

---

119. Ibid.

120. Such an outlook matches that held by Jews throughout the Old Testament; indeed, in his explanation of Joshua 6:1–27, Butler concludes that after Israel's battles and travails, "again she found her identity. The identity still rested in the God who gave victory to his people. Now the people were called on to see that being people of God meant obeying the word of God. Battle plans and life plans were laid out not by man but by God. Even the general of the army had to get his battle plans from his Commander-in-Chief." Butler, *Joshua*, 72.

Bibliography

Abelard, Peter. "Peter Abelard on the Love of Christ in Redemption." In *The Christian Theology Reader*, edited by Alister E. McGrath, 299–300. Chichester, UK: Wiley-Blackwell, 2011.

Aghiororgoussis, Maximos. "Christian Existentialism of the Greek Fathers: Persons, Essence, and Energies in God." *Greek Orthodox Theological Review* 23 (1978) 15–41.

Alison, James. *Joy of Being Wrong: Original Sin through Easter Eyes*. New York: Crossroad, 1998.

Anderson, Paul N. *The Fourth Gospel and the Quest for Jesus: Modern Foundations Re-Considered*. London: T. & T. Clark, 2006.

Anderson, Walter Truett. *Reality Isn't What It Used to Be: Theatrical Politics, Ready-to-Wear-Religion, Global Myths, Primitive Chic and Other Wonders of the Postmodern World*. San Francisco: Harper & Row, 1990.

Angel, Andrew Richard. "*Crucifixus Vincens:* The 'Son of God' as Divine Warrior in Matthew." *Catholic Biblical Quarterly* 73 (2011) 299–317.

Anselm. *Cur Deus Homo*. Edinburgh: John Grant, 1909.

Anthony, Metropolitan, of Sourozh. *God and Man*. London: Darton, Longman & Todd, 1971.

Athanasius. *On the Incarnation*. London: Mowbray, 1944.

Atlan, Henri. "Founding Violence and Divine Referent." In *Violence and Truth: On the Work of René Girard*, edited by Paul Dumouchel, 198–208. Stanford: Stanford University Press, 1988.

Aulén, Gustaf. *The Faith of the Christian Church*. London: SCM, 1954.

———. *Christus Victor: An Historical Study of the Three Main Types of the Idea of the Atonement*. Eugene, OR: Wipf & Stock, 1931.

Aune, David E. *Revelation 6–16*. Word Biblical Commentary 52b. Nashville: Thomas Nelson, 1998.

Avalos, Hector. *Fighting Words: The Origins of Religious Violence*. Amherst: Prometheus, 2005.

Ayer, A. J. *Language, Truth and Logic*. Harmondsworth, UK: Penguin, 1971.

Bailey, Kenneth E. *Poet & Peasant and Through Peasant Eyes: A Literary-Cultural Approach to the Parables of Luke*. Grand Rapids: Eerdmans, 1976.

Barker, Margaret. *The Revelation of Jesus Christ: Which God Gave to Him to Show to His Servants What Must Soon Take Place*. Edinburgh: T. & T. Clark, 2000.

Barrett, C. K. *The Holy Spirit and the Gospel Tradition*. London: SPCK, 1947.

Barth, Karl. *Church Dogmatics, Volume II—The Doctrine of God, Part 1*. Peabody, MA: Hendrickson, 2010.

———. *Church Dogmatics, Volume III—The Doctrine of Creation, Part 3*. Peabody, MA: Hendrickson, 2010.

Bartlett, Anthony W. *Cross Purposes: The Violent Grammar of Christian Atonement*. Harrisburg, PA: Trinity, 2001.

Bauckham, Richard. *The Climax of Prophecy: Studies on the Book of Revelation*. Edinburgh: T. & T. Clark, 1993.

———. *The Theology of the Book of Revelation*. Cambridge: Cambridge University Press, 1993.

Beale, Gregory K. "Eschatology." In *Dictionary of the Later New Testament & Its Developments*, edited by Ralph P. Martin and Peter H. Davids, 330–45. Leicester, UK: InterVarsity, 1997.

———. *The Book of Revelation—A Commentary on the Greek Text*. Carlisle, UK: Paternoster, 1999.

Beasley-Murray, George R. "Revelation, Book of." In *Dictionary of the Later New Testament & Its Developments*, edited by Ralph P. Martin and Peter H. Davids, 1025–38. Leicester, UK: InterVarsity, 1997.

———. *John*. Word Biblical Commentary 36. Dallas, TX: Word, 1987.

Beck, Richard, and S. Taylor. "The Emotional Burden of Monotheism: Satan, Theodicy, and Relationship with God." *Journal of Psychology and Theology* 36 (2008) 151–60.

Beilby, James, and Paul R. Eddy, eds. *The Nature of the Atonement: Four Views*. Downers Grove, IL: IVP Academic, 2006.

Bell, Richard H. *Deliver Us from Evil: Interpreting the Redemption from the Power of Satan in New Testament Theology*. Tübingen: Mohr Siebeck, 2007.

Belousek, Darrin W. Snyder. *Atonement, Justice, and Peace: The Message of the Cross and the Mission of the Church*. Grand Rapids: Eerdmans, 2012.

Bergman, Jan, and Elsie Johnson. "Πνάφ." In *Theological Dictionary of the New Testament*, vol. 1, edited by G. Johannes Botterweck and Helmer Ringgren, 348–60. Grand Rapids: Eerdmanns, 1974.

Bietenhard, Hans. "ἐκ-βάλλω." In *The New International Dictionary of New Testament Theology*, vol. 1: A-F, edited by Colin Brown, 453–54. Exeter, UK: Paternoster, 1975.

Blumenthal, David R. "Confronting the Character of God: Text and Praxis." In *God in the Fray—A Tribute to Walter Brueggemann*, edited by Tod Linafelt and Timothy Kandler Beal, 38–54. Minneapolis: Fortress, 1998.

———. *Facing the Abusing God: A Theology of Protest*. Louisville, KY: Westminster John Knox, 1993.

Bobrinskoy, Boris. "God in Trinity." In *The Cambridge Companion to Orthodox Christian Theology*, edited by Mary B. Cunningham and Elizabeth Theokritoff, 49–62. Cambridge: Cambridge University Press, 2008.

Boersma, Hans. *Violence, Hospitality and the Cross: Reappropriating the Atonement Tradition*. Grand Rapids: Baker Academic, 2006.

Boling, Robert G. *Joshua*. Anchor Bible. New York: Doubleday, 1982.

Borchert, Gerald L. "Wrath, Destruction." In *Dictionary of Paul and His Letters*, edited by Gerald F. Hawthorne et al., 991–93. Downers Grove, IL: InterVarsity, 1993.

Borg, Marcus J. *Conflict, Holiness and Politics in the Teachings of Jesus*. London: Continuum, 1984.

――――. "Executed by Rome, Vindicated by God," In *Stricken by God? Nonviolent Identification and the Victory of Christ*, edited by Brad Jersak and Michael Hardin, 150–63. Grand Rapids: Eerdmans, 2007.

Bouteneff, Peter. "Christ and Salvation." In *The Cambridge Companion to Orthodox Christian Theology*, edited by Mary B. Cunningham and Elizabeth Theokritoff, 93–106. Cambridge: Cambridge University Press, 2008.

Boyd, Gregory A. *God at War—The Bible and Spiritual Conflict*. Downers Grove, IL: IVP Academic, 1997.

――――. "Christus Victor View." In *The Nature of the Atonement: Four Views*, edited by James Beilby and Paul R. Eddy, 23–49. Downers Grove, IL: IVP Academic, 2006.

Bray, Michael. "A Time for Revolution? A Time to Kill?" In *Princeton Readings in Religion and Violence*, edited by Mark Juergensmeyer and Margo Kitts, 56–61. Princeton, NJ: Princeton University Press, 2011.

Breytenbach, Cilliers. "Satan." In *Dictionary of Deities and Demons in the Bible*, edited by Karel van der Toorn et al., 726–32. Grand Rapids: Eerdmans, 1999.

Brown, Joanne Carlson, and Rebecca Parker, "For God So Loved the World?" In *Christianity, Patriarchy, and Abuse: A Feminist Critique*, edited by Joanne Carlson Brown and Carole R. Bohn, 1–30. New York: Pilgrim, 1989.

Brown, Robert McAfee. *Religion and Violence*. Philadelphia: Westminster, 1973.

Bruce, F. F. *The Spreading Flame*. Exeter, UK: Paternoster, 1964.

Brueggemann, Walter. *Divine Presence Amid Violence: Contextualizing the Book of Joshua*. Milton Keynes: Paternoster, 2009.

――――. *Theology of the Old Testament: Testimony, Dispute, Advocacy*. Minneapolis: Fortress, 1997.

Büchsel, Hermann Martin Friedrich. "thymós." In *Theological Dictionary of the New Testament*, edited by Gerhard Kittel and Gerhard Friedrich, 339. Grand Rapids: Eerdmans, 1985.

Buffacchi, Vittorio. *Violence and Social Justice*. Basingstoke, UK: Palgrave Macmillan, 2007.

Bultmann, Rudolf. *The History of the Synoptic Tradition*. Oxford: Basil Blackwell, 1963.

――――. "Is Exegesis Without Presuppositions Possible?" In *New Testament and Mythology and Other Basic Writings*, edited by Schubert M. Ogden, 145–53. Philadelphia: Fortress, 1984.

――――. *Jesus Christ and Mythology*. London: SCM, 1958.

――――. "New Testament and Mythology: The Problem of Demythologizing in the New Testament Proclamation." In *New Testament and Mythology and Other Basic Writings*, edited by Schubert M. Ogden, 1–43. Philadelphia: Fortress, 1984.

――――. "On the Problem of Demythologizing." In *New Testament and Mythology and Other Basic Writings*, edited by Schubert M. Ogden, 95–130. Philadelphia: Fortress, 1984.

Burrell, David B. *Knowing the Unknowable God: Ibn-Sina, Maimonides, Aquinas*. Notre Dame, IN: University of Notre Dame Press, 1986.

――――. "Rene Girard: Violence and Sacrifice." *Cross Currents* 38 (1988–89) 443–47.

Bushnell, Horace. *The Vicarious Sacrifice: Grounded in Principles Interpreted by Human Analogies*. Eugene, OR: Wipf & Stock, 2004.

Butler, Trent C. *Joshua*. Word Biblical Commentary 7. Nashville: Thomas Nelson, 1983.

Caird, George Bradford. *The Language and Imagery of the Bible*. London: Duckworth, 1980.

Cairns, David. *A Gospel Without Myth? Bultmann's Challenge to the Preacher*. London: SCM, 1960.

Calvin, John. *Institutes of the Christian Religion*. Philadelphia: Westminster, 1975.

———. *Tracts and Treatises on the Doctrine and Worship of the Church*, vol. 2. London: Oliver & Boyd, 1849.

Camfield, F. W. "The Idea of Substitution in the Doctrine of the Atonement." *Scottish Journal of Theology* 1 (1948) 282–93.

Casey, Maurice. "Culture and Historicity: The Cleansing of the Temple." *Catholic Biblical Quarterly* 59 (1997) 306–32.

Castelo, Daniel. *The Apathetic God: Exploring the Contemporary Relevance of Divine Impassibility*. Eugene, OR: Wipf & Stock, 2009.

Cavanaugh, William T. *The Myth of Religious Violence: Secular Ideology and the Roots of Modern Conflict*. Oxford: Oxford University Press, 2009.

Chalke, Steve, and Alan Mann. *The Lost Message of Jesus*. Grand Rapids: Zondervan, 2003.

Chase, Kenneth R. "Introduction." In *Must Christianity Be Violent?*, edited by Kenneth R. Chase and Alan Jacobs, 9–19. Grand Rapids: Brazos, 2003.

Chilton, Bruce D. "[ὡς] φραγέλλιον ἐκ σχοινίων (John 2:15)." In *Templum Amicitiae: Essays on the Second Temple Presented to Ernst Bammel*, edited by William Horbury, 330–44. Sheffield, UK: JSOT Press, 1991.

Chryssavgis, John. "The Origins of the Essence-Energies." *Phronema* 5 (1990) 15–31.

Cicero, Marcus Tullius. "In Defence of Gaius Rabirius." In *Murder Trials*, 255–90. Harmondsworth, UK: Penguin, 1975,

Collins, Adela Yarbro. *Crisis and Catharsis: The Power of the Apocalypse*. Philadelphia: Westminster, 1984.

———. *The Combat Myth in the Book of Revelation*. Eugene, OR: Wipf & Stock, 2001.

Combes, Isobel A. H. *The Metaphor of Slavery in the Writings of the Early Church: From the New Testament to the Beginning of the Fifth Century*. Sheffield, UK: Sheffield Academic, 1998.

Conrad, Edgar W. "Ban." In *The Oxford Companion to the Bible*, edited by Bruce M. Metzger and Michael David Coogan, 73.Oxford: Oxford University Press, 1993.

Cooper, David E. *Metaphor*. Oxford: Basil Blackwell, 1986.

Cotterell, Peter. *Mission and Meaninglessness: The Good News in a World of Suffering and Disorder*. London: SPCK, 1990.

Cotterell, Peter, and Max Turner. *Linguistics and Biblical Interpretation*. Downers Grove, IL: InterVarsity, 1989.

Cremer, Hermann. *Die christliche Lehre von den Eigenschaften Gottes*. Charleston, SC: BiblioBazaar, 2009.

Croy, N. Clayton. "The Messianic Whippersnapper: Did Jesus Use a Whip on People in the Temple (John 2:15)?" *Journal of Biblical Literature* 128 (2009) 555–68.

Cunningham, Mary B., and Elizabeth Theokritoff, "Who Are the Orthodox Christians?" In *The Cambridge Companion to Orthodox Christian Theology*, edited by Mary B. Cunningham and Elizabeth Theokritoff, 1–18. Cambridge: Cambridge University Press, 2008.

Cupitt, Don. *Explorations in Theology, 6*. London: SCM, 1979.

Dale, Robert William. *The Atonement*. Rev. ed. Oswestry, UK: Quinta, 1875.

Dalley, Stephanie, trans. "The Epic of Gilgamesh." In *Myths from Mesopotamia: Creation, the Flood, Gilgamesh, and Others*, 228–77. Oxford: Oxford University Press, 1989.

Davis, Charles T. "Seeds of Violence in Biblical Interpretation." *The Destructive Power of Religion: Violence in Judaism, Christianity, and Islam*, vol. 1, *Sacred Scriptures, Ideology, and Violence*, edited by J. Harold Ellens, 35–53. Westport, CT: Praeger, 2004.

Dawkins, Richard. *The God Delusion*. London: Random House, 2006.

Dodd, C. H. *The Epistle to the Romans*. London: Hodder & Stoughton, 1932.

Dow, Graham. "The Case for the Existence of Demons." *Churchman* 94 (1980) 199–208.

Dozeman, Thomas B. *God at War: Power in the Exodus Tradition*. Oxford: Oxford University Press, 1996.

Driver, John. *Understanding the Atonement for the Mission of the Church*. Scottdale, PA: Herald, 1986.

Dunn, J. D. G. *Christology in the Making: A New Testament Inquiry into the Origins of the Doctrine of the Incarnation*. London: SCM, 1980.

———. *Romans 1–8*. Word Biblical Commentary 38. Dallas, TX: Word, 1988.

———. *The Theology of Paul the Apostle*. Edinburgh: T. & T. Clark, 1998.

Duriez, Colin. "Voldemort, Death Eaters, Dementors, and the Dark Arts: A Contemporary Theology of Spiritual Perversion in the Harry Potter Stories." In *The Lure of the Dark Side: Satan and Western Demonology in Popular Culture*, edited by C. Partridge and E. Christianson, 182–95. London: Equinox, 2009.

Ebeling, Gerhard. *Introduction to a Theological Theory of Language*. London: Collins, 1973.

Edwards, David L., with John Stott. *Essentials—A Liberal-Evangelical Dialogue*. London: Hodder & Stoughton, 1988.

Eliade, Mircea. *The Sacred and the Profane: The Nature of Religion*. San Diego: Harvest, 1957.

Ellens, J. Harold. "Religious Metaphors Can Kill." In *The Destructive Power of Religion: Violence in Judaism, Christianity, and Islam*, vol. 1, *Sacred Scriptures, Ideology, and Violence*, edited by J. Harold Ellens, 255–72. Westport, CT: Praeger, 2004.

———. "The Violent Jesus." In *The Destructive Power of Religion: Violence in Judaism, Christianity, and Islam*, vol. 3, *Violence in Judaism, Christianity, and Islam*, edited by J. Harold Ellens, 15–37. Westport, CT: Praeger, 2004.

Gracia Fay Ellwood. *Batter My Heart*. Wallingford, PA: Pendle Hill, 1988.

Enslin, Morton S. "The Pontic Mouse." *Anglican Theological Review* 27 (1945) 1–16.

Evans, Craig Alan. "Jesus' Action in the Temple: Cleansing or Portent of Destruction?" *Catholic Biblical Quarterly* 51 (1989) 237–70.

Ferdinando, Keith. "Screwtape Revisited: Demonology Western, African, and Biblical." In *The Unseen World: Christian Reflections on Angels, Demons and the Heavenly Realm*, edited by Anthony N. S. Lane, 103–32. Carlisle, UK: Paternoster, 1996.

Feuerbach, Ludwig. *The Essence of Christianity*. New York: Dover, 2008.

Fichte, Johann Gottieb. "Über den Grund unseres Glaubens an eine göttliche Weltregierung." *Philosophische Journal* 8 (1798) 1–20.

Fiddes, Paul S. *Freedom and Limit—A Dialogue between Literature and Christian Doctrine*. London: Macmillan, 1991.

———. *Participating in God—A Pastoral Doctrine of the Trinity*. London: Darton, Longman and Todd, 2000.

————. *Past Event and Present Salvation: The Christian Idea of Atonement*. London: Darton, Longman & Todd, 1989.

————. "Salvation." In *The Oxford Handbook of Systematic Theology*, edited by J. Webster et al., 176–96. Oxford: Oxford University Press, 2007.

————. *The Promised End—Eschatology in Theology and Literature*. Oxford: Blackwell, 2000.

Finlan, Stephen. *Options on Atonement in Christian Thought*. Collegeville, MN: Liturgical, 2007.

————. *Problems with Atonement*. Collegeville, MN: Liturgical, 2005.

Fish, Varda. "Noah and the Great Flood: The Metamorphosis of the Biblical Tale." *Judaica Librarianship* 5 (1990) 74–78.

Fleming, Chris. *René Girard: Violence and Mimesis*. Cambridge, UK: Polity, 2004.

Flew, Anthony. "Theology and Falsification." In *Reason and Responsibility: Readings in Some Basic Problems of Philosophy*, edited by J. Feinberg, 48–49. Belmont, CA: Dickenson, 1968.

Foucalt, Michel. *Discipline and Punish: The Birth of the Prison*. London: Penguin, 1991.

Friedrich, Gerhard. "εὐαγγέλιον." In *Theological Dictionary of the New Testament*, vol. 2, edited by Geoffrey W. Bromiley, 707–37. Grand Rapids: Eerdmans, 1967.

Gaston, Lloyd. *No Stone on Another: Studies in the Significance of the Fall of Jerusalem in the Synoptic Gospels*. Leiden: Brill, 1970.

Gibson, John C. L. *Language and Imagery in the Old Testament*. Peabody, MA: Hendrickson, 1998.

Girard, René. *Deceit, Desire, and the Novel*. Baltimore: Johns Hopkins University Press, 1965.

————. *I See Satan Fall Like Lightning*. Maryknoll, NY: Orbis, 1999.

————. *Job the Victim of His People*. London: Athlone, 1987.

————. *The Scapegoat*. Baltimore: Johns Hopkins University Press, 1986.

————. *Things Hidden Since the Foundation of the World*. London: Continuum, 1987.

————. *Violence and the Sacred*. London: Continuum: 1988.

Goldingay, John. *Models for Scripture*. Carlisle, UK: Paternoster, 1994.

————. *Old Testament Theology*, vol. 2, *Israel's Faith*. Milton Keynes: Paternoster, 2006.

————. *Theological Diversity and the Authority of the Old Testament*. Grand Rapids: Eerdmans, 1987.

Gorringe, Timothy. *God's Just Vengeance: Crime, Violence and the Rhetoric of Salvation*. Cambridge: Cambridge University Press, 1996.

Gopin, Marc. *Between Eden and Armageddon: The Future of World Religions, Violence and Peacemaking*. Oxford: Oxford University Press, 2000.

Green, Joel B. "The Death of Jesus and the Ways of God. Jesus and the Gospels on Messianic Status and Shameful Suffering." *Interpretation* 52 (1998) 24–37.

————. "Kaleidoscopic Response." In *The Nature of the Atonement: Four Views*, edited by James Beilby and Paul R. Eddy, 110–16. Downers Grove, IL: IVP, 2006.

Green, Joel B., and Mark D. Baker. *Recovering the Scandal of the Cross: Atonement in New Testament and Contemporary Contexts*. Milton Keynes: Paternoster, 2003.

Green, Michael. *I Believe in Satan's Downfall*. Grand Rapids: Eerdmans, 1981.

Grimsrud, Ted. *Instead of Atonement: The Bible's Salvation Story and Our Hope for Wholeness*. Eugene, OR: Cascade, 2013.

Gunton, Colin E. *Act and Being: Towards a Theology of the Divine Attributes*. London: SCM, 2002.

————. *A Brief Theology of Revelation*. Edinburgh: T. & T. Clark, 1995.

————. *Christ and Creation*. Carlisle, UK: Paternoster, 1992.

————. "Christus Victor Revisited: A Study in Metaphor and the Transformation of Meaning." *The Journal of Theological Studies* 36 (1985) 129–45.

————. *The Actuality of Atonement: A Study of Metaphor, Rationality and the Christian Tradition*. Edinburgh: T. & T. Clark, 1998.

————. *The Christian Faith—An Introduction to Christian Doctrine*. Oxford: Blackwell, 2002.

Hamerton-Kelly, Robert G. *Sacred Violence: Paul's Hermeneutic of the Cross*. Minneapolis: Augsburg Fortress, 1992.

————. "Sacred Violence and Sinful Desire: Paul's Interpretation of Adam's Sin." In *The Conversation Continues: Studies in Paul and John in Honor of J. Louis Martyn*, edited by R. J. Fortua and B. R. Gaverta, 35–54. Nashville: Abingdon, 1990.

Hanson, Paul D. "War and Peace in the Hebrew Bible." *Interpretation* 38 (1984) 341–62.

Hanson, R. P. C. "The Attractiveness of God." In *The Attractiveness of God: Essays in Christian Doctrine*, 1–9. London: SPCK, 1973.

————. "The Grace and the Wrath of God." In *The Attractiveness of God: Essays in Christian Doctrine*, 138–54. London: SPCK, 1973.

————. *The Search for the Christian Doctrine of God*. Edinburgh: T. & T. Clark, 1988.

Hardin, Michael E. "Out of the Fog: New Horizons for Atonement Theory." In *Stricken by God? Nonviolent Identification and the Victory of Christ*, edited by Brad Jersak and Michael Hardin, 54–76. Grand Rapids: Eerdmans, 2007.

————. "Violence: René Girard and the Recovery of Early Christian Perspectives." *Brethren Life and Thought* 37 (1992) 107–20.

Häring, Hermann. "Overcoming Violence in the Name of Religion (Christianity and Islam)." In *Religion as a Source of Violence*, edited by Wim Berken and Karl-Josef Kuschel, 81–92. London: SCM, 1997.

Harnack, Adolf Von. "Marcion and the Marcionite Churches." In *Encyclopedia Britannica*, 9th ed., 15:533–35. Edinburgh: A&C Black, 1888.

Harris, R. Laird, et al., eds. *Theological Wordbook of the Old Testament*. Vols. 1 and 2. Chicago: Moody, 1980.

Harris, Sam. *The End of Faith: Religion, Terror and the Future of Reason*. London: Simon & Schuster, 2004.

Harrison, Nonna Verna. "The Human Person as Image and Likeness of God." In *The Cambridge Companion to Orthodox Christian Theology*, edited by Mary B. Cunningham and Elizabeth Theokritoff, 78–92. Cambridge: Cambridge University Press, 2008.

Hart, Trevor. *Faith Thinking: The Dynamics of Christian Theology*. London: SPCK, 1995.

————. *Regarding Karl Barth: Essays Toward a Reading of his Theology*. Carlisle, UK: Paternoster, 1999.

Hastings, Adrian. "Devil." In *The Oxford Companion to Christian Thought*, edited by Adrian Hastings, 164–66. Oxford: Oxford University Press, 2000.

Hauck, Friedrich. "βαλλω." In *Theological Dictionary of the New Testament*, vol. 1, edited by Gerhard Kittel and Gerhard Friedrich, 526–29. Grand Rapids: Eerdmans, 1964.

Hauerwas, Stanley. "Explaining Christian Nonviolence: Notes for a Conversation with John Milbank." In *Must Christianity by Violent? Reflections on History, Practice, and Theology*, edited by Kenneth R. Chase and Alan Jacobs, 172–82. Grand Rapids: Brazos, 2003.

Hawk, Lewis Daniel. *Joshua*. Berit Olam: Studies in Hebrew Narrative and Poetry. Collegeville, MN: Liturgical, 2000.

Hayes, John H. "Atonement in the Book of Leviticus." *Interpretation* 52, no. 1 (1998) 5–15.

Hays, Richard B. *The Moral Vision of the New Testament: Community, Cross, New Creation*. Edinburgh: T. & T. Clark, 1996.

Hegel, Georg Wilhelm Friedrich. *Science of Logic*. Translated by A. V. Miller. New York: Prometheus, 1969.

Heidel, Alexander. *The Babylonian Genesis: The Story of the Creation*. Chicago: Phoenix, 1942.

Heim, S. Mark. *Saved from Sacrifice: A Theology of the Cross*. Grand Rapids: Eerdmans, 2006.

Helm, Paul. "Are They Few that Be Saved?" In *Universalism and the Doctrine of Hell*, edited by N. M. de S. Cameron, 257–81. Carlisle, UK: Paternoster, 1992.

———. *The Providence of God*. Leicester, UK: InterVarsity, 1993.

Herion, Gary A. "Wrath of God (OT)." In *The Anchor Bible Dictionary*, vol. 6, edited by David Noel. Freedman, 989–96. New York: Doubleday, 1992.

Herzog, W. R., II. "Temple Cleansing." In *Dictionary of Jesus and the Gospels*, edited by Joel B. Green and Scot McKnight, 817–21. Leicester: InterVarsity, 1992.

Heschel, Abraham Joshua. *The Prophets*. New York: Harper-Collins, 2001.

Hesse, F. "The Evaluation and the Authority of the Old Testament Texts." In *Essays in Old Testament Interpretation*, edited by Claus Westerman, 285–313. London: SCM, 1963.

Heyer, C. J. den. *Jesus and the Doctrine of the Atonement: Biblical Notes on a Controversial Topic*. Translated by John Bowden, London: SCM, 1998.

Hilary, Saint, Bishop of Poitiers. *The Trinity*. Translated by S. McKenna. Washington, DC: Catholic University of America Press, 1954.

Hilborn, David. "Atonement, Evangelism and the Evangelical Alliance: The Present Debate in Context." In *The Atonement Debate*, edited by David Hilborn et al., 15–33. Grand Rapids: Zondervan, 2008.

Hill, David. *Greek Words and Hebrew Meanings: Studies in the Semantics of Soteriological Terms*. Cambridge: Cambridge University Press: 1967.

Hitchens, Christopher. *God Is not Great: How Religion Poisons Everything*. London: Atlantic, 2007.

Hjelm, Titus. "Celluloid Vampires, Scientization, and the Decline of Religion." In *The Lure of the Dark Side: Satan and Western Demonology in Popular Culture*, edited by Christopher Partridge and Eric Christianson, 105–21. London: Equinox, 2009.

Hoffman, Joshua, and Gary S. Rosenkrantz. *The Divine Attributes*. Oxford: Blackwell, 2002.

Holliday, L. R. "Will Satan Be Saved? Reconsidering Origen's Theory of Volition in Peri Archon." *Vigiliae Christianae* 63 (2009) 1–23.

Holmes, Stephen R. *The Wondrous Cross: Atonement and Penal Substitution in the Bible and History*. London: Paternoster, 2007.

Horsley, Richard A. *Jesus and the Spiral of Violence: Popular Jewish Resistance in Roman Palestine*. Minneapolis: Fortress, 1993.

Houtart, François. "The Cult of Violence in the Name of Religion: A Panorama." In *Religion as a Source of Violence*, edited by Wim Beuken and Karl-Josef Kuschel, 1–9. London: SCM, 1997.

Hughes, Gerard J. *The Nature of God*. London: Routledge, 1995.

Hunsinger, George. "The Politics of the Nonviolent God: Reflections on René Girard and Karl Barth." *Scottish Journal of Theology* 51, no. 1 (1998) 61–85.

Hurtado, Larry W. *One God, One Lord: Early Christian Devotion and Ancient Jewish Monotheism.* London: SCM, 1988.

Hutchens, S. M. "Terrible Salvation: A Dark Meditation on God and Hannibal Lecter." *Touchstone* (2007) 5–6.

Imasogie, Osadolor. *Guidelines for Christian Theology in Africa.* Achimota, Ghana: Africa Christian, 1993.

Jacobs, Alan. "Afterword." In *Must Christianity Be Violent?*, edited by Kenneth R. Chase and Alan Jacobs, 224–35. Grand Rapids: Brazos, 2003.

James, Frank A., III. "The Atonement in Church History." In *The Glory of the Atonement: Biblical, Historical and Practical Perspectives*, edited by Charles E. Hill and Frank A. James III, 209–19. Downers Grove: InterVarsity, 2004.

Jantzen, Grace M. *Violence to Eternity: Death and the Displacement of Beauty.* Vol. 2. London: Routledge, 2009.

Jenson, Robert W. *Systematic Theology.* Vol. 2, *The Works of God*, Oxford: Oxford University Press, 1999.

Johnson, E. "Divine Anger." In *Theological Dictionary of the Old Testament*. Vol. 1, edited by G. Johannes Botterweck and Helmer Ringgren, 356–60. Grand Rapids: Eerdmans, 1974.

Johnson, Luke Timothy. "Powers and Principalities." *Commonweal* 138 (2011) 14–17.

Johnson, Mark. "Philosophy's Debt to Metaphor." In *The Cambridge Handbook of Metaphor and Thought*, edited by Raymond W. Gibbs Jr., 39–52. Cambridge: Cambridge University Press, 2008.

Jones, Gareth Lloyd. "Sacred Violence: The Dark Side of God." *Journal of Beliefs and Values*, 20, no. 2 (1999) 184–99.

Juergensmeyer, Mark. "Religious Justifications for Violence." In *Princeton Readings in Religion and Violence*, edited by Mark Juergensmeyer and Margo Kitts, 7–12. Princeton, NJ: Princeton University Press, 2011.

———. *Terror in the Mind of God: The Global Rise of Religious Violence.* Berkeley, CA: University of California Press, 2000.

Jüngel, Eberhard. *God as the Mystery of the World.* Grand Rapids: Eerdmans, 1983.

Kaeuper, Richard W. *Chivalry and Violence in Medieval Europe.* Oxford: Oxford University Press, 1999.

Kaiser, Christopher B. *The Doctrine of God: An Historical Survey.* London: Marshall, Morgan & Scott, 1982.

Kang, Sa-Moon. *Divine War in the Old Testament and in the Ancient Near East.* Berlin: de Gruyter, 1989.

Kass, Leon R. *The Beginning of Wisdom: Reading Genesis.* New York: Free, 2003.

Kelly, J. N. D. *Early Christian Doctrines.* London: A&C Black, 1958.

Kelsey, Morton T. *Myth, History and Faith: The Remythologizing of Christianity.* New York: Paulist, 1974.

———. "The Mythology of Evil." *Journal of Religion and Health* 13 (1974) 7–18.

Kierkegaard, Søren. *Fear and Trembling.* Translated by Alastair Hannay. London: Penguin, 1985.

Kille, Andrew D. "'The Bible Made Me Do It': Text, Interpretation, And Violence." In *The Destructive Power of Religion: Violence in Judaism, Christianity, and Islam*, vol. 1: *Sacred Scriptures, Ideology, and Violence*, edited by J. Harold Ellens, 55–73. Westport, CT: Praeger, 2004.

Kirwan, Michael. *Discovering Girard*. Cambridge, MA: Cowley, 2005.

———. *Girard and Theology*. London: T. & T. Clark, 2009.

Kittay, Eva Feder. *Metaphor: Its Cognitive Force and Linguistic Structure*. Oxford: Clarendon, 1987.

Klein, William W., et al. *Introduction to Biblical Interpretation*. Dallas, TX: Word, 1993.

Koch, Klaus. "Is There a Doctrine of Retribution in the Old Testament?" In *Theodicy in the Old Testament*, edited by James L. Crenshaw, 57–87. Philadelphia: Fortress, 1983.

Kooi, Cornelis van der. *As in a Mirror: Jean Calvin and Karl Barth on Knowing God—A Diptych*. Boston: Brill, 2005.

Kreitzer, Larry J. "Parousia." In *Dictionary of the Later New Testament & Its Developments*, edited by Ralph P. Martin and Peter H. Davids, 856–75. Leicester, UK: InterVarsity, 1997.

Küng, Hans. *Does God Exist? An Answer for Today*. London: Collins, 1980.

———. *Credo: The Apostle's Creed Explained for Today*. London: SCM, 1992.

Lakoff, George, and Mark Johnson. *Metaphors We Live By*. Chicago: The University of Chicago Press, 1980.

Lakoff, George, and Mark Turner. *More than Cool Reason: A Field Guide to Poetic Metaphor*. Chicago: University of Chicago Press, 1989.

Langton, Edward. *Essentials of Demonology: A Study of Jewish and Christian Doctrine Its Origin and Development*. London: Epworth, 1949.

Lawrence, Bruce B. "General Introduction: Theorizing Violence in the Twenty-First Century." *On Violence: A Reader*, edited by Bruce B. Lawrence and Aisha Karim, 1–15. Durham, NC: Duke University Press, 2007.

Levi, Primo. *Moments of Reprieve*. London: Penguin, 1986.

Lewis, C. S. *Surprised by Joy*. Orlando: Harvest, 1955.

Lilley, J. P. U. "Understanding the Herem." *Tyndale Bulletin* 44, no. 1 (1993) 169–77.

Lincoln, Andrew T. *The Gospel According to Saint John*. New York: Continuum, 2005.

Lind, Millard C. *Yahweh Is a Warrior: The Theology of Warfare in Ancient Israel*. Scottdale, PA: Herald, 1980.

Lohfink, Norbert. *Great Themes from the Old Testament*. Translated by R. Walls, Chicago: Franciscan Herald, 1982.

Lorberbaum, Yair. "The Rainbow in the Cloud: An Anger-Management Device." *Journal of Religion* 1 (2009) 498–540.

Lüdemann, Gerd. *The Unholy in Holy Scripture: The Dark Side of the Bible*. London: SCM, 1997.

Lyon, Ardon. "John Wisdom." In *The Oxford Companion to Philosophy*, edited by Ted Honderich, 912. Oxford: Oxford University Press, 1995.

Mabee, Charles. "Reflections on Monotheism and Violence." In *The Destructive Power of Religion: Violence in Judaism, Christianity, and Islam*, vol. 4, *Contemporary Views on Spirituality and Violence*, edited by J. Harold Ellens, 111–18. Westport, CT: Praeger, 2004.

Macquarrie, John. "Demonology and the Classic Idea of Atonement." Pts. 1 and 2. *Expository Times* 68, no. 1 (October 1956) 3–6; (November 1956) 60–63.

———. *God-Talk: An Examination of the Language and Logic of Theology*. London: SCM, 1967.

———. *Jesus Christ in Modern Thought*. London: SCM, 1990.

———. *Paths in Spirituality*. London: SCM, 1972.

————. *Principles of Christian Theology*. London: SCM, 1977.

————. *The Scope of Demythologizing: Bultmann and his Critics*. London: SCM, 1960.

Madsen, Catherine. "Notes on God's Violence." *CrossCurrents* 51, no. 2 (2001) 229–56.

Marshall, I. Howard. *Aspects of the Atonement: Cross and Resurrection in the Reconciling of God and Humanity*. London: Paternoster, 2007.

————. "Historical Criticism." In *New Testament Interpretation*, edited by I.Howard Marshall, 126–138. Carlisle, UK: Paternoster, 1977.

————. "Myth." In *The New Dictionary of Theology*, edited by J. I. Packer and David F. Wright, 449–51. Leicester: InterVarsity, 1988.

Marion, Jean-Luc. "Evil in Person." In *Prolegomena to Charity*, translated by S. E. Lewis. New York: Fordham University Press, 2002.

Martell, Yann. *Beatrice and Virgil*. London: Canongate, 2010.

Matson, Mark A. "The Temple Incident: An Integral Element in the Fourth Gospel's Narrative." In *Jesus in Johannine Tradition*, edited by R. T. Fortua and T. Thatcher, 145–54. Louisville, KY: Westminster John Knox, 2001.

Mayes, Andrew David Hastings. *Deuteronomy*. London: Marshall, Morgan & Scott, 1979.

Mayhew, Peter. *A Theology of Force and Violence*. London: SCM, 1989.

McCabe, Herbert. *God Matters*. London: Mowbray, 1987.

McDonald, Brian. "Violence and the Lamb Slain: An Interview with René Girard." *Touchstone* 16 (2003) 40–43.

McFague, Sallie. "Is God in Charge? Creation and Providence." In *Essentials of Christian Theology*, edited by William Carl Placher, 101–15. Louisville, KY: Westminster John Knox, 2003.

————. *Metaphorical Theology: Models of God in Religious Language*. London: SCM, 1982.

————. *Models of God: Theology for an Ecological, Nuclear Age*. Philadelphia: Fortress, 1987.

McKnight, Scot. *The King Jesus Gospel: The Original Good News Revisited*. Grand Rapids: Zondervan, 2011.

Michaels, J. Ramsey. *The Gospel of John*. Grand Rapids: Eerdmans, 2010.

Michel, Andreas. "Sexual Violence against Children in the Bible." In *The Structural Betrayal of Trust*, edited by Regina Ammicht-Quinn et al., 51–71. London: SCM, 2004.

Middleton, J. Richard. "Created in the Image of a Violent God? The Ethical Problem of the Conquest of Chaos in Biblical Creation Texts." *Interpretation* 58 (2004) 341–55.

Middleton, J. Richard, and B. J. Walsh. *Truth Is Stranger than It Used to Be: Biblical Faith in a Postmodern Age*. London: SPCK, 1995.

Milbank, John. *Being Reconciled: Ontology and Pardon*. London: Routledge, 2003.

————. "Violence: Double Passivity." In *Must Christianity Be Violent?*, edited by Kenneth R. Chase and Alan Jacobs, 183–200. Grand Rapids: Brazos, 2003.

————. *Theology and Social Theory: Beyond Secular Reason*. Cambridge, UK: Blackwell, 1991.

Miller, Patrick D. "God the Warrior: A Problem in Biblical Interpretation and Apologetics." *Interpretation* 19 (1965) 39–46.

————. *The Divine Warrior in Early Israel*. Cambridge: Harvard University Press, 1973.

Mills, David. *Atheist Universe: The Thinking Person's Answer to Christian Fundamentalism.* Berkeley, CA: Ulysses, 2006.

Moberly, R. W. L. "God Is not a Human that He Should Repent (Num 23:19 and 1 Sam 15:29)." In *God in the Fray: A Tribute to Walter Brueggemann,* edited by Tod Linafelt and Timothy Kandler Beal, 112–23. Minneapolis: Fortress, 1998.

Moltmann, Jürgen. *The Coming of God: Christian Eschatology.* London: SCM , 1996.

———. *The Crucified God.* London: SCM, 1974.

———. *The Future of Creation.* London: SCM, 1979.

Morris, Leon. *The Atonement: Its Meaning and Significance.* Downers Grove: InterVarsity, 1983.

———. *The Gospel According to John.* Grand Rapids: Eerdmans, 1995.

Moser, Paul K. *The Severity of God: Religion and Philosophy Reconceived.* Cambridge: Cambridge University Press, 2013.

Mouw, Richard J. "Violence and the Atonement." In *Must Christianity Be Violent?,* edited by Kenneth R. Chase and Alan Jacobs, 159–71. Grand Rapids: Brazos, 2003.

Muchembled, Robert. *A History of the Devil: From the Middle Ages to the Present.* Cambridge: Polity, 2003.

Murdoch, Brian. *The Medieval Popular Bible: Expansions of Genesis in the Middle Ages.* Cambridge, UK: Brewer, 2003.

Nelson-Pallmeyer, Jack. *Is Religion Killing Us? Violence in the Bible and the Quran.* Harrisburg, PA: Trinity, 2003.

Neufeld, Thomas R. Yoder. *Jesus and the Subversion of Violence: Wrestling with the New Testament Evidence.* London: SPCK, 2011.

Newbigin, Lesslie. *The Gospel in a Pluralist Society.* London, SPCK, 1989.

Nicole, Roger. "Postscript on Penal Substitution." In *The Glory of the Atonement: Biblical, Historical and Practical Perspectives,* edited by Charles E. Hill et al., 445–52. Downers Grove, IL: InterVarsity, 2004.

Niditch, Susan. *War in the Hebrew Bible: A Study in the Ethics of Violence.* Oxford: Oxford University Press, 1993.

Niebuhr, Reinhold. *Moral Man and Immoral Society.* London: Charles Scribner's Sons, 1942.

Noble, Thomas A. "The Spirit World: A Theological Approach." In *The Unseen World: Christian Reflections on Angels, Demons and the Heavenly Realm,* edited by Anthony N. S. Lane, 185–223. Carlisle, UK: Paternoster, 1996.

Noll, Stephen F. "Thinking about Angels." In *The Unseen World: Christian Reflections on Angels, Demons and the Heavenly Realm,* edited by Anthony N. S. Lane, 1–27. Carlisle, UK: Paternoster, 1996.

Norris, Christopher. "Modernism." In *The Oxford Companion to Philosophy,* edited by Ted Honderich, 583. Oxford: Oxford University Press, 1995.

Northey, Wayne. "The Cross: God's Peace Work—Towards a Restorative Peacemaking Understanding of the Atonement." In *Stricken by God? Nonviolent Identification and the Victory of Christ,* edited by Brad Jersak and Michael Hardin, 356–77. Grand Rapids: Eerdmans, 2007.

Nyssa, Gregory of. "The Great Catechism." In *A Select Library of Nicene and Post-Nicene Fathers of the Christian Church,* edited by P. Schaff and H. Wace, 471–509. Grand Rapids: Eerdmans, 1954.

O'Brien, Peter T. "Principalities and Powers: Opponents of the Church." *Evangelical Review of Theology* 16 (1992) 353–84.

Otto, Rudolf. *The Idea of the Holy*. Oxford: Oxford University Press, 1923.

Pannenberg, Wolfhart. *Systematic Theology*. Vol. 1. Grand Rapids: Eerdmans, 1988.

Paul, Robert S. *The Atonement and the Sacraments*. London: Hodder & Stoughton, 1961.

Perrin, Norman. *Jesus and the Language of the Kingdom: Symbol and Metaphor in New Testament Interpretation*. London: SCM, 1976.

Perry, Michael. "The Demonic and Exorcism in the Bible." In *Deliverance: Psychic Disturbances and Occult Involvement*, edited by Michael Perry, 136–48. London: SPCK, 1987.

———. "Taking Satan Seriously." *The Expository Times* 1 (1990) 105–12.

Pfau, Julie Shoshana, and David R. Blumenthal. "The Violence of God: Dialogic Fragments." *CrossCurrents* 51, no. 2 (2001) 177–200.

Phillips, Gary A. "The Killing Fields of Matthew's Gospel." In *The Labour of Reading: Desire, Alienation, and Biblical Interpretation*, Semeia Studies 36, edited by Fiona C. Black et al., 249–66. Atlanta: Society of Biblical Literature, 1999.

Pinker, Steven. *The Better Angels of Our Nature: The Decline of Violence in History and Its Causes*. London: Penguin, 2011.

Placher, William Carl. "Christ Takes Our Place: Rethinking Atonement." *Interpretation* 53, no. 1 (1999) 5–20.

———. "Is God in Charge? Creation and Providence." In *Essentials of Christian Theology*, edited by William C. Placher, 93–100. Louisville, KY: Westminster John Knox, 2003.

Poland, Lynn. "The Idea of the Holy and the History of the Sublime." *The Journal of Religion* 72 (1992) 175–97.

Polanyi, Michael. *Personal Knowledge: Towards a Post-Critical Philosophy*. London: Routledge, 1958.

Prigent, Pierre. *Commentary on the Apocalypse of St. John*. Tübingen: Mohr Siebeck, 2004.

Pyper, Hugh S. "Demythologizing." In *The Oxford Companion to Christian Thought*, edited by Adrian Hastings and Hugh Pyper, 159–60. Oxford: Oxford University Press, 2000.

———. "Person." In *The Oxford Companion to Christian Thought*, edited by Adrian Hastings, 532–33. Oxford: Oxford University Press, 2000.

Rad, Gerhard von. *Holy War in Ancient Israel*. Grand Rapids: Eerdmans, 1991.

———. *Old Testament Theology*. Vol. 1, *The Theology of Israel's Historical Traditions*. London: Oliver & Boyd, 1957.

Rahner, Karl. *Theological Investigations*. Vol. 4. London: Darton, Longman & Todd, 1966.

Ranieri, John J. *Disturbing Revelation: Leo Strauss, Eric Voegelin, and the Bible*. Columbia, MO: University of Missouri Press, 2009.

Raphael, Melissa. *Rudolf Otto and the Concept of Holiness*. Oxford: Clarendon, 1997.

Rashdall, Hastings. *The Idea of the Atonement in Christian Theology*. London: Macmillan, 1919.

Rauser, Randal. *Faith Lacking Understanding: Theology "Through a Glass Darkly."* Milton Keynes, UK: Paternoster, 2008.

Rawlinson, Alfred Edward John. *The Gospel According to St. Mark*. London: Methuen, 1925.

Ray, Darby Kathleen. *Deceiving the Devil: Atonement, Abuse and Ransom*. Cleveland: Pilgrim, 1998.

Richardson, Alan. *Introduction to the Theology of the New Testament*. New York: SCM, 1958.

Ricoeur, Paul. *The Rule of Metaphor: Multi-Disciplinary Studies of the Creation of Meaning in Language*. London: Routledge & Kegan Paul, 1978.

———. *The Symbolism of Evil*. New York: Harper & Row, 1967.

Riddell, Michael. *Threshold of the Future: Reforming the Church in the Post-Christian West*. London: SPCK, 1998.

Rieger, Nathan. "Good News for Postmodern Man: Christus Victor in the Lucan Kerygma." In *Stricken by God? Nonviolent Identification and the Victory of Christ*, edited by Brad Jersak and Michael Hardin, 378–403. Grand Rapids: Eerdmans, 2007.

Riley-Smith, Jonathan. "Christian Violence and the Crusades." In *Religious Violence between Christians and Jews: Medieval Roots, Modern Perspectives*, edited by Anna Sapir Abulafia, 3–20. New York: Palgrave, 2002.

Ritschl, Albrecht. *The Christian Doctrine of Justification and Reconciliation: The Positive Development of the Doctrine*. Eugene, OR: Wipf & Stock, 2004.

Robbins, Anna M. "Atonement in Contemporary Culture." In *The Atonement Debate*, edited by D. Tidball et al., 329–44. Grand Rapids: Zondervan, 2008.

Rollins, Wayne G. "The Myth of Redemptive Violence or The Myth of Redemptive Love." *The Destructive Power of Religion: Violence in Judaism, Christianity, and Islam*, vol. 4, *Violence in Judaism, Christianity, and Islam*, edited by J. Harold Ellens, 175–86. Westport, CT: Praeger, 2004.

Römer, Thomas. *Dark God: Cruelty, Sex, and Violence in the Old Testament*. New York: Paulist, 2013.

Rorty, Richard. *Contingency, Irony and Solidarity*. Cambridge: Cambridge University Press, 1989.

Russell, Jeffrey Bunton. *The Prince of Darkness: Radical Evil and the Power of Good in History*. Ithaca, NY: Cornell University Press, 1988.

Sabatino, Charles J. "Projection as Symbol: Rethinking Feuerbach's Criticism." *Encounter* 48 (1987) 179–93.

Sanders, Ed Parish. *Jesus and Judaism*. Philadelphia: Fortress, 1985.

Sanders, John. *Atonement and Violence: A Theological Conversation*. Nashville: Abingdon, 2006.

Schleiermacher, Friedrich. *On Religion: Speeches to Its Cultured Despisers*. New York: Harper & Row, 1958.

———. *The Christian Faith*. London: T. & T. Clark, 1999.

Schlier, Heinrich. *Principalities and Powers in the New Testament*. London: Burns & Oates, 1961.

Schmiechen, Peter. "Christ the Goal of Creation." In *Saving Power: Theories of Atonement and Forms of the Church*, 222–52. Grand Rapids: Eerdmans, 2005.

Schreiner, Thomas R. "Penal Substitution View." In *The Nature of the Atonement: Four Views*, edited by James Beilby and Paul R. Eddy, 67–98. Downers Grove, IL: IVP Academic, 2006.

Schroeder, Christopher. "Standing in the Breach: Turning Away the Wrath of God." *Interpretation* 52, no. 1 (1998) 16–23.

Schwager, Raymund. *Must There Be Scapegoats? Violence and Redemption in the Bible.* New York: Crossroad, 1987.

———. "Religion as the Foundation of an Ethic of Overcoming Violence." In *Religion as a Source of Violence?,* edited by W. Beuken and K-J. Kuschel, 119–128. London: SCM, 1997.

Scott, Ernest F. *The Crisis in the Life of Jesus: The Cleansing of the Temple and Its Significance.* New York: Scribner, 1952.

Seibert, Eric A. *Disturbing Divine Behavior: Troubling Images of God.* Minneapolis: Fortress, 2009.

———. *The Violence of Scripture: Overcoming the Old Testament's Troubling Legacy.* Minneapolis: Fortress, 2012.

Shapiro, Susan E. "Failing Speech: Post-Holocaust Writing and the Discourse of Postmodernism." *Semeia* 40 (1987) 65–91.

Sheriffs, Deryck. *The Friendship of the Lord: An Old Testament Spirituality.* Carlisle, UK: Paternoster, 1996.

Sloyan, Gerard S. *The Crucifixion of Jesus: History, Myth, Faith.* Minneapolis: Fortress, 1995.

Smalley, Stephen S. *1,2,3 John.* Word Biblical Commentary 51. Nashville: Thomas Nelson, 2007.

Soggin, Jan Alberto. *Joshua.* London: SCM, 1972.

Soskice, Janet Martin. *Metaphor and Religious Language.* Oxford: Clarendon, 1985.

Southern, Richard W. *Saint Anselm: A Portrait in a Landscape.* Cambridge: Cambridge University Press, 1990.

Spence, Alan. *The Promise of Peace: A Unified Theory of Atonement.* Edinburgh: T. & T. Clark, 2006.

Stählin, Gustav. "The Wrath of Man and the Wrath of God in the New Testament." In *Theological Dictionary of the New Testament,* vol. 5, edited by Geoffrey W. Bromiley, 419–47. Grand Rapids: Eerdmans, 1967.

Stead, Christopher. *Divine Substance.* Oxford: Clarendon, 1977.

Steffen, Lloyd. *The Demonic Turn: The Power of Religion to Inspire or Restrain Violence.* Cleveland: Pilgrim, 2003.

Stenger, Victor J. *God the Failed Hypothesis: How Science Shows that God Does not Exist.* New York: Prometheus, 2007.

Stibbe, Mark W. G. *John's Gospel.* New York: Routledge, 1994.

Stott, John. *Obeying Christ in a Changing World.* Vol. 1, *The Lord Christ.* London: Fountain, 1977.

———. *The Cross of Christ.* Downers Grove, IL: InterVarsity, 1986.

Strecker, Georg. "εὐαγγέλιον." In *Exegetical Dictionary of the New Testament,* vol. 2, edited by Horst Balz and Gerhard M. Schneider, 70–74. Grand Rapids: Eerdmans, 2000.

Tan, C. E. L. "Humanity's Devil." *Evangelical Review of Theology* 34 (2010) 136–54.

Tidball, Derek. "Penal Substitution: A Pastoral Apologetic." In *The Atonement Debate,* edited by D. Tidball et al., 345–60. Grand Rapids: Zondervan, 2008.

Tillich, Paul. *Systematic Theology.* 3 vols. Chicago: University of Chicago Press, 1951–63.

———. *What Is Religion?* New York: Harper, 1963.

Tirosh-Rothschild, Hava. "Sefirot as the Essence of God in the Writings of David Messer Leon." *Association for Jewish Studies Review* 7–8 (1982–83) 409–24.

Tracy, David. "Metaphor and Religion: The Test Case of Christian Texts." In *On Metaphor*, edited by Sheldon Sacks, 89–104. Chicago: The University of Chicago Press, 1978.

Turner, H. E. W. *Jesus, Master and Lord: A Study of the Historical Truth of the Gospels.* London: Mowbray, 1957.

Turner, Laurence A. *Genesis.* Sheffield, UK: Sheffield Academic, 2000.

Twelftree, Graham. *Christ Triumphant: Exorcism Then and Now.* London: Hodder & Stoughton, 1985.

Unger, Merrill Frederick. "The Babylonian and Biblical Accounts of Creation." *Biblioteca Sacra* 109 (1952) 304–17.

Urban, Wilber Marshall. *Language and Reality.* London: Allen & Unwin, 1939.

Vanhoozer, Kevin J. "Theology and the Condition of Postmodernity: A Report on Knowledge (of God)." In *The Cambridge Companion to Postmodern Theology*, edited by Kevin J. Vanhoozer, 3–25. Cambridge: Cambridge University Press, 2003.

Volf, Miroslav. "Divine Violence?" *Christian Century* 116, no. 27 (1999) 972–74.

———. *Exclusion and Embrace: A Theological Exploration of Identity, Otherness, and Reconciliation.* Nashville: Abingdon, 1996.

———. *Free of Charge: Giving and Forgiving in a Culture Stripped of Grace.* Grand Rapids: Zondervan, 2005.

Vries, Hent de. *Religion and Violence: Philosophical Perspectives from Kant to Derrida.* Baltimore: Johns Hopkins University Press, 2002.

Walker, Andrew. *Enemy Territory: The Christian Struggle for the Modern World.* London: Hodder & Stoughton, 1987.

———. *Telling the Story: Gospel, Mission and Culture.* London: SPCK, 1996.

Ware, Owen. "Rudolph [sic] Otto's Idea of the Holy: A Reappraisal." *Heythrop Journal* 1 (2007) 48–60.

Watt, Jan G. van der. "Soteriology in the New Testament: Some Tentative Remarks." In *Salvation in the New Testament: Perspectives on Soteriology*, edited by J. G. van der Watt, 505–22. Leiden: Brill, 2005.

Weaver, J. Denny. "Narrative Christus Victor: The Answer to Anselmian Atonement Violence." In *Atonement and Violence: A Theological Conversation*, edited by J. Sanders, 1–32. Nashville: Abingdon, 2006.

———. *The Nonviolent Atonement.* Grand Rapids: Eerdmans, 2001.

———. "Violence in Christian Theology." *CrossCurrents* 51, no. 2 (2001) 150–76.

Weil, Simone. *Waiting for God.* New York: Harper & Row, 1951.

Wenham, Gordon J. *The Book of Leviticus.* Grand Rapids: Eerdmans, 1979.

———. *Genesis 1–15.* Word Biblical Commentary 1. Milton Keynes: Word, 1987.

Westermann, Claus. *Genesis 1–11: A Commentary.* Minneapolis: Augsburg, 1984.

———. "The Complaint Against God." In *God in the Fray: A Tribute to Walter Brueggemann*, edited by Tod Linafelt and Timothy Kandler Beal, 233–41. Minneapolis: Fortress, 1998.

Wiles, Maurice. "Creeds." In *The Oxford Companion to Christian Thought*, edited by Adrian Hastings, 144–46. Oxford: Oxford University Press, 2000.

Williams, Anna N. "Contemplation: Knowledge of God in Augustine's De Trinitate." In *Knowing the Triune God: The Work of the Spirit in the Practices of the Church*, edited by James J. Buckley and David S. Yeago, 121–46. Cambridge, MA: Eerdmans, 2001.

Williams, Daniel H. *Retrieving the Tradition and Renewing Evangelicalism*. Cambridge, MA: Eerdmans, 1999.

Williams, Rowan. "Girard on Violence, Society and the Sacred." In *Wrestling with Angels: Conversations in Modern Theology*, edited by Mike Higton, 171–85. Cambridge, MA: Eerdmans, 2007.

———. *On Christian Theology*. Oxford: Blackwell, 2000.

Wils, Jean Pierre. "Violence as an Anthropological Constant? Towards a New Evaluation." In *Religion as a Source of Violence?*, edited by Wim Beuken and Karl-Josef Kuschel, 110–18. London: SCM, 1997.

Wink, Walter. *Engaging the Powers: Discernment and Resistance in a World of Domination*. Minneapolis: Fortress, 1992.

———. *Naming the Powers: The Language of Power in the New Testament*. Philadelphia: Fortress, 1984.

———. *The Powers That Be: Theology for a New Millennium*. New York: Doubleday, 1998.

———. *Unmasking the Powers: The Invisible Forces that Determine Human Existence*. Philadelphia: Fortress, 1986.

Winter, Michael. *The Atonement: Problems in Theology*. London: Chapman, 1995.

Wood, L. J. "הָרַם." In *Theological Wordbook of the Old Testament*, edited by R. Laird Harris et al., 324–25. Chicago: Moody, 1980.

Wolterstorff, Nicholas. *Justice in Love*. Grand Rapids: Eerdmans, 2011.

Wright, Archie T. *The Origin of Evil Spirits: The Reception of Genesis 6:1–4 in Early Jewish Literature*. Tübingen: Mohr Siebeck, 2005.

Wright, Nigel G. *A Theology of the Dark Side: Putting the Power of Evil in Its Place*. Carlisle, UK: Paternoster, 2003.

Wright, N. T. *Jesus and the Victory of God*. London: SPCK, 1996.

———. *Surprised by Hope: Rethinking Heaven, the Resurrection, and the Mission of the Church*. New York: Harper Collins, 2008.

Wright, Tom. *Simply Jesus*. London: SPCK, 2011.

Yoder, John Howard. "If Abraham Is Our Father." In *The Original Revolution: Essays on Christian Pacifism*, 85–104. Eugene, OR: Wipf & Stock, 1998.

———. *The Politics of Jesus*. Cambridge, MA: Eerdmans, 1972.

Young, Jeremy. *The Violence of God and the War on Terror*. London: Darton, Longman & Todd, 2007.

Zbikowski, Lawrence M. "Metaphor and Music." In *The Cambridge Handbook of Metaphor and Thought*, edited by Raymond W. Gibbs Jr., 502–24. Cambridge: Cambridge University Press, 2008.

Žižek, Slavoj. *Violence*. New York: Picador, 2008.

Lightning Source UK Ltd.
Milton Keynes UK
UKOW06f1302061017
310511UK00006B/230/P